FORENSICS SERIES VOLUME 1

Duo Practice and Competition

• • •

Thirty-five 8–10 Minute
Original Comedic Plays

Published by Smith and Kraus, Inc.
177 Lyme Road, Hanover, NH 03755
www.SmithKraus.com

First Edition: August 2003
10 9 8 7 6 5 4 3 2 1
Manufactured in the United States of America

Cover design by Lisa Goldfinger,
featuring actors Colleen Kehoe and Ricky Staub
Text design by Julia Hill Gignoux, Freedom Hill Design

Library of Congress Cataloguing-in-Publication Data
Lhota, Barbara.
Forensics series: duo practice and competition /
by Barbara Lhota and Janet B. Milstein.
p. cm. — (Young actors series)
Contents: v.1 Thirty-five 8–10 minute original comedic plays —
v.2 Thirty-five 8–10 minute original dramatic scenes.
ISBN 1-57525-308-9 (v1) 1-57525-309-7 (v2)
1. Dialogues, English. 2. Acting. 3. Forensics (public speaking)
I. Title: Duo practice and competition. II. Milstein, Janet B. III. Title. IV.
Young actor series.
PN2080.L53 2003
812'.608—dc21   2003042486

FORENSICS SERIES VOLUME 1

Duo Practice and Competition

• • •

Thirty-five 8–10 Minute Original Comedic Plays

By Barbara Lhota and Janet B. Milstein

YOUNG ACTORS SERIES

A Smith and Kraus Book

ACKNOWLEDGMENTS

Lisa Herceg, for her understanding throughout
and her editing of the scene intros

Merel Marine

Dr. James M. Brandon

Jaye Morrison

David Scheidecker

Michael Graupmann

Darlene F. Olson

Cody Duncan

Tia Maxwell

Ricky Staub

Emily Casey

Joanna Ericson

The Milsteins

Elizabeth Monteleone

Julia Hill Gignoux

Lisa Goldfinger

and

Eric Kraus and Marisa Smith for their belief,
support, and incredible patience

Contents

Introduction

As an acting teacher, I am constantly being asked to recommend monologues to students. Every acting teacher, I imagine, faces this on a regular basis. However, a strange thing started to happen. After class, some students began asking me to recommend scenes. "For what in particular?" I asked.

"For my forensics competition," they'd reply.

"Forensics?! What in the world is that?"

"Oh, it's my speech team. We do competitions that are called duo or duet — like acting class — scenes with only two people."

"Sure, there are tons of wonderful scenes —"

"But it has to be eight minutes long."

Another voice interjected, "Mine has to be ten."

"OK . . ." I began again.

"And there can't be any swearing or bad language," added the first student.

"And I'm sick of the old classical stuff and British comedies," uttered the second.

"And something with cool blocking in it."

"We can't move at all in mine. I need something that's good without blocking."

"And it should be balanced between the actors, not focused more on one."

"Yeah, and my partner is a guy."

"Mine is a girl."

"What scenes should we do?"

I paused. "Well, that about narrows it down to . . . not much."

"Exactly," they sighed.

I went home after a third similar conversation thinking that something should be done about this. There should be books out there for them. I wondered if there were. I happened to be living with a roommate at the time, who also happens to be a gifted writer. "Hey Barb, have you ever heard of forensics? It's like a speech team thing?"

"Oh, yeah, I did it all through high school and college. In fact, I was president of my forensics team in high school." Ah, the small-world-thing works its magic. I went on to explain my students' dilemma and my idea to put together books of material for them.

We plunged in together and did a good deal of research on what was out there — basically nothing. Sure there were some books on the different types of speeches and how to teach those, but there were no books for the duo/duet competitions. I saw a lot of students were purchasing ten-minute play collections, hoping the material would be appropriate.

Barb and I compiled our research, explained it all to the very patient and always-eager-to-learn Eric Kraus (of Smith and Kraus). We decided there was a tremendous need for books of this nature.

So, voilà—Volume 1! The plays in this book are the result of Barb's and my arguments turned comedy, our life dramas turned comedy, and our bleary-eyed nights of delirium turned comedy. Not to mention much hard work and dedication.

Whether the rules of your league permit eight minutes, ten minutes, or, the more rare, twelve minutes, you will find many pieces in this book to fit your needs. The language is tame, but if it causes a problem with your guidelines, a word here or there can easily be cut or replaced. In addition, the pieces do not require any props and will work with or without blocking. The characters are rich, the roles are balanced, and the situations are sure to make you giggle if not guffaw. This book is also a great source of fresh new material for scene study classes and ten-minute play competitions.

This is the first volume of what we believe will be a very successful series of forensics books. We hope we have accomplished our mission: to save you valuable searching time and provide you with original award-winning material. We wish you the best of luck in all your competitions. And most of all—have fun!

Janet B. Milstein

Tips from the Pros: What Coaches, Directors, and Judges Think

To make this book more useful, we talked to high school and college coaches, directors, and judges to get their opinions on the duo forensics event. We asked a series of questions—a survey of sorts. We found their tips enlightening. They suggest how to rehearse and prepare for a performance. In addition, their tips offer some insight about what to expect at a competition.

• • •

WHAT DO YOU LIKE ABOUT THE DRAMATIC DUO EVENT?

It provides a "slice of life" opportunity to explore experiences and viewpoints students may otherwise never encounter and helps them to understand the problems of others.

— Merel K. Marine

I like that it is the only "individual" event that requires a partner. This one peculiar factor makes the event so important as the speaker develops the skills of timing, teamwork, and, when someone misses a cue, improvisation.

— Dr. James M. Brandon

It gives young actors a chance to develop characters with a variety of emotional levels; it also allows them some freedom to analyze the motivations of the characters in-depth and with less restriction.

— Jaye Morrison

I think that learning how to perform with a partner is a really important acting skill and communication tool. This was always my favorite event because it allowed me as a performer to share my time on stage with someone else and also allowed me to play off of someone else. Learning how to build a scene and how to react to another performer's energy is an important skill that cannot be learned in solo interpretation events.

— Michael Graupmann

The oral interpretation of dramatic literature without "acting it out" is an opportunity and an artistic challenge that is exciting as well as fun!

— Darlene F. Olson

WHAT ARE THE RULES?

Time limits? Eight minutes for most high school competitions and ten minutes for most college competitions.

Movement? The answers here varied from none at all to unlimited. If you are not permitted to move, you have the opportunity to show off your vocal skills and imagination. The key is to follow your league's rules for each individual competition to the letter. Some coaches and judges complained that rules were frequently and unfortunately ignored. Because of that, some scenes that were better than others in presentation received lower scores than their competitors. If you do not follow the rules of a sport, you most likely will be penalized or disqualified no matter how much talent you possess.

Are set pieces allowed? Again, answers varied here from none at all, to a table and chair, to just chairs. Follow your individual league's rules. Some judges commented that if you are allowed to use furniture — use it creatively. Let the blocking enhance and clarify the story.

Should the script be held or memorized? It tends to vary from league to league.

Script in hand, and the script should be used during the performance (i.e., It *can* be used as a prop, but it *must* be looked at from time to time. This is another rule too often ignored.).

— Dr. James M. Brandon

Memorized!

— Merel K. Marine

Scripts need to be memorized but also black binders held to give recognition to the authors.

— Michael Graupmann

HOW DO YOU CREATE AN INTRO FOR DUO COMPETITION?

The student should be speaking in his or her own voice; the intro should include both speakers, and it should reflect the tone and intent of the piece. Introductions should be accessible, but not overly explanatory.

— Dr. James M. Brandon

I usually like to use part of the scene or the result of an improv as an attention catcher or teaser and then follow with a brief out-of-character shared narrative intro. I also like to incorporate singing when the talent and theme make it appropriate.

— Merel K. Marine

I try to give the audience a sense of who the characters are and draw them into the scene immediately. Often the scene begins, and then a *short* intro, which includes the title and author, is given.

— Jaye Morrison

I always make sure to give a helpful bit of outside knowledge first. This can be historical, literary, or scientific information that applies. Then I relate this nugget of insight to the relationship in the piece, perhaps giving plot or character background that needs to be known beforehand. Extra points for creativity, humor, and elegant phrasing.

—Michael Graupmann

I prefer a very brief introduction to the scene. If we don't need background information to understand the scene, don't give it to us. Also, don't smack us in the face with the theme. Show us, don't tell us. Remember: The shorter the intro, the more time you have to perform.

— Dan Foss

WHAT DO THE JUDGES LOOK FOR IN THIS EVENT?

I feel some judges too often concern themselves with the rule book. However, communication of text and hopefully subtext are important. Quality of the literature should be important, and acting skill is important. I personally rate the extent to which I am emotionally moved as most important, followed by creative and appropriate composition, blocking, and naturalness of performance.

— Merel K. Marine

Who knows? Depth of character? Acting ability? But unfortunately, often good, original scripts and acting itself become secondary to the emotional "umph" of the script.

— David Scheidecker

Commitment to the playwright's literature — to interpret the playwright's intention or purpose first and foremost. Authentic, practiced interpretation beginning and ending with vocal and physical suggestions of the two characters.

— Darlene F. Olson

Confidence. Poise. A student who uses the full range of his or her voice. A student who is believable. A student who can give the appearance of spontaneity. A student who has selected and performed material that is within his or her range. A student who clearly enjoys what he or she is doing. *Energy!*

— Dr. James M. Brandon

I want to see two characters complete a journey in eight minutes. Have the actors worked together to create a believable relationship? Have they demonstrated a clear understanding of their characters' goals?

— Dan Foss

WHAT SORT OF REHEARSAL SCHEDULE WOULD YOU RECOMMEND FOR THIS TYPE OF COMPETITION?

It depends on the student, but before the first read-through of the piece before an audience, the student *must* complete, at minimum, an hour of rehearsal for every minute of stage time. So a ten-minute duo should be rehearsed at least ten hours before ever approaching an audience. This ten-hours does *not* include mere read-throughs and line memorization time.

— Dr. James M. Brandon

Depending on the amount of scenes with which one has to rehearse, I recommend one rehearsal per week at the following schedule:

    First rehearsal: Half-hour read-through and discussion/
       improvisation
    Second rehearsal: One-hour blocking session
    Third rehearsal: One-hour off-script review of blocking
       and polish/ business
    Fourth rehearsal and all subsequent rehearsals:
       Alternate half-hour and one-hour sessions, depending
       on problems. Include special rehearsal sessions to keep
       things fresh.

— Merel K. Marine

I believe that a great deal of work needs to go into the initial staging and blocking of a duo, for the purpose of getting both partners comfortable and able to manipulate the text to suit their own needs. When the words and actions feel natural and spontaneous, they are at the desired level of performance. . . . Nothing seems less inspired than over-practiced duo. For this reason, I think students have to know their own work habits.

— Michael Graupmann

I want to see my duet scene partners three to four times a week for an hour at a time. This gives us the time to review the judges' critiques from the previous weekend and give attention to that feedback in our rehearsals.

— Dan Foss

DO YOU HAVE ANY TIPS ON HOW TO KEEP THE PIECE FRESH SINCE IT IS PRESENTED SO FREQUENTLY?

(A) Switch roles. (B) Mute acting (communicate the script via facial expressions and movement only). (C) Rehearse as a humorous scene to find the humor that should exist in all scenes. Don't be afraid to be outrageous. (D) Improv problems that may have existed between characters prior to the opening of the scene. (E) Give each character a secret subtext to carry throughout the scene. This is never to be shared with the partner. This should provide interpretation variety from rehearsal to rehearsal or performance to performance.

— Merel K. Marine

Remember that judges want you to succeed and provide you with feedback that will improve your performance. Don't discount comments with which you may not necessarily agree. Try everything your judges recommend in rehearsal. Even if it doesn't work for you, you may still learn something new about your character from attempting a different approach.

— Dan Foss

Pick it up before each tournament and try to read it again "for the first time." You'll be surprised at what you find.

— Dr. James M. Brandon

We sometimes switch roles. We often alter blocking. Sometimes we add vocal music in the intro. We do many dramatic exercises to help discover the characters and make them fuller during the season.

— David Scheidecker

Experiment casting each scene as a different movie genre: mystery, sci-fi, farce, musical, and so forth. Finding new hidden meaning will reveal a wealth of new life to a piece.

— Michael Graupmann

We try to expand their thinking — think outside the box; try new things with delivery and blocking.

— Jaye Morrison

Never settle into your performance so much that it doesn't change — even if you're winning! Often judges will see you more than once in a season. We love to find that even the best scenes have progressed and improved. Look for new moments each time you rehearse or perform. Watch for what your scene partner is giving you and ensure that you are returning the favor!

— Dan Foss

• • •

We would like to thank those who kindly offered their helpful advice. In the pages that follow, we hope you find a scene that sets your soul ablaze — that you simply *must* do. Be sure to check out the other books in our Forensics Series. Good luck in all competitions and remember—have *fun!*

Barbara Lhota and Janet B. Milstein

SHIPSHAPE

Renee, twenty-seven, has brought herself to the Ship-Shape Weight Loss Program because she gained a lot of weight after bearing her first child several years back. The problem is that Renee hates restrictive programs. Karl, the coach of the local ShipShape Program, is doing his occasional heart-to-hearts with current weigh-ins to see how they are faring with the daily Stack-O-Snack cards. Renee, being a longtime poker fan, has made some major alterations to the rules of the program. She waits impatiently to be weighed in, with a mountainous chip on her shoulder, when Karl finally approaches, waving her weekly logbook.

CHARACTERS
Renee: 27, overweight member of ShipShape Weight
    Loss Program
Karl: late 20s, the coach of the local ShipShape Program

SETTING
ShipShape Weight Loss Center

TIME
The present

RENEE: *(Impatiently looking at her watch.)* Jeez, this line was long today, huh? I was supposed to pick up my kid half an hour ago.
KARL: Every few weeks us coaches like to really talk to people. Get a feel for how well one is following the ShipShape Program. We do it right while we weigh in. I'm Karl.
RENEE: Well, Karl, I sucked this week at ShipShake . . . Shape. Thinking about my thighs shakin' not shapin'. Here's my log. *(Handing him her logbook.)* I'm just here to see how fat I am and get out of here quick.

KARL: *(Wagging finger.)* Uh, uh, uh. We're all weight-endowed, hoping to be weight-reduced. We don't use the F-word.

RENEE: That depends on what that scale says, doesn't it? And I'm not talking the F-A-T word if you know what I mean, Karl.

KARL: I'm glad to see you have a little sense of humor. Now, what did you have a problem with this week?

RENEE: Eating. Now, my car's at a meter. Can I . . . *(Starts to step on scale.)*

KARL: *(Blocks the scale.)* No, no, no. Now, let's slow down. Let's breathe. *(Looking at her.)* Breathe.

RENEE: I don't want to.

KARL: Why not?

RENEE: I've been doing it naturally for years. I have it down to a science.

KARL: Now, come on, we don't need to rush everywhere. It just gets us all worked up.

RENEE: No, it's the *lack* of rushing that gets me worked up. The ticketing of the car that gets me really, really worked up.

KARL: OK, I hear your frustration. And I understand. I've been through this. I have. The first couple of weeks, it's hard to understand the program fully. It's hard to change old habits.

RENEE: Oh God! *(Sighs.)* Now you have me sighing . . . breathing. Are you happy? Can I step on the scale now or what?

KARL: Before you step on the scale, it's good, it's healthy to talk about things here a little bit . . . uh . . . *(Looking for the name tag.)* Where's your name tag?

RENEE: I'm not staying for the meeting.

KARL: Not staying for the meeting? *(To others around.)* Do you hear this? She's not staying for the meeting. *(To Renee.)* As you can see, frowns abound at that.

RENEE: Well, turn the mob against me, why don't you? I can't stay for the meeting, OK? My two-year-old daughter is wreaking havoc on my sister's new couch right this second.

KARL: Yes, but these fat grams are wreaking havoc on your

ShipShape Spirit. Stealing your soul every second of your life. Which is more important — your sister's stupid couch or your soul?

RENEE: My sister's couch is not stupid. It's not even a couch. It's like a, like a sofa. And it's absolutely gorgeous! And uninsured!

KARL: And what about your soul?

RENEE: Well, I was baptized and confirmed. I know I use a lot of profanity and only show up to church on major holidays. But still, I'd like to think I'm semicovered.

KARL: What's your name?

RENEE: Renee.

KARL: *(Elongating it.)* Renee. That's a beautiful name.

RENEE: Cut the crap. Get to the point.

KARL: How did you do dealing our Stack-O-Snack cards this week?

RENEE: Stacking was fine. Real good. It was the snacking that got a little out of hand.

KARL: So did you stay within your allotted cards per day?

RENEE: Uh . . . more or less.

KARL: More or less? Can you elaborate on that?

RENEE: I just drew a couple of extra cards.

KARL: Extra cards? But, but you can't draw extra cards. Renee, you're only allotted eleven cards per day.

RENEE: I know but that's so odd. Eleven is so odd. I thought I'd go with a nice even twelve instead.

KARL: But that's not the program.

RENEE: Well, la-de-da. There's no room to be flexible?

KARL: Well, you'll gain that way.

RENEE: Oh come on. It was just one card. One measly, green-vegetable-crud card.

KARL: *(Relieved.)* OK. Well . . . I'm glad it was a vegetable card at least.

RENEE: Yeah. Except that I didn't use it for vegetables.

KARL: What?!

RENEE: I hate vegetables. That's why I had to make green wild.

KARL: Wild?

RENEE: I had to.

KARL: You can't suddenly make a card wild. Green is supposed to be a green leafy vegetable.

RENEE: Yeah. But that's so limiting.

KARL: It's supposed to be, Renee!

RENEE: I said wild! Wild. It didn't mean you *couldn't* have a green leafy vegetable.

KARL: So did you?

RENEE: No! Would you? Given the choice? *(Beat.)* Wait, the chocolate cake had vegetable oil in it. That counts. That's how they make vegetable oil, isn't it? With green leafy vegetables?

KARL: This is a scientific program, Renee. It's scientifically designed for weight loss. You receive eleven cards. A perfect, color-coded mix of each of the four basic food groups.

RENEE: Yeah. That's why I wanted to shake it up a bit.

KARL: Shake it up? We don't shake it up.

RENEE: That's painfully obvious, hon.

KARL: Well, that's how you do it. The same group of cards every day.

RENEE: So who always wants to be dealt the same hand day after day? Boorrring. Some days you want to win. Some days you don't mind . . . winning more.

KARL: Renee. This is not a winning game.

RENEE: That's not what your commercials say, is it?

KARL: I mean, it's a winning game but not like you're describing.

RENEE: I know. I just played a lot of cards when I was a kid. Actually, I had a little gambling issue. That's probably why I discarded a few.

KARL: Discarded? No! You can't discard. Discarding is not part of the program.

RENEE: Jeez, you're uptight. Haven't you ever played Five Card Draw? You know, you discard a few cards you don't like, and pick up the same number as you discarded.

KARL: That's cheating!

RENEE: No it's not! It's how you play the game.

KARL: But you won't have a perfect mix of the four food groups.

RENEE: Picky, picky! This way you could get a better hand. A dairy flush! A carb full-house.

KARL: I don't think you grasp the program, Renee. You only pick additional cards — one to two cards — if you've completed twenty-five minutes of activity.

RENEE: I did. I went to the laundromat.

KARL: *Rigorous* activity.

RENEE: You haven't seen my laundromat. This elderly woman tried to steal my dryer. She strangled me with her wet nylons. I had to wrestle her to the ground. I earned those two cards.

KARL: I don't think you're taking this seriously enough, Renee. Do you really want to lose weight?

RENEE: Yes. But I think the card concept gets me competitive. I want to have a great hand.

KARL: Wouldn't ya rather have a great bod? Huh?! *(She frowns.)* Besides, you're not playing against anybody.

RENEE: Well, how fun is that? No wonder I think the Ship-Shape Program sucks. Maybe we should be playing against each other. Ever think of that, huh? Make it like a real game.

KARL: Oh yeah, sure, then we can just go crazy and play War, or Go Fish. *(Getting frustrated.)* Trading in all our cards every which way with each other so that we have no nutritional value whatsoever and become big honking lardballs. Is that what you want?!

RENEE: Wow. You're angry.

KARL: No, I'm not. I'm fine. I'm good. I'm Karl.

RENEE: Yes, you're also pissed. This program makes you really tense, doesn't it?

KARL: No, I love it. I love it. I really love it. I've lost sixty pounds on it. This is what I think the problem is, Renee. You see, I've isolated this to a card problem here. I think playing cards isn't a good concept for you to think about. Let's use a shopping concept.

RENEE: Oh great. I love shopping. I'm a shop-a-holic.

KARL: You are given a salary of eleven cards per day. No more. No less. Each time you use a card, you purchase food. Once the cards—in other words, the money—are gone. No more food.

RENEE: What about credit?

KARL: There is no credit.

RENEE: How about a loan? Say I borrow twenty percent of tomorrow's cards for today?

KARL: There is no credit.

RENEE: Well, how un-American is that? How can you work the system?

KARL: You don't. You commit to the program as is. You just try it for this week and see what results it yields.

RENEE: All right.

KARL: All right?

RENEE: Yeah. I'll do what you say. I'll do the eleven-card thing. Fine. My meter's probably expired by now.

KARL: OK. So now, when you step on the scale, I don't want you to have any false expectations.

RENEE: Fine.

KARL: You were getting used to the program — settling into it — so you wouldn't have lost weight yet. Don't want to build up false impressions. But you will. You hold onto your faith.

RENEE: All right. All right, Karl. Would you let me get on the scale now?

(Karl nods and gestures to it. Renee sucks in her stomach loudly.)

RENEE: *(Handing stuff to Karl.)* Here take my sweater and my hat. And my ring. I just don't want it to give me a false reading. *(Renee steps on the scale.)*

KARL: *(Karl's face drops.)* Oh boy. Oh my —

RENEE: That bad?

KARL: No, this couldn't be right.

RENEE: How bad is it? How bad could it be?

KARL: You lost ten pounds.

RENEE: *(Disappointed.)* Oh great! Lost? *(Realizing.)* That's good! I lost!

KARL: No, it isn't. There must be something wrong with the scale.

RENEE: *(Smacks Karl.)* Don't you dare touch that scale, Karl!

KARL: *(Shaking his hand at her.)* But you didn't follow the program. You had extra cards everywhere. Wild cards! It just can't be.

RENEE: My grandma taught me how to play Five Card Draw. She was really good. I told you.

KARL: This isn't a game, fat girl!

RENEE: Watch it, dog breath. Or I'll be using the other F-word while I rearrange your face. You're just jealous that I lost ten pounds! Admit it. *(Singsongy, dancing around.)* Sometimes you gotta shake it up, Karl.

KARL: Shake it up? I'll shake you up. How much would I like to suck down some chocolate cake and peanut butter crackers? But nooooo! I have to follow the program to the letter. I love eating. I love snacks! And all the while I have to convince you people that the program works. It's all about your cards, your feelings, your activity points. You, you, you! Where am I in the deck? I'm the discarded joker. The one you yell at when you gain a few measly pounds. Gain because *you* decided you don't *like* eleven cards. "What's an extra card here and there?" And then someone like you ruins everything by losing! By cheating. I am the butt of the joke.

RENEE: Personally, Karl, I would use the A-word in this situation.

ALL TAI'D UP

Dale, twenty-two, a recent graduate in archaeology, has reached the end of his rope. He decides to visit Anita, twenty, a psychic and physiognomist (a facial reader) out of desperation. In the past few weeks, his relationship with his girlfriend, Lea, has become disastrous — mostly because she seems to hate him. Anita, a third-generation psychic and biology major, uses the money from her psychic sessions to pay her way through college. Unfortunately, she not only has no talent in this area she also doesn't fake it very well. Dale has just rung the bell, and Anita has buzzed him in.

CHARACTERS
Dale: 22, a recent graduate of archaeology
Anita: late 20s, a physiognomist (a facial reader and student

SETTING
Anita's family's psychic storefront

TIME
The present

DALE: Hi. I'm glad you're still open.
ANITA: Uh, we're not open. In fact, we just closed.
DALE: What? But the blinking "Psychic" sign says ten.
ANITA: Yeah, but the nonblinking me says "last appointment nine-thirty."
DALE: *(Looking at his watch.)* It *is* nine-thirty. See? I have nine-thirty. In fact, it's nine-twenty-nine according to my watch. And my watch is very good — a Swiss, precision-controlled watch synchronized with the National Weather Service.
ANITA: *(Pointing to her watch.)* Mine's a *gift* I received when I ordered a ridiculous amount of magazines I didn't want. Now it's a constant reminder of pushy people. Hint, hint.

DALE: I'm not being pushy. I'm just desperate.

ANITA: And this matters to me because . . .

DALE: I have a lot of money.

ANITA: Would you like to take a seat?

DALE: I can't. My life is a mess. It's this woman I'm very serious about.

ANITA: Can we go back to the lotta money thing again?

DALE: *Was* very serious about. I don't know. Everyone keeps saying that she's, that something is going on with this, this tai chi guy. I need to know what to do.

ANITA: Oh, I get it. Sigma, Sigma Pi, right? This is some lame initiation. I don't need this.

DALE: What?!

ANITA: I know what you all pulled at the laundromat yesterday. That poor girl. She nearly had a heart attack when that guy started knocking on the dryer window. Now, she's terrified of Clingfree sheets! Rule number one: Don't put freshman in dryers, understand? I hate frat boys! Even if you are cute.

DALE: But I'm not a frat boy. I couldn't get in. Not that I wanted to. I graduated from G.W. last year with a degree in archaeology. I'm twenty-two. I'm nice. I work at the museum. With rocks.

ANITA: Oh, well that assures me of your character. I'll call a stalagmite tomorrow for a reference.

DALE: Did you just say I was cute or did I mishear you?

ANITA: Yes.

DALE: To which?

ANITA: Never mind. *(Beat.)* Do you know if Beck's sells used books?

DALE: You're a student as well as a psychic?

ANITA: Yeah. Well . . . was. I'm not a psychic anymore. Tonight was my last night.

DALE: Last night? How? Once a psychic, always a psychic. Isn't that how it works? It's a gift.

ANITA: Yeah, I know. But it's really my mother's and her

mother's and her mother's mother's gift. Mine was more like a gift certificate. You use it a couple times and that's it.

DALE: So you don't have to be perfect at this, Zelda. I just need a little sound advice.

ANITA: I'm not Zelda. That's my mother. I'm Anita. It doesn't even sound like a psychic.

DALE: *(Shrugs.)* It's not as bad as Martha. That has no psychic ring.

ANITA: My mother's a genius. So is my aunt Ruby. I'm just not as good at this crap, OK? I can't feel vibes. I don't hear voices. And the only aura I ever saw turned out to be a strobe light in a smoky bar. Truth is I *suck.*

DALE: Well, I'm sure you don't suck.

ANITA: I suck. I really suck.

DALE: Are you sure you suck? You look intuitive.

ANITA: *(Intrigued.)* I do? Really? *(Shakes her head.)* I do not.

DALE: Yes, you do. You really, really do.

ANITA: I do? *(Flirting.)* Want to grab a drink tomorrow?

DALE: I, I can't. Even if I want to. *(She stares at him.)* Not that I don't because I do. Very much like your . . . drinks. I like drinks. But I have a fiancée. Well, not exactly a fiancée — a soon-to-be fiancée if she doesn't dump me. You see I need some sound advice.

ANITA: From a psychic?

DALE: My relationship, my whole life hangs in the balance.

ANITA: Oh sure. No pressure. I'm really sorry, uhhh? *(Referring to his name.)*

DALE: Dale.

ANITA: Dale? *(He nods.)* That's so cute. Look, Dale, I'm not good at this. And it sounds like you need a therapist, not a psychic. It would be completely unethical for me to give you advice.

DALE: But cost is no object.

ANITA: Of course, who said I was ethical? That'll be fifty bucks. Take a seat.

DALE: Fifty bucks?! I can't afford that.

ANITA: I thought you said cost was no object?

DALE: It isn't. Just as long as it's no more than seven.

ANITA: What?!! No more than seven?! Even for regulars, we charge twenty.

DALE: I'm sorry. I can't help it. I'm broke. My girlfriend has been forcing me to fix up my place. She says I have to up-scale if she's going to stay with me.

ANITA: Upscale? What kinda snot-faced brat is she?

DALE: Exactly. That's exactly what I say — sort of . . . in a nicer way. I don't know why I always have to spend money to make her happy. I'm a neat guy. I keep my laundry off the floor. And I do our laundry every week.

ANITA: Our? You do her laundry? *(He nods.)* You're sick.

DALE: She has me setting up my living environment so that it brings flow or energy or peace or something. It's, uh, this Chinesey thingy called uh funk, funk, funk —

ANITA: Feng Shui?

DALE: *(Smacking his hands.)* That's it! It's supposed to be all about peace.

ANITA: And marketing.

DALE: Buying a seventy-five dollar water fountain didn't bring me peace. She insists we run it all night long. I have to pee every half-an-hour with its tinkling.

ANITA: Tinkling?

DALE: Well, you know what I mean.

ANITA: It's all crap. *(Chinese accent.)* "Do put a plant or living thing in the southwest corner of the room." I kill plants.

DALE: So do I. Decaying plants do not equal peace. She's on me all the time about the living thing in the southwest corner.

ANITA: I always keep a *living thing* in my southwest corner. It does keep the peace.

DALE: It does?

ANITA: Yep, my roommate. I tried to kill her, but she has other living things over there, protecting her. Molding coffee mugs, fish, her boyfriend. It's just useless.

DALE: You're funny. But I'm serious. She blames me for her low energy. She said I don't have a well-defined main entrance to my place. I have to define it. It's the mouth of my chi. She says I have bad chi 'cause of my mouth problem. Do you think I have bad chi?

ANITA: No, I think you have great chi. *(Flirting more.)* You have a nice mouth too.

DALE: You too — I mean, you do? She says the door problem is damaging her energy.

ANITA: Tell her if the door is a problem, maybe she'd be more comfortable on the other side of it.

DALE: I know. You're right. My friends say she's rotten to me now. She hates my cat. She used to love my cat. Poor thing sheds a lot. She's nervous with all the knick-knacks and New Age music. Maybe I should do something drastic like get rid of her. What do your vibes say?

ANITA: Get rid of her.

DALE: But she's so friendly and cuddly. I love her.

ANITA: Not the cat, Dale. The chick.

DALE: The chick?

ANITA: The chick, the snot-faced brat. She's messing with your relationship with your cat. That's wrong.

DALE: But don't you need to consult the tarot cards, the tea leaves, the crystal balls?

ANITA: Yes, that's what you could use here, Dale — balls.

DALE: You do the crystal ball?

ANITA: I meant . . . never mind. Look, I don't do all that stuff. I'm a physiognomist.

DALE: Oh. Of course. That's great then. What is that?

ANITA: Facial reading.

DALE: You read faces? How does one read a face?

ANITA: Sit down. And I'll show you. *(Starting her routine.)* Now relax. Just relax. Relax. *(She stares at him intently.)* Relax!

DALE: How can I relax? I feel like you're staring at me.

ANITA: Of course I am. That's how you do it.

DALE: Well, what do you see? You see anything about my girlfriend?

ANITA: No, no. I'm seeing blue. Is blue something significant to you?

DALE: Blue . . . blue . . . Um, well, my room is white and the basement I work in is green . . . Blue, um . . . I have been . . . blue. That's it! I've been feeling so blue!!

ANITA: Well, that's just . . . that's really stretching. Let's see what else I get.

DALE: I've been feeling really blue because I wanted to ask my girlfriend to marry me this Thanksgiving, but I think I realized that was a bad idea when she told me she hated me.

ANITA: Yeah, I'd say that doesn't sound too promising.

DALE: So what else does my face say about my girlfriend?

ANITA: It says, it says, um . . . you have nice eyes.

DALE: Does my girlfriend think that?

ANITA: Who cares. She's irritating. *(Looking at him more closely.)* Oh my God.

DALE: What? What? It says she's seeing someone else, doesn't it?

ANITA: It does? *(Realizing.)* Oh yes, it does. This, this wrinkle here. Right in this wrinkle.

DALE: She gave me a wrinkle?

ANITA: She did! It's a guy, a guy she knows who's like some, some big —

DALE: Nah, the guy I'm thinking of is short.

ANITA: Fat —

DALE: Nah, he's kinda lean too.

ANITA: Fat eating it says . . . type of guy.

DALE: He does like burgers. I saw him with a burger. You're good. You're really, really good.

ANITA: Thanks, cutie. But let's face it. I'm making this crap up. I suck.

DALE: No, no, you're doing really well. You just have to warm up.

ANITA: Warm up? No. I wouldn't know a fortune if came

wrapped in a cookie. I'm just too insensitive. Just today I told a guy he'd meet a woman and then probably die in the next month wearing an ugly toupee. I should've left that part out.

DALE: His dying?

ANITA: No, the toupee. Oh yeah. I probably should have left out the dying part too, huh? See, I'm insensitive.

DALE: That's not true. You've been very sensitive to me. And you can see what's going on with me too. You've already made me feel better about it.

ANITA: About what? Your stupid, mean girlfriend who's sleeping with her Tai Chi instructor?

DALE: Tai Chi instructor? How did you know?

ANITA: I don't know. Probably because you said it when you walked in. Tai Chi. Feng Shui. Lotta chi chi goin' on to me.

DALE: They're definitely having an affair?

ANITA: It looks pretty certain to me, Dale. And a guy like you . . . you don't deserve that.

DALE: No, I certainly don't.

ANITA: You're a good catch. You're cute. You're a guy with a cat. And you work in a museum —

DALE: With rocks.

ANITA: Rocks. Exactly. She's a boulder on your back.

DALE: She's why I have such a blue aura.

ANITA: Black and blue. You don't need that. You deserve someone better.

DALE: I know. I know. Someone in science and, and —

ANITA: Anatomy. Anatomy is always good.

DALE: You know what I see?

ANITA: What?

DALE: *(He looks in her eyes.)* I see something in you now . . . I see something red and new —

ANITA: My new car! You're good too.

DALE: You have a new car? And it's red? Really?

ANITA: No, it's old. But I just got it back from the shop so it's like new.

DALE: But it's red?

ANITA: No, it's blue but it does have red rust. It's a bug.

DALE: I love bugs.

ANITA: Me too. Just the drivable kind though.

DALE: I'm seeing this red car and you and me and maybe a few drinks?

ANITA: Oh really? *(She looks at him devilishly.)* Aren't you quite the psychic now?

DALE: Maybe I've found my new calling.

ANITA: You have. *(She smiles and takes his arm.)*

CRYPTIC VIBES

Robin, twenty-four, a painting contractor, and Gloria, twenty-six, a manager at a local art gallery, have been friends for the past two years and have been dating for the last four months. Robin has unexpectedly shown up at Gloria's house tonight to confess his secret. He has just, within the last few days, accepted that he is gay. Gloria, too, has something she needs to share with Robin. In the last week, she has begun to fall for her new next-door neighbor, Jack. She wants to break it off with Robin because it's just not happening between them. Neither suspects that the other has such news. They each are terrified that the breakup will destroy the other. Gloria is making dinner for Jack when Robin arrives.

CHARACTERS
Robin: 24, a painting contractor
Gloria: 26, a manager at a local art gallery

SETTING
Gloria's kitchen, which opens onto the living room

TIME
The present

ROBIN: *(Entering nervously.)* I'm sorry, I didn't call. I couldn't wait. I had to see you.
GLORIA: *(Nervous and annoyed.)* Robin?! I didn't expect you. Um. Hi!
ROBIN: This is . . . I just . . . this is very important, Gloria, please. I think we should sit.
GLORIA: Sit? Like down? I don't think sitting is a good idea right now.
ROBIN: I've been walking by the lake, thinking. Every night just thinking and thinking.

GLORIA: Oh, honey. Don't do that. You're not made for that.

ROBIN: It's mostly about us, Gloria.

GLORIA: Us? Really? Us?

ROBIN: No, now, now it's not bad. Exactly. Surprising, and a bit serious.

GLORIA: Serious? Not serious. Oh, no, no, Robin. Not serious. This is not a good time.

ROBIN: Of course I must propose that we —

GLORIA: No, no, no proposing anything now! I'm cooking dinner. Pitting olives, peeling potatoes, ripping peas. It's not good timing.

ROBIN: You're going to hate me, Gloria. *(Reflecting.)* Ripping peas, did you say? You're cooking? Since when do you cook?

GLORIA: Since . . . now. I just thought I'd try it, but . . . I'm sorry that you must be going.

ROBIN: Going? Oh no, not yet. You're learning to cook for me, aren't you?

GLORIA: No. I mean, well, I-I wouldn't exactly . . .

ROBIN: And you hate it don't you? *(She nods.)* And all this cooking is for me?

GLORIA: Well, I wouldn't go so far as to say that. I wouldn't call it cooking, I mean.

ROBIN: Oh, I'm certain it's delicious. What is it?

GLORIA: Burnt. Actually. Burnt is what it is.

ROBIN: Oh, well, I'm sure it's not *all* burnt. *(Looking.)* Well. Burnt is good. I'm not complaining.

GLORIA: We'll probably have to go out.

ROBIN: Oh, no! We can't. We have to talk here. In private.

GLORIA: No! I mean, not tonight. When I said we have to go out just now, it wasn't you and me. I meant, I had plans with a person. I was cooking for a — a friend-person, Robin.

ROBIN: Oh? A friend?

GLORIA: Yes. My friendly neighbor.

ROBIN: Your neighbor? Oh, good. Good. Sheila?

GLORIA: No. Uhhhh . . . well, he fixed my light last week. I felt like I owed him.

ROBIN: He? *(Beat.)* Oh she's a he, huh? Mr. Woods?

GLORIA: No. I, uh . . . not Woods. It's uh, remember the new guy in 17C — the, the really built guy with the *(Getting into it.)* gorgeous, incredibly lush . . . well, average-looking . . . we made fun of him? He had a very ugly cat? You probably don't remember —

ROBIN: Jack?

GLORIA: You know his name?

ROBIN: It's funny that you mentioned him.

GLORIA: Funny?

ROBIN: Well, I ran into Jack in the hall a few days ago when you got off late.

GLORIA: Oh. You talked to Jack?

ROBIN: Yes, in the hall. And for a few hours at his place. It was like therapy.

GLORIA: Really?

ROBIN: It turns out he's a hell of a guy. Very interesting and sensitive.

GLORIA: Interesting that you didn't tell me, sweetie. Sensitive . . . great. How sensitive?

ROBIN: Interesting that you didn't happen to mention that you invited him to dinner either.

GLORIA: What did you talk about? I wouldn't think you'd have a whole lot in common.

ROBIN: Oh, you'd be surprised. I guess you've realized he's not the jock we first thought.

GLORIA: Yes, I noticed he knew a great deal about art. He asked me about my gallery. He came up to my studio. He loved my *Woman with Grapefruits* painting.

ROBIN: Well, they're impressive grapefruits, honey. Great grapefruits.

GLORIA: Yes, he loved them. He bought a miniature Kafka my student painted. Still, he plays football and drinks milk out of the carton. He's kinda jock-ey.

ROBIN: I know, I *love* that. I mean, that he's not stuffy. It turns out he teaches English and has a thing for antique candelabras. He wants his kitchen redone in dusty blue and avocado. My guys are going to repaint it for him. He actually said "dusty blue and avocado."

GLORIA: Did he?

ROBIN: He knows his decor lingo. He also collects English flatware.

GLORIA: Well, how "Antiques Roadshow" of him. So what else did you talk about, Robin?

ROBIN: Well, funny that you ask.

GLORIA: You keep saying that but nothing's very ha ha yet.

ROBIN: Well, I just meant that it's odd we mentioned him.

GLORIA: *We* didn't mention him. I did. Because he happens to be stopping by. For dinner. Now.

ROBIN: He's the reason I'm here, Gloria. I mean, certain things came up out of our —

GLORIA: That lousy good-for-nothing! He told you everything, didn't he, Robin?

ROBIN: Well — I — he — you know. He said it was based on a vibe.

GLORIA: A vibe? My God. I gave him a lot more than a vibe. I gave him a whole viiibration.

ROBIN: Oh my God! You told him to ask me? You told him to confront me for you?

GLORIA: What?! No, I was going to tell you everything, Robin. I swear. I don't know what came over me. I just couldn't help it. I got so completely ravenous.

ROBIN: I understand. I understand your need to know and your suspicions all along. I should have known myself by my obsessions — fine china, *Martha Stewart* magazine.

GLORIA: No, I should have been honest about everything. I . . . *(Beat.) Martha Stewart* magazine? What are you talking about?

ROBIN: The relief. The relief of having the truth out there. I feel so much better that you know.

GLORIA: Know what?

ROBIN: I thought you'd fall apart.

GLORIA: Me fall apart? I was afraid *you'd* fall apart.

ROBIN: Me? Why am I falling apart?

GLORIA: Because I practically — I lusted after . . . well, he already told you . . .

ROBIN: Just because I'm gay, it doesn't mean I'm falling apart.

GLORIA: What?!

ROBIN: Excuse me. Did you just use the word *lusted*?

GLORIA: Never mind that, you Martha groupie. You're telling me you're gay? You're gay?!! *(Beat.)* Wait. Don't tell me Jack's gay too?

ROBIN: Well, who would care if he was, hmmm? You were confessing, weren't you? Cheater!

GLORIA: Cheater? You can't call me a cheater! How could I cheat on a gay man?!

ROBIN: That doesn't count. You didn't *know* that I was gay.

GLORIA: Ohhh, details! Let's not stray from the subject at hand. Are you saying that Mr. Jack sings in your choir?

ROBIN: No. He sings in yours. He's just very in touch with his vibe.

GLORIA: Oh, I bet he is.

ROBIN: So why did you put Jack up to raising the crux?

GLORIA: Put Jack up to what? Raising the *what*?

ROBIN: The crux, the question, the point.

GLORIA: I didn't put Jack up to raising anything, honey, because I raised the gay question months ago. Remember? And you told me, swore to me, you told me men did nothing for you! Now, all you want to do is raise the crux. You told me how much you loved my body, my spirit — me. "You're so attractive, Gloria." Well, you're so full of crap! You're gay? When were you going to tell me? We've been dating for four months, pal!

ROBIN: And you've been cheating with Jack for weeks!

GLORIA: That's not true! I wouldn't say weeks. Maybe *a* week.

ROBIN: Did you think nothing of what we had together?

GLORIA: *(Irritated.)* Meeee? You weren't even in the right ocean. You don't even like my fish. I told you you were gay.

I knew it. From the beginning. Didn't I call that? What was wrong with *my* vibe? You only listen to guys' vibes?

ROBIN: You don't count. You think everyone is gay when you first meet them, Gloria.

GLORIA: Yeah. And you are! See? It pays to think that way.

ROBIN: I wanted to tell you gently.

GLORIA: Oh, yeah, real gently. Just stick it between the hot guy's thing for dusty avocado and English pottery —

ROBIN: Flatware.

GLORIA: Whatever!! The point is that you should have told me directly a long time ago. Instead of lying all over the place.

ROBIN: Lying?! I wasn't lying. If I was lying, I was lying to myself.

GLORIA: While you were lying next to me. Don't I count?

ROBIN: I understand your condemnation, Gloria.

GLORIA: What are you now? Some sort of New Age thera- pist? I can't believe Jack didn't tell me about you either.

ROBIN: How many times have you "talked" to this guy?

GLORIA: None of your beeswax, Mr. Gay Boyfriend.

ROBIN: Did you feel it?

GLORIA: Feel what? In particular?

ROBIN: My gayness, of course?! Is that why you had an affair?

GLORIA: Had an affair? He taught me proper downward dog position. *(Robin's mouth drops. Gloria is disgusted.)* Yoga! We're talking yoga! Don't be disgusting!

ROBIN: Oh lovely. So, he's been over every night.

GLORIA: Not every night. Just three times this week. I told you. He fixed my lightbulb!

ROBIN: Oh, yeah! Lit ya right up I bet, Ms. Yogi Poodle.

GLORIA: Don't fake jealousy. You're not even interested in me. Or my sisters. You think of kissing me and pictures of stale white bread fill your mind.

ROBIN: Tostada chips dipped in mild salsa. You're kinda feisty, but fat.

GLORIA: *(Appalled.)* What?! Fat?! You have a lot of nerve! I'm a very attractive woman.

ROBIN: Oh, who told you that besides me? Mr. Jack?

GLORIA: Well, if you must know, he complimented my posture.

ROBIN: *(Softer.)* Ohhh. Sweetheart. Is he not into you?

GLORIA: Well, apparently, he's more into talking about pottery with you. I flirted with him like a madwoman. Didn't make any headway. It's disgusting!

ROBIN: *(Going to hug her.)* Oh honey!

GLORIA: Don't you dare feel sorry for me, you lousy . . . gay guy.

ROBIN: To tell you the truth, sweetie, I don't think he's interested in your type.

GLORIA: So he *is* gay?! Fine. Give me a gun. Is everyone gay? I fully expect my cat to come out tomorrow.

ROBIN: No, I think he's into, ya know, women that are extremely . . . athletic.

GLORIA: What are you trying to say? I could tone up a bit. How athletic are we talking? Suzanne Somers . . . sort of ab-building, thigh-crunching, bun-toning —

ROBIN: Muscle-bulking, gender-confusing, facial hair–growing —

GLORIA: Oh. Ewwwy. That's not pretty.

ROBIN: Bingo! You got it.

GLORIA: Well. I never liked his cleft chin anyway. There were hairs in it.

ROBIN: I know. Uck. He's got terrible cuticles too. We could do much better. *(Pause.)* So are you still mad at me?

GLORIA: Yes.

ROBIN: You are still very sexy to me, ya know?

GLORIA: Please.

ROBIN: I mean it.

GLORIA: That means a whole lot coming from a homo like you. *(She smiles at him.)* So you want to hang out with me tonight? I'll dump the jock.

ROBIN: Absolutely. We're done with that namby-pamby, ugly cat-owning nimrod.

GLORIA: Good. What are we going to do about dinner?

ROBIN: Well, we aren't eating your black, decaying, burnt opus out there.

GLORIA: Leo's?

ROBIN: Where else?

GLORIA: Ya know, I always wondered why on Saturday nights I wanted to eat a whole bag of cookie dough with you and do your nails. Now, everything makes perfect sense.

ROBIN: I love you madly, you know.

GLORIA: Oh, hush up, you big ole poop.

READY STEADY

Larry, thirties, is training Gretchen, twenties, to be an expert telemarketer for BNA America Credit Card. Gretchen is reluctant to follow the training because BNA's methods don't make complete sense to her. In addition, she doesn't want to be a nag, like the barrage of telemarketers she has to deal with day in and day out. However, Larry is persistent, for he knows the best way to go about things. He does, of course, have five years' experience as a refusal reverser. As the scene opens, Larry is beginning his training session.

CHARACTERS
Larry: 30s, BNA Customer Service Telemarketing
    trainer
Gretchen: 20s, trainee

SETTING
BNA phone cubical

TIME
The present

LARRY: OK, Gretchen, my name is Larry, and I'll be training you today. We'll be using something called a CATI *(Pronounced caddie.)* system. Now, a CATI system is a fancy name for a —
GRETCHEN: Computer-assisted telephone interviewing system.
LARRY: Wow-wee! You've worked in customer service before, haven't you?
GRETCHEN: No.
LARRY: Well then you're extremely knowledgeable and well-read about customer service.
GRETCHEN: Well, it's on this paper you gave me.
LARRY: Oh. *(Laughs.)* I forgot that was written there. Silly me. Smart you for looking. OK, well, basically this baby is an

expensive computer that assists us in making our courtesy calls faster and more efficiently. Today, you can expect to be calling close to one hundred and twenty-four of our most reliable customers. Now, these are not cold calls. Not cold calls. We never do cold calls here at BNA. We don't believe in it. I assume you know what a cold call is?

GRETCHEN : Um . . . where they hang up on you?

LARRY: *(Laughs.)* No, that's a typical call. Let me explain in more detail. Basically, when you cold call, you are calling people who you don't know and who may not be interested in what you're selling. We, on the other hand, call only our very reliable customers — those individuals that have a BNA America credit card. We're calling tonight — as a courtesy — to see if they want our preferred partner's Ready Steady Clean Way System. We'll be giving them a *huge* discount. Any questions so far, Gretchen?

GRETCHEN : Uh . . . well, I . . .

LARRY: We have a script here that you will —

GRETCHEN: I, I don't understand something.

LARRY: OK. No problem. That's great! Not understanding is great! BNA believes in not understanding. There is no question too dumb for us.

GRETCHEN: I don't understand the difference between cold calling and what we're doing. I mean, the reliable people I call will be interested in the Ready Steady Clean Way System?

LARRY: Well, maybe, but not necessarily. That's why we're calling them.

GRETCHEN: Oh. But you said when you cold call, which we're *not* doing, you are calling people who may not be interested in what you're selling.

LARRY: Uh-huh. That's true. Very good definition of a cold call. Good.

GRETCHEN: So it's just a cold call of your current customers. Isn't it?

LARRY: *(Pause.)* That may be one way of looking at it. But we're offering them a *huge* discount. You see?

GRETCHEN: Uh-huh.

LARRY: And there is no charge for Ready Steady because it's through one of our preferred partners. It doesn't cost anything so what does it matter about their interest in it or not? There's no expense!

GRETCHEN: Ever?

LARRY: Well, no, not ever! For the first thirty days of course it's free and then . . . Listen, think of it this way, for our customers, it's like hearing about a great deal through a best friend. The friend's recommending it. You know how that is? I bet you recommend great deals to your best friend on CD players and DVDs and trendy clothes all the time. Don't you?

GRETCHEN: My best friend has been deaf since birth and lives in Berlin. Telecommunication is difficult.

LARRY: *(Beat.)* Well, then . . . that example isn't so good. Listen, I think you'll find that this floor-cleaning system sells itself with no trouble. I'd want to try it for free, wouldn't you?

GRETCHEN: We have carpets.

LARRY: Yes, but if you didn't . . . huh? Huh?

GRETCHEN: Well, I don't think so because I hang up when people call from my credit card trying to sell me stuff.

LARRY: Well, of course — duh! With stuff! I understand. I resent that too! But Ready Steady is *not* stuff. *(Laughs.)* It's something needed. Everybody has to clean their hardwood floors, right?

GRETCHEN: I guess. Unless they have carpets or a maid or live with their mother or something.

LARRY: Well, see? OK. Right. Then they can either purchase it for their mother or maid or be the stingy, money-pinching people they are. No problem either way. See?

GRETCHEN: Uh-huh.

LARRY: See, you just come to me with your questions, Gretch.

I do have answers. And just so you feel more relaxed, I have nearly a decade in the CS field — customer service. And five years as a BNA Advanced Account Manager. *(He smiles nodding at her.)* Five years.

GRETCHEN: That's nice.

LARRY: You betcha! Advanced Account Manager is the official title. But the more inside lingo is that I'm a refusal reverser. In fact, I'm one of their *top* refusal reversers. Do you know what that is?

GRETCHEN: A person who reverses refusals?

LARRY: You are good! I had a feeling about you. You're gonna be an RR someday too. But that doesn't happen overnight. It takes work and dedication. But oh is it amazing. Do you know, people will call wanting to refuse these offers and even sometimes cancel our credit card? In a matter of seconds, I have them begging to stay on and buy more. From no to yes in seconds. You just get that good.

GRETCHEN: But what if they have a lot of debt?

LARRY: Well . . . that's their problem, isn't it? Anyway, then they'll pay it monthly and establish good credit so they can buy a house some day. It's very U.S.A.

GRETCHEN: But due to the credit card's high interest rate, average customers pay four to five times more than the original price of the item. It can get people into a lifelong cycle of debt.

LARRY: *(Thinks. Shrugs.)* Again, their problem. Now, before we get into some mock phone calls, let me ask you if you feel you have a good sense of the Ready Steady features?

GRETCHEN: I guess.

LARRY: Ohhh. Now, now. That's not very enthusiastic. We're all about colorful voices here. Really having power behind your answers and a conviction to them. So let's try this again. Do you have a good sense of the product's assets, Gretchen?

GRETCHEN: *(Just louder.)* I guess!

LARRY: OK. *(Beat.)* We'll work on that. Now, let's start with the product. Why don't you tell me about it?

GRETCHEN: *(Reading from literature without emotion.)* It's a revolutionary dusting, polishing, and waxing system that recreates the radiant splendor and luster of your hardwood floors.

LARRY: OK, OK . . . OK. It, it lacked a little color. It was a little beige. You want to grab people and get them to feel the polishing of the floor. You don't want to be reading and let them think your dog just died or something.

GRETCHEN: She did.

LARRY: What?

GRETCHEN: Rhonda died this past Sunday.

LARRY: Your dog? I'm so sorry. I had no idea.

GRETCHEN: It's OK. She was old and gassy. She didn't have control of her bodily functions anymore.

LARRY: Oh. *(Beat.)* Let's let sleeping dogs . . . lie.

GRETCHEN: It was for the best, for all of us. Go ahead.

LARRY: Well, I, I just wanted you to add expression to your voice. Maybe let the words sound like what they are . . . let the "revolutionary" sound . . . like a revolution. Let the polishing sound, sound . . . polishy. Why don't you try it again?

GRETCHEN: *(Reading from literature, emphasizing words strangely.)* A revolutionary dusting, polishing, and waxing system that recreates the radiant splendor and luster of your hardwood floors.

LARRY: Hum. OK, OK. OK. Why don't we just have you say what the Ready Steady Clean Way System is in your own words? Sometimes that, that helps create foundation. So . . . what is the Ready Steady Clean Way System to you, Gretch?

GRETCHEN: It's um . . . it's like a mop.

LARRY: A mop. Uh-huh. And this mop . . . ?

GRETCHEN: It can be used for mopping . . . and sort of dusting and stuff and it's got a feature.

LARRY: A feature. Yes, yes . . . go on . . .

GRETCHEN: But that costs extra.

LARRY: No, no, let's —

GRETCHEN: But it's cool —

LARRY: Good, good, good —

GRETCHEN: Because then you don't need a stepladder. It can reach up high.

LARRY: Good, good! Go on . . .

GRETCHEN: Real, real high. Really hellishly, nosebleed-like —

LARRY: Oh-kay. Hold it there. I wouldn't advise words like hellishly or bleeding anything in any of the calls. They, they just don't go over well. OK? *(She nods.)* OK, let's, um, why don't we just dive right in and get all wet with a mock call. I'll be playing a reliable BNA customer. You read from the script on the computer screen and I'll push the computer buttons so you can see how it all works. OK?

GRETCHEN: OK.

LARRY: OK. First things first. You would push the dial button here. Then you'd hear . . . dialing. *(Doing imitation.)* Beep, beep, beep, beep, beep, beep, beep. *(Pretending to be a woman on the other end.)* Kennedy residence. Hello? *(He looks at Gretchen and points to the screen.)*

GRETCHEN: What? What do I push?

LARRY: *(Whispers.)* Read.

GRETCHEN: *(Very cardboard.)* Hello. May I speak to Ms. Blank?

LARRY: Kennedy. Yes, this is Ms. Kennedy.

GRETCHEN: How are you this morning, afternoon, or evening?

LARRY: *(Under his breath.)* You pick one. *(Answering.)* Well, I'm fine. How are you?

GRETCHEN: I'm good. Thank you. My name's blank and I'm glad to find you at home Ms. Blan — Kennedy because I have good news. I'm calling on a — for very special customers like you Ms. Blank — ooh. On behalf of your BNA account to announce an astounding offer from one of your, I mean, one of *our* preferred partners.

LARRY: Uh-huh. That sounds great. What is it?

GRETCHEN: It's a *(Trying to have expression.)* revolutionary dusting, polishing, and waxing system that recreates the radiant splendor and luster of your hardwood floors.

LARRY: Well, what is that exactly? In your own words, dear?

GRETCHEN: Huh? Oh. It's, it's a, a, a mop — but one with this doohickey reach feature that's not that expensive.

LARRY: Wow! That sounds great! How do I get it?

GRETCHEN: All you have to do is say yes, right now, and you can have it for free. For thirty days you can use this system for free. I know you'll love the shine and luster it restores to your floors almost like magic.

LARRY: But what if I use it and don't like it, honey?

GRETCHEN: If you are not completely satisfied, no explanation necessary, just return Ready Steady and the entire cost of the system will be refunded to your card.

LARRY: How much is it, dear?

GRETCHEN: It's only thirty-nine ninety-five.

LARRY: Oh. That's way too expensive!

GRETCHEN: Oh. OK. Bye.

LARRY: No. No! *(Pointing to the screen.)* Read the screen. If *no* or *too expensive*, read the rebuttal. Let's try this again. "Oh. That's too expensive, dear!"

GRETCHEN: Well don't you worry, Mrs., uh, Kennedy because I'm so sure you'll love this system and I don't want you to have to clean without it, so I'll tell you what I'll do. I can divide the cost of the Ready Steady Clean Way System into four low, low payments of nine ninety-five per month.

LARRY: Oh, that's a little better, honey, but it still seems a tiny bit high.

GRETCHEN: Because you are such a good customer, and because we are so confident that you will love this system, we want to make this easy for you. We don't want you to struggle here at BNA. So . . . due to your excellent customer status, we're going to offer you a fifteen percent discount. What do you think about that?

LARRY: Wow! You guys are great.

GRETCHEN: *(Breaking character.)* This doesn't seem very real. I would have hung up on myself.

LARRY: What do you mean? Of course it does.

GRETCHEN: I'm just saying this script on the screen here is too fakey.

LARRY: No, it's not. I wrote it myself. It's professional. It's won awards.

GRETCHEN: Well why don't I offer the discount right away? Try to be as up-front as I can? That's what *I* would want.

LARRY: Welll, you, you, you. And um-hmm like that's going to work. We only have seventy-some years in the business. But what do we know? Little Miss Telequeen knows it all.

GRETCHEN: Let me just try it on a call. If it doesn't work, fine, I'll do whatever you want.

LARRY: Fine. We're open to suggestions here at BNA . . . no matter how stupid.

GRETCHEN: You think I'm going to fall on my face, don't you?

LARRY: Me? No, no. OK . . . Just punch the dial — I'll do it. You read. *(Getting ready to punch the button.)* Ready? Here we go. *(He pushes. Makes dialing sound again.)* Beep, beep, beep, beep, beep, beep, beep.

GRETCHEN: Hello? May I speak to Mrs. Handson? . . . You're Mrs. Handson? *(Sounding startled.)* Oh . . . Well, you didn't exactly sound like . . . Oh. A sex change? Well, well that's, that's —

LARRY: *(Whispers.)* Oh God, he's playing with you. Here comes the hang-up.

GRETCHEN: *(Still on phone.)* Great . . . Who am I? . . . Oh, I'm uh, uh —

LARRY: *(Whispering.)* Gretchen — Gretchen.

GRETCHEN: I'm Gretchen. I'm calling with your BNA account . . . It's, I'm uh, calling because we want to sell you this dust-mop thing.

LARRY: Dust-mop thing?

GRETCHEN: *(Looking at Larry.)* Huh? . . . Oh, oh I'm sorry. My training instructor is giving me a hard time about how I described —

LARRY: *(Waving his hands.)* No, no, no!

GRETCHEN: *(On the phone.)* Can you hear that? He's really uptight . . . So anyway . . . What? Hardwood floors? You do?! But it's really overpriced.
(Larry ducking down, mouthing — "Are you crazy?!!")

GRETCHEN: But it does have this doohickey reach thing for hard-to-reach areas . . . You do? . . . Then you could really use that. Hey, everybody has hellishly high corners to clean, right? *(Larry hitting his head.)* Gives you a nosebleed up that high.

LARRY: *(Whispers.)* No bleeding. No blood.

GRETCHEN: It really restores the total luster to them — like brand new . . . Huh? Uh, well, it's uh . . . fifty-nine ninety-five. *(Larry squints, bracing himself.)* You will?! . . .
(Larry jumps up and declares victory in several poses.)

GRETCHEN: *(In phone.)* Great! *(Larry gives her a thumbs-up.)* And since you're such a valuable customer, Mrs. Handson, there's a few extra items some of our preferred partners are offering that I'd like to tell you about . . . Oh, now, just think of me as a best friend giving a recommendation —
(Larry kneels and kisses her hand as she continues.)

SPARE SOMETHIN'?

Sammy, thirties, a drunk who always has a story to get some spare change, spots the well-dressed Lorna heading toward the train station and grasps the opportunity to hit her up for some money. His story today is simple — his car ran out of gas while he was here visiting his poor, sick mother in a run-down nursing home. Now, he has no gas to take his mother back to his home so that he can care for her. The problem with his story is that no one will stop long enough to hear it. It's been a rough morning for Sammy. Last night, he had to sleep on a steam grate in front of the library. And now, most of the early morning business people are ignoring his pleas for help. But Lorna's different. She takes an interest. Unfortunately, Sammy is in for a lot more than he bargains for when he realizes that Lorna is a mental patient at the nearby Rock Creek Facility.

CHARACTERS
Sammy: 30s, a drunk on the street
Lorna: 30s, a mental patient at the nearby Rock
    Creek Facility

SETTING
Urban street near subway station

TIME
The present

SAMMY: *(Quick wave good-bye to someone.)* God bless ya anyway. *(Seeing Lorna.)* Hey, ma'am, can I ask ya somethin'?
LORNA: That depends entirely on the something, doesn't it? I can't be expected to answer all questions at all times.
SAMMY: No, I wouldn't expect, I don't expect you to —
LORNA: If you asked me a geographic question — for instance,

where is Zimbabwe in proximity to Mozambique — I wouldn't be able to answer it, would I?

SAMMY: No, I guess . . .

LORNA: And that wouldn't be any good. If you were looking for Zimbabwe.

SAMMY: Oh, ma'am, I'm not gonna ask ya nothin' geology-like.

LORNA: Geology? That's not geology. Geology is quite different from geography.

SAMMY: Geology, geography. I get that all confused.

LORNA: I loved geology class. I loved the earth, and it's burning center. The fiery oven inside. Burning and churning. Didn't you love that? The center of the earth. The fire. We all learned about that in grade school. Remember the fire?

SAMMY: No. I remember when this dude Roger pulled the fire alarm and the nuns got really pissed.

LORNA: Geology is the study of the rocks, the minerals, the fossils, the . . . *(Change in face.)* stones. I say no to stones. I don't like stones. Not any of them. Too plain and hard. *(Singsongy.)* Sticks and stones will break your bones but names will never hurt you. Have you heard that before?

SAMMY: Uhh —

LORNA: It's completely untrue, you know. Absolutely. Names can hurt you. *Words* can hurt you.

SAMMY: Are you playin' with me?

LORNA: Especially if they're elongated. Long, elongated words can make you absolutely crazy.

SAMMY: Oh-kay. *Not* playin'.

LORNA: *(Intensely to him.)* Are you crazy?

SAMMY: Uh, no. I'm broke, ma'am. Just broke. Not crazy. *(Waves.)* And I think I best be going now 'cause I don't want to keep ya. *(Waves and starts to move.)* Bye.

LORNA: *(Following him.)* Going? Where?

SAMMY: Where? I'm just, just on the go. Going to see my mother.

LORNA: Your mother? How sweet.

SAMMY: Sweet? Yes! I'm sweet. *(Realizes it still might be worth a try.)* It's just my poor, sick mother. Too bad my car broke down, and I don't have any money — none to take her home with me. To my warm, comfy home where I'd care for her every minute of every day. I just miss her so much.

LORNA: I wish they'd taken me home. I have lots of money. I always hated staying at my aunt's. I hated her wallpaper.

SAMMY: Yes, that's terrible. What did you just say?

LORNA: I wish they'd taken me home.

SAMMY: Oh, I know, ma'am. They should have. They should be shot. No, after that, what did you say?

LORNA: I hated her wallpaper. It talked too much.

SAMMY: I understand. I had the same problem with my ex. No, I meant *after* you said you wanted to go home. *Before* the freaky wallpaper.

LORNA: Oh. *(Thinking.)* Um. I have lots of money.

SAMMY: That's it! That's what I thought you said. So, you do? Well, isn't that strange?

LORNA: Is it? Strange?

SAMMY: Well, just 'cause I happen to be able to use a little money right now. Just, just for my mother. I wasn't gonna ask, but since you say you have lots. She's very sick.

LORNA: Oh, my mother was sick too. Very sick.

SAMMY: Oh. That's terrible. So you know how it is then. I'm sorry about that.

LORNA: Yes. She watched too much TV. Too many commercials.

SAMMY: Oh, I know what you mean. Then you sit and rot all day — no exercise — get stains on your teeth.

LORNA: The waves from the TV and the commercials made her very sick.

SAMMY: Uh huh. The waves. *(Thinking.)* They's tricky, them waves.

LORNA: What is your mother sick with?

SAMMY: Sick with? Well, she would be sick with, uh . . . she's got a bad, a bad . . . a bad . . . heart.

LORNA: What's so bad about it?

SAMMY: It's uh, it's uh, uh, not pumping as it should be.

LORNA: It isn't?

SAMMY: No. It's a little slow. The doctor says it's just a little slow.

LORNA: *(Suspiciously.)* Slow?

SAMMY: Or it might be fast. Now that I come to think of it, it's fast. It's real fast —

LORNA: High blood pressure?

SAMMY: High blood pressure! That's it! High blood pressure medicine.

LORNA: I've heard of that condition. It's not good.

SAMMY: Nope. Not good. She needs constant care. That's straight from the doctor. I just want to bring her home to be with me. To love her and take care of her and nursery her.

LORNA: That's good-hearted of you. You are a good man.

SAMMY: Oh well, that's kind of you to say. But I am her only son and she's not well.

LORNA: Is your place decorated warmly?

SAMMY: Oh. Yeah. Real warm. Cozy like a bug. And no wallpaper. All my walls are silent.

LORNA: That's great. I'd be happy to give you *all* of my money.

SAMMY: All? Well, I, I, I don't need *all* of it, ma'am. I don't want —

LORNA: I don't need it. I have family money.

SAMMY: Oh? Yes, but I don't need — I am not a greedy man — how much are we talkin' about?

LORNA: Millions.

SAMMY: Millions?!

LORNA: I have hundreds of thousands myself.

SAMMY: Really?! Oh well, isn't that's nice? Still I wouldn't want — You wouldn't happen to have a bankcard handy?

LORNA: No. We have to go to the graveyard first.

SAMMY: Grave-what?

LORNA: My father would like to meet you first.

SAMMY: Meet me? For what? He's in a grave?

LORNA: Yes! He died. And he *still* insists on approval of all men I date. It's ridiculous.

SAMMY: Date? I — this — we are not. Things are gettin' freaky here. Let's rewind the tape.

LORNA: Then we could ask my nurse or my day-worker at Rock Creek for the bankcard. I'm off to work . . . it's supervised, but it's very important work.

SAMMY: The nurse or the day-who at Rock Creek? Rock Creek? *(She nods. He steps back.)* Ohhh. Rock Creek the place for really, really . . . They let you out in the public? I mean, you have a job? How nice. I don't know what's wrong with me. You're all dressed up. I don't want to keep you from your train.

LORNA: But what about the money for the medicine?

SAMMY: I forgot. I think I have some in my pocket here. *(He searches.)* I, look, I do.

LORNA: So why did you stop me?

SAMMY: I was gonna ask somethin'. Maybe the time. But I can see the clock on the tower now.

LORNA: You said you'd ask me a question. The only question I can't answer is a geology question because it reminds me of stones, which remind me of my childhood. I didn't have a very good childhood.

SAMMY: Yeah. I figured. Mama got sick on TV waves and Daddy in the grave telling you who to date. That's tough. That's harsh. I understand, but I got to go now.

LORNA: But any other question, any other question is fine. I want to answer.

SAMMY: I don't remember my question anyway. I was probably just asking for directions to the drugstore. And now I see the drugstore. *(Points.)* See. I'm fine. I'm good. Have money in my pocket. There's the store. I'm happy. I found the store. Nice talkin' to you.

LORNA: That store is northeast from here though.

SAMMY: Uh-huh. Yes. Thank you.

LORNA: Sometimes if I walk northeast for too long I burst into hysterical fits of laughter. *(Laughing.)* You know how it is. So you were saying . . . ?

SAMMY: I wasn't saying anything. I didn't say nothin'. I'm mindin' my own business. Askin' no questions. No questions here. None.

LORNA: You may ask me what I want in life.

SAMMY: Oh, no, I'm not. I'm not askin'. I'm not nosy.

LORNA: Oh come on. You'd like to know what I want. But how would I answer? My conversation would be a series of pauses because it's hard to know what you want. Long pauses. And then I'd finally answer. But after that answer, I would get sad and desperate and sorrowful. *(Tearfully.)* Because generally there is a great gaping canyon between what people want and what they can manage to get in life. Don't you think?

SAMMY: Ya know what I think? You want to know what I really think?

LORNA: What?

SAMMY: You're crazy. You are one crazy bird. You look all dressed up, like you're steppin' out of a Christian Du Jour Catalogue, but you are one crazy loon-toon lady, OK.
(Long pause. Lorna doesn't move. She appears frozen.)

SAMMY: I'm sorry. I didn't mean any offense, really. I just . . . I'm sorry, I had a bad morning. I didn't mean to take it out on you. It's just none of them folks say they can even spare a dime or nickel. Come on. I know you had a hard childhood, but I had a hard night. I slept on a steam grate. And that's bad for your back. You got to go to a gynopractor to fix it. You see, my car ran outta gas here when I was visiting my sick . . . Are you OK? *(He whistles to try to get her eyes to follow him. He goes to touch her but she stands frozen.)* Oh, I'm very sorry. *(Bending down to look in her eyes.)* I hope I didn't do this to you. Hello? *(Waves his hand over her eyes.)* Hello? *(He looks at her.)* Hi. It's, it's just my car broke down and my mama is . . . *(She moans quietly.)* OK, OK, I'm lyin', OK. You're right. You got me. You called me out now. God's gonna get me too. I'm a little bit of an alcoholic, it's true, but I'm workin' on that. I didn't want to harm you now. I just. Ya know, I just, I just wanted a little bit of spare change. But that was rude. And I don't need it now. Especially since I know you're, no offense there, very, very mentally crazy. So I hope you're all right. I'm gonna go over by the store now. Nice talkin' to you. Have a good day. *(He starts to leave.)*

LORNA: That wasn't a question.

SAMMY: Oh God, good. You're alive. Good!

LORNA: That was not phrased as a question. Are you aware of that? Ask the question!

SAMMY: *(Starts to move.)* I don't want to. I'm gonna go, ma'am. I don't want to bug you. *(Waves.)* Bye now. Bye.

LORNA: *(Following him, grabbing his hand.)* You're not bugging me! I love you!

SAMMY: What? You — no, no, no, you don't! Let go of my hand. You don't even know me, ma'am. Did I tell you I'm an alcoholic? No money. I have bad habits. Bad. I eat very poorly. I don't shower. And my breath don't smell too good neither.

LORNA: I want you to meet my dad.

SAMMY: Well, but see, but see here, I don't want to meet him. He's dead, lady. Dead! He's dead! For two, me, you — no, no — no together. *(Looking at how she's gripping his hand.)* I'm no good. Did I tell you I'm homeless? I got nothin'. I'm an alcoholic! I'm a li-ar too! No sick mother, no car, no high blood pressure. Except maybe mine right now.

LORNA: I don't care about any of that. I love you. I want you to have my money.

SAMMY: *(Trying to shake her off.)* But I don't want your money! Please, I don't want it! Please, leave me alone. Go on — get! *(She releases him.)*

LORNA: *(Trying to hand him her money.)* Take my money.

Take all my spare change. Take my body too. *(Trying to reach out to him as he starts to move away.)*

SAMMY: No! Stay away now. You are freaking me out. *(Pointing to her.)* I don't know this lady. I swear! I asked her for nothing!

LORNA: *(She persists.)* We'll run off together. Daddy will love you!

SAMMY: *(Starting to back away.)* Now, don't be followin' me! Cut that out. I ain't headin' nowhere but trouble. You stay back! Stay back now! Lady, you are scarin' me. I'll call the police. *(To himself.)* I'm calling the police?

LORNA: But . . . *(Looks longingly in Sammy's direction.)* I love you.

SAMMY: *(Calling out, running.)* Mr. Officer?!! Mr. Officer?!! Heeeeeelp!!

OPPOSITE SPIRITS

Frank, seventeen, is one of the finest young adults at St. Mary's High School in Rhode Island. Besides being a straight-A student, he's won the school science contest, presided over the treasury portion of the faculty-student council and is the student most responsible for his Mind Bender Team making it into nationals three years running. It's Frank's senior year, and the faculty is seriously considering him for valedictorian of his class. The only problem is Frank has been getting in trouble all of a sudden — skipping classes, throwing regular trash in the recycle bins, even smoking. He has no real friends. He's fallen into a funk because he's realizing he's never gone to a big dance, a party, or even a football game. Jessie is Frank's antithesis. She's a straight-C student, though she tests way above her grades. The only class she excels in is English, and that's because she's an avid reader. She has a regular seat saved in detention because she tends to rile teachers. Unlike Frank, Jessie, seventeen, never misses a social event. She goes to all major dances, parties, and football games, typically accompanied by her boyfriend, Kip, of the famed high school band, the Shampoo Boys. It is the end of the day, and Jessie and Frank are caught in detention together alone. Sister Pat has gone down the hall to attend to some things in her office. She informed them that she would return shortly.

CHARACTERS
Larry: 17, straight-A student, loner
Gretchen: 17, straight-C student, social

SETTING
St. Mary's High School; a classroom used for
    detention

TIME
The present

*(Jessie watches Frank as he quietly considers a trigonom-
etry problem. Jessie clears her throat. Frank is obviously
deep in thought. Jessie clears her throat again with a bit
more rhythm and musicality to it. Again, Frank doesn't
react. She turns toward Frank and clears her throat in
a manner that sounds much like she is trying to dislodge
a full-sized rodent. Frank still doesn't turn.)*

JESSIE: Hey. *(Beat.)* Hey!
   *(Frank turns around to look at her. He points to himself as
   if to ask, "Me?")*
JESSIE: Who do you think I'm calling to, Einstein?
FRANK: God bless you.
JESSIE: Huh?
FRANK: Didn't you sneeze?
JESSIE: No.
FRANK: Oh. I thought you had sneezed, and I didn't say any-
   thing. I was into this trig problem. I didn't want to be rude.
JESSIE: No, no sneeze. I cleared my throat though. *(Moving in
   toward him.)* It felt like something was stuck. *(Frank nods
   in understanding.)* It turns out it was. I had a full-sized ro-
   dent to dislodge from the back of my throat. Isn't that some-
   thing? The department of health has really gotten lax, huh?
   Must have been the cafeteria lunch special.
FRANK: *(Not sure what to make of this.)* Umm. Oh.
JESSIE: I'm kidding, Frank.
FRANK: Oh.
JESSIE: *(Beat.)* That's so weird.
FRANK: Weird?
JESSIE: Saying "God bless you" for a sneeze. Why do we do
   that?
FRANK: Well . . . your heart stops beating and your breathing
   pauses momentarily. Actually, every major organ and artery
   shuts down for the exact moment of the sneeze and you are
   closest to being dead as you'll ever be.
JESSIE: Well hell, that's the least we could do then. I thought

I read somewhere that we say that because, like in the eighteenth century or somethin', sneezing was ridding yourself of really rude spirits that somehow possessed you.

FRANK: Evil spirits. Do you think we ought to be talking?

JESSIE: Yes. I don't know why everyone assumes that all spirits are evil. I mean, what happens if you rid yourself of a spirit who was a lot more exciting than yourself? What a screwup. All the friends, who really liked the spirit, are going to split. They'll think you're like this major dud. But the spirit guy. He was rockin'. It's kind of like being in high school, huh?

FRANK: We aren't supposed to be talking in detention.

JESSIE: Relax, Frankie, we're the only ones here.

FRANK: I know, but Sister Pat said she'd be back —

JESSIE: Oh, Pat-schmat. *(Beat. He nods.)* Besides, I know Sister Pat. I've spent the better part of four years in detention. When she says she's going to her office to grade papers, what she really means is she's going to her office to liquefy.
(Frank looks confused.)

JESSIE: Toss 'em. *(Still confused.)* Push her pedals. Kick back a few?

FRANK: You mean drink? Alcohol?

JESSIE: No, Kool-Aid.

FRANK: Come on. No way!

JESSIE: Why do you think she shakes so much? She just tells you it's her heart medication.

FRANK: How do you know? I've worked with her for three years off and on with student treasury, and she's never . . . I mean, she's always been clear thinking and . . .

JESSIE: Let me ask you. Does she ever stand within three or four feet of you when she talks to you? She's always addressing the group, right?

FRANK: I don't know.

JESSIE: She drinks. Trust me. She doesn't get in close 'cause you'd smell it. I caught her once. And anyway, why would I lie?

FRANK: Because it's more fascinating than the truth.

JESSIE: Oooh. Aren't we clever? Anyway, forget Pat. I was making a point. About spirits. High school spirits. You put on this face, this front, this spirit to be like . . . I don't know — cool and then you graduate and you're suddenly in life. You gotta make dinner or order out, but the point is that you have to have money. In order to make good money, you have to study something probably practical, yet futuristic — biotech engineering or computer dweebiness. Meanwhile, you start thinking about things. The job you'll have, the man you'll marry — if you marry, kids, which dental plan. Like with me — I have really bad teeth so you got to. Sure, you go to a few parties in college. Maybe drink a lot, but in your second year, you realize that your two best friends flunked out and if you don't get a handle on this, you'll be dead or worse, you'll be one of those zombies you see in New York that has drool that extends from your lip to the sidewalk — flowing down —

FRANK: *(Grossed out.)* Uuuh.

JESSIE: Yeah. So you get real serious. And there's no time to be cool anymore. Unless you're some egomaniac pop star. The spirit's drummed out of you. Never to return. And all your friends disappear. You know?

FRANK: Aren't you in my psychology class?

JESSIE: All that about the futility of our future life and that's all you can say?

FRANK: Are you flunking out? You only come half the time.

JESSIE: You see, that's the point I was making, Frank. High school is the last time you have to really enjoy yourself. Afterwards, all choices made will be responsible ones.

FRANK: Don't say that. That sounds terrible.

JESSIE: Why not? It's true.

FRANK: I don't like it.

JESSIE: Why? You don't think you've enjoyed it sufficiently?

FRANK: I bet you skipped all kinds of classes and are *still* managing to graduate.

JESSIE: I have a "very disappointing" two point oh. Didn't apply myself. So you didn't enjoy it, did you?

FRANK: Why are you talking to me?

JESSIE: I'm fascinated by you, Frank. We're opposites, like opposite spirits, or pretend to be.

FRANK: You keep saying my name like you know me or something.

JESSIE: Frank, you are the most likely candidate for valedictorian. You won that brainy thing a couple years in a row. I know who you are. Everybody does.

FRANK: Well, I know who you are too, but that's not my point. My point is the exaggerated degree of familiarity. You think because we're in detention together, you and I are suddenly friends.

JESSIE: Why not?

FRANK: Why not? Because you've never given me the time of day before this. I sat in front of you sophomore year in English, and you looked right through me. I was in your track-and-field gym class last year and you never even acknowledged my presence. I fell flat on the field, and you acted as if my crumpled, bloody body was an additional hurdle to leap over. You never even paused. Now, just because I decide to suck down some nicotine in the lavatory, we're best friends?

JESSIE: So who am I? *(Frank is confused.)* You said you knew who I was before. Who am I?

FRANK: What? . . . Jessica — or Jessie Martin.

JESSIE: Yes, but what does that mean? What does it represent to you? You represent the "perfect student" to me. What do I represent?

FRANK: I don't know. Party girl. Popular. Fun. You're Kip Hendrick's girlfriend.

JESSIE: Thanks. I was afraid you'd say that. So you were smoking? That's not good. Didn't you almost have a coronary on the field?

FRANK: Asthma attack.

JESSIE: Same difference. That scared me. I get nervous over blood and stuff. That's why I didn't stop to help you. You really shouldn't smoke.

FRANK: *(Sarcastically.)* Really? No. I hadn't heard that. I'm glad you mentioned it.

JESSIE: OK, no need for that. I do remember you from those classes. I just didn't talk to you before because the opportunity didn't arise. It wasn't a snub — nothing personal. My life was about being cool. Besides, you were kinda different back then — last year and all that.

FRANK: How so?

JESSIE: I don't know. More nerdy.

FRANK: Thanks. Thanks a lot. That's just what I needed to hear.

JESSIE: No offense. I mean, nerdy *now* is usually well-paid *later*. At least you aren't fake like a lotta popular types.

FRANK: Yeah, like you? Like the way you'll be to me tomorrow?

JESSIE: Look, I'm not going to change how I am tomorrow. That was then. I was Miss Thang. I was the Shampoo Boy's inspiration. The really cool girlfriend. Kip's girlfriend — the fun, party girl, girlfriend. It's really pathetic. At least your identity is your own.

FRANK: Was? Was his Miss Thang?

JESSIE: Yeah. Didn't you know? Big news here. Kip dumped my butt. Dumped me and signed a contract to become a pop star.

FRANK: No way. Really?

JESSIE: Really. He gets this like big contract from this agent. Quits the band. The agent wants him in New York pronto — going to make him a pop idol. That's cool. We had always planned on going to New York. I was going to waitress. He was gonna do the band thing. We'd live in the Village. Get a loft or something. I was going to take dance classes so I could maybe do musicals someday or join some weird dance troop or whatever. But then he just said, out of the blue . . . Oh well, just screw him!

FRANK: What did he say?

JESSIE: I don't know, something like I don't love you. I don't love you and I don't want you, and it's over. I guess I was really stupid.

FRANK: No, no, I thought you guys were solid. He seemed like he was crazy about you.

JESSIE: Crazy to mess around with me regularly. Until he got bored of me. And I'm such an idiot I thought it would never end, so I was a major screwup for four years. I could have gotten good grades, especially in English. Mom always told me that.

FRANK: At least you had a lotta fun. Good grades aren't everything.

JESSIE: Yeah, they are to colleges. I'll be lucky to make a junior college now. That stupid egomaniac. You know he got the words to their big hit, "Dead Fish Do Float" from me!

FRANK: I thought so.

JESSIE: You did?

FRANK: Yeah, it always reminded me of that poem you wrote in English class — "Dangerous Parks." It had the same cadence to it. And it was thematically both ironic and sweet.

JESSIE: Wow! I can't believe you remembered my poem. Amazing. (Beat.) Why are you in trouble all of a sudden? You aren't freaking, are you? I mean, smoking? Smoking is really not your style.

FRANK: No, but I wanted to try it once or twice. And I wanted to be caught too.

JESSIE: Why?

FRANK: For the experience. Last week my mother started asking me who I was taking to prom. Not only did I not have an answer, I didn't even have a friend I could complain about it to. I've never even kissed a girl. Now, *that's* pathetic. I flipped through the yearbook to see if maybe there was some girl I hadn't thought of — quiet and shy like me. All those pictures — parties, dances, toilet papering the courtyard on Halloween . . . I don't know. I just suddenly felt depressed. Four years and no friends. No dances, no parties, no dates, no friends. What's wrong with me? This last week I just stopped following rules. I threw regular trash in the recycle bin, wore ripped T-shirts, mooned a group of freshman girls.

JESSIE: No way!

FRANK: Yeah. It was fun. It's like if I believed in evil spirits like they used to, I'd say some spirit got into me. Something that wanted to see what it was like to be a real teenager — to be risky and crazy and rebellious. I guess I hoped it would *turn* me into a real teenager — "a real boy," like everyone else, and then a friend or friends would appear.

JESSIE: I feel the same way. Sorta. But opposite . . . like something way too good came into me now. I made it to my Lit class every day this week. Isn't that disgusting? And my friends, though I seem to have many, are not all that good of friends. Most of them disappeared when Kip dumped me.

FRANK: Really? That sucks. *(She nods.)* Maybe we could be friends?

JESSIE: Yeah. *(Beat.)* Oh my God! You're Brian Johnson and I'm Ally Sheedy.

FRANK: What are you talking about?

JESSIE: Brian Johnson . . . Anthony Michael Hall. Boy, his career took a dive, didn't it? The brainy perfect student guy. *(Frank is still confused.)* The brainy guy from that old movie *The Breakfast Club*.

FRANK: Oh yeah, I remember that. Ally Sheedy's the really weird one with the sandwich. Now she's had a pretty good career.

JESSIE: Well, basket cases always do.

FRANK: But I think you're too popular to be just a basket case. You're sort of a mix — the Molly Ringwald popular girl, the basket case and, and —

JESSIE: Judd Nelson, the criminal. I can't be boxed in. Oh God. You don't have a gun in your locker, do you?

FRANK: No! Why?

JESSIE: That's what Brian's problem was. He flunked an exam and wanted to kill himself.

FRANK: That's a bit extreme.

JESSIE: True. So you've never wanted to kill yourself?

(Pause.)

FRANK: You?

JESSIE: Two weeks ago. I just never thought of myself as some girl who wrapped her life around a guy. My mother did that when I was a kid, and she absolutely fell apart when my dad left. Of course, it never occurred to me that Kip wouldn't love me anymore. I grabbed some sleeping pills the Saturday after he ended it, but then . . . I thought about my mom — how much she loves me. I thought about how Kip would just use it for material, and then I just said "Screw it! No way!" I have something to give to this world. I don't know what it is yet, but I'll find it someday. *(Pause.)* So what about you? You didn't answer.

FRANK: My uncle did it. I hated him for it. My mother cried for weeks blaming herself. I was real close to him. He'd take me to the Cape every summer. He seemed to have everything. A lot of people say we're alike. I hate that. I do. He was real smart. Worked for IBM. Had a cool place in Boston, but he didn't have many friends. He was a loner. He'd put in personal ads all the time, but girls weren't impressed. He treated them too nice. They never liked him. Why is that, Jessie? Why do girls always hate nice guys?

JESSIE: They don't. They just don't tend to like guys who don't like themselves enough. But if you respect yourself enough not to be a pushover, that's good. You can be nice. Girls will eventually respond to that.

FRANK: Yeah, I suppose. Maybe someday. Maybe someday when I'm even less of a nerd. I just don't want to end up like him. You know?

JESSIE: You won't. You already respect yourself enough to take a few chances. Trying out a new dangerous life for a week or two. It's cool.

FRANK: I guess.

JESSIE: You want to go to the prom with me?

FRANK: Yeah, right.

JESSIE: No, I mean it. I didn't know who I'd go with. Turned down a couple requests. I just didn't like 'em all that much. I've never talked to someone so easily, Frank . . . without being fake and all that. It would be great. And it's fitting to our spirit changes. Makes you seem a bit more wild and me a bit more straightlaced. I like it. Do you?

FRANK: Well . . . Yeah. I just . . . well, yeah . . . Heck yeah!

JESSIE: OK. Good. That works. *(She moves in.)*

FRANK: What are you doing?

JESSIE: I'm going to kiss you. What does it look like?

FRANK: Here?

JESSIE: Yes.

FRANK: But Sister Pat.

JESSIE: You can kiss her afterwards.
(She kisses him.)

JESSIE: What's that look for? You look so serious. I'm happy, Frank. Are you?

FRANK: *(Nods.)* Yeah. Yeah. I'm happy.

JESSIE: Good. 'Cause don't look now, but Sister Pat is standing in the doorway ready to ream us.

FRANK: Oh shhhh —
(Jessie covers his mouth to stop the expletive.)

SHHHHH!

Alice and Nate, thirties, a married couple who just moved to Miami, go to bed early after a long day unpacking their house. Nate needs the sleep because he will be starting his first day of residency at the University of Miami hospital tomorrow. Alice plans to wake up early to start filling out paperwork for her job as a government social worker. They both are overly nervous about making friends, the new environment, and doing well in their positions in Miami. Alice has been particularly concerned since a friend mentioned how dangerous Miami was. She turns over. A strange look comes over her face. She tries to close her eyes, but they pop open. She sits up and begins to tap Nate's shoulder.

CHARACTERS
Alice: 30s, Nate's wife
Nate: 30s, Alice's husband

SETTING
Their brand-new house in Miami

TIME
The present

ALICE: *(Tapping quietly at first, she whispers.)* Nate. Nate. *(Louder.)* Nate!
NATE: *(Springing up, panicked.)* What, what?!
ALICE: Shhh.
NATE: Shhh? Why shhh? I have to get up in less than six hours.
ALICE: Did you hear something?
NATE: Yeah, you yelling "Nate!"
ALICE: Shhh.
NATE: Don't shhh me unless you tell me why we're shhshing!
ALICE: *(Whispers.)* I heard something.
NATE: *(Whispering now.)* You did? What did your hear?

ALICE: *(Whispers.)* I don't know. *(Pause. They both look around.)* I. Don't. Know.

NATE: I don't hear anything. If you don't know, you probably didn't really.

ALICE: Shhh!

NATE: Don't do that.

ALICE: Well, I don't hear it now. Anyway, I meant before. Did you hear something before that?

NATE: You mean when I was in a deep and sound and pleasant sleep? No.

ALICE: My God, we just lay down. How do you crash so fast?

NATE: It's very easy. You lie down. You close your eyes. And then you don't speak. At all!

ALICE: I don't speak all the time. Sometimes I don't speak when we lie down now. I know you think I do it all the time. I do do it sometimes. Sometimes I talk to relax myself. I think I must be —

NATE: *(Annoyed.)* Alice?!

ALICE: Be riled up from the move.

NATE: Breathe.

ALICE: *(She takes a deep breath.)* Don't you think I'm riled up from the move?

NATE: The two pots of coffee didn't help.

ALICE: Well, I had to unpack the kitchen. I'm just worried about liking Miami.

NATE: Oh no! We cannot have this discussion now, Alice. It's midnight. I'm nervous about everything too. It's a move. Of course we're nervous. But it's my first day tomorrow. Making a good impression in a residency is really important. I need to be well rested. I need to have brainpower. I need to exude confidence and well-restedness.

ALICE: In other words, "I need you to shut up."

NATE: Exactly.

ALICE: OK. I understand.

NATE: I love you, honey, and I'm sorry I have to tell you to shut up.

ALICE: I love you too, sweetie. *(She smiles.)* And you're right. If I hear any more strange noises, I'll just pretend I don't.

NATE: Thanks honey.

ALICE: Or just cover my ears. *(Beat.)* I'll think — *(Covering ears.)* La, la, la, la, la. I know it's an iffy neighborhood, but how iffy can it be, right? I'm sure it's nothing. It's so weird because everything we own is scattered all over our living room and the window is wide open —

NATE: *(Getting up.)* Uhp, I'm going to go down!

ALICE: No! *(Grabbing him.)* Wait! I don't want you to go down there.

NATE: Oh come on!

ALICE: I just wanted to see if we heard anything together.

NATE: I know you, Alice, and you are not going to let me get any sleep unless I go down there.

ALICE: I'm sorry. I'm sorry. *(She grabs his hand.)* Lie back down. You're right. I'm being ridiculous. The only reason I'm paranoid at all is because of Sue.

NATE: Sue?

ALICE: She pointed out that a disproportionate amount of cops-and-robbers shows take place in Miami, signaling that it's a high-crime area.

NATE: What are you talking about?!

ALICE: *CSI Miami, Miami Vice* —

NATE: That's ridiculous — *Miami Vice?!* That's been off the air for years. Besides, did it ever occur to you that the reason they chose Miami over a place like Detroit, which you survived for twenty-two years, is because stars can wear sexy clothes and look good in a very beautiful setting? That it has nothing to do with crime at all? It's Hollywood.

ALICE: Well, actually it's Miami. But a lot of weirdness goes down in Florida. You have to admit. Anthrax was here. Lots of riots. Terrorists *like* Florida.

NATE: So do geriatric people. Are you scared of them too?!

ALICE: Occasionally. OK. I see your point. Let's just go to sleep, honey.

NATE: *(Holding out his hands.)* Why don't you wear your earplugs?

ALICE: But then if something does happen, I won't hear it.

NATE: Exactly.

(She reluctantly takes them and puts them in her ears. They both lie down and close their eyes. Nate opens his eyes suddenly. He looks around the room. He closes his eyes again, but they pop open surprised by something. He sits up.)

NATE: Huh!

ALICE: *(Loudly because she can't hear herself with the earplugs in.)* What's the matter?

NATE: Shhh.

ALICE: *(Pulling the earplugs.)* Oooh, I told you! I told you. You heard something, didn't you?

NATE: Shhh! *(They look around. Whispering.)* It's mumbling. Like people talking.

ALICE: *(Whispers, terrified.)* There's two of them?!

NATE: Ya know, I think it's just coming from outside.

ALICE: What are you talking about?! You don't know. You have no sense of sound direction. Remember when we were at that house and we heard that dog and you told me he was chained up and that he wasn't in attack mode and the lady with that hair agreed, but then the mean dog ran after me? Remember that?

NATE: That wasn't a sound direction problem! It was a sight problem. And it wasn't a dog. It was a poodle.

ALICE: Well! All your senses are pretty lousy. Remember the smelly green thing in the attic?

NATE: OK, OK, you're right. But shhh. I want to hear it for a sec. *(They are silent.)*

ALICE: I think it stopped.

NATE: Wait, shhh . . . *(Beat.)* There. There it is again. Mumbling. Do you hear?

ALICE: *(She nods.)* Definitely in the downstairs direction. Oh my God! My *Wham* —

NATE: Shhh!!

ALICE: *(Whispering.)* My Wham CD collection is down there!

NATE: Oh please God let them take it.

ALICE: *(Hits him.)* Hey! How mean!

NATE: What I meant is I have a brand new Sony digital stereo with a mega sound system, which you use regularly to play your collection on, if you remember. I think my stereo system is worth a little more than your girlie eighties techno band crap.

ALICE: So! Mr. Fancy-Pants Doctor. Is this how it's going to be from now on? I'm the lowly social worker wife with the silly eighties CD collection?

NATE: No! No, I'm just saying the stereo is more expensive than anything we have.

ALICE: And expensive is everything? Nothing has sentimental value?

NATE: OK, you're right. You're right. I'm sorry. I'm going down there.

ALICE: *(Pulling him out of the way.)* No, you don't! I'm going down!

NATE: *(Grabbing.)* You certainly are not!

ALICE: Why not?

NATE: Because it's dangerous. I love you. And I am going down.

ALICE: No, you aren't. *(Pulling him out of the way.)* I love you too!

NATE: Ow!

ALICE: What?

NATE: You pinched my arm when you did that.

ALICE: Sorry. I survived in Detroit for twenty-two years. You said it yourself. I'm the tough one.

NATE: Yeah, but I'm the guy.

ALICE: From a suburb! Fair Oaks. That even sounds pansy. I was born to walk tough. I was stuck in a closet at seven when a burglar broke into the neighbor's house.

NATE: So what does that prove?!

ALICE: I don't know! What do a bunch of teenage geriatric-muggers got over me, huh?

NATE: Guns.

ALICE: *(Beat.)* Good point.

NATE: And who says they're teenagers? I think we ought to call the police.

ALICE: And say what? We hear mumbling in the direction of our living room. We think.

NATE: Why not?!

ALICE: 'Cause we just moved here.

NATE: So!

ALICE: Well, I don't want them to think we don't like the neighborhood.

NATE: Who cares?!

ALICE: When I lived in Detroit, and people in the suburbs came to the city, they were always calling the cops. It was really insulting.

NATE: I don't care if it's insulting! If you get mugged on the street, you don't hand over your wallet and say, "Don't worry, I won't mention anything about this. I don't want to ruin your neighborhood's reputation."

ALICE: Well . . . no.

NATE: I'm going to go down there.

ALICE: Oh no you don't!

NATE: Why?!

ALICE: A few minutes ago, you didn't even hear anything, Mr. Fancy Pants! Give me one good reason I shouldn't go down first?!

NATE: I have a more expensive insurance policy on me.

ALICE: Like that would mean anything to me! *(Beat.)* How much are we talkin' about?

NATE: It's big money. Will you let me go down by myself now?

ALICE: *(Beat.)* No! I'm going with you. I don't care how much you leave behind. I don't care about your stupid money. I'm crazy about you, you big lug!

NATE: Aww. I love you too, honey. This does actually make me scared. Like what if something . . .

ALICE: No, don't think that. I love you too! Huge bunches of love! *(She hugs him.)* Umm! *(He goes to kiss her.)* Don't start now! We've got to strategize. Now, once you get to the bottom of the stairs, grab the chair in the hallway. I'll grab one of your golf clubs by the hall closet.

NATE: Grab the iron, not the putter. *(She looks at him.)* It's better for this kind of thing.

ALICE: If you see something or hear something, move quickly. You'll be closest to the phone, so grab it.

NATE: Where is the phone now?

ALICE: Right next to the radio in the nook.

NATE: Oh. OK . . . Radio?

ALICE: *(Realizing something.)* Ray-dee-oh.

NATE and ALICE: The radio!!

NATE: Did you turn off the radio before we went to bed?

ALICE: I thought you were going to do it?!

NATE: I was . . . but . . . I was listening to the weather and . . .

ALICE: You forgot.

NATE: Nothing's stolen. Your Wham collection's safe. We're alive.

ALICE: Thank God. *(Beat.)* OK. Well, try and get some sleep sweetheart. *(She gives him a quick kiss.)* Good night.

NATE: Good night.

ALICE: *(Beat.)* How come there's no big insurance policy when *I* die? I'm not worth it to you?!

NATE: Alice!

ALICE: What?

NATE: Stuff in your earplugs!

THE EVIL FLUFF BALL

Angelica, the cat, is very upset about the new addition to the family. She would like to destroy the new little kitten that the family has brought into their happy household. When the family is out of the house, Angelica tries to convince the family dog, Roofus, to go in on a plot. As the scene begins, Roofus is staring out the kitchen window. Angelica is cleaning herself.

CHARACTERS
Angelica: the cat
Roofus: the dog

SETTING
Angelica and Roofus's house

TIME
The present

ANGELICA: Have they left, Roofus? What do you see?

ROOFUS: Nothin'.

ANGELICA: Well, did they leave in the vehicle or what, Roofus?

ROOFUS: I guess. I'm hungry.

ANGELICA: You guess? Well, did they or didn't they? I guess if you want something done, you have to jump on the windowsill yourself.

ROOFUS: Hey um, are you talking to me?

ANGELICA: Yes, put the bowl aside and concentrate. I thought we were going to plot the kill. Isn't that what we said yesterday?

ROOFUS: You don't talk to me. You never talk to me. Are you *really* talking to me?

ANGELICA: Yes! I'm talking to you. I'm saying words directed at you. My whiskers are moving. I'm calling out your name — Roofus. Is there any other Roofus in the house?

ROOFUS: *(Thinking slowly.)* Well now, let me think —

ANGELICA: There's nothing to think about! There's no other Roofus here. There's only you, me, and the new one — *(Saying name with disdain.)* Fuzzie.

ROOFUS: I thought her name was Fluffy?

ANGELICA: Who cares?!

ROOFUS: You seem a little hyper, Gel?

ANGELICA: Don't call me Gel. How many times have I had to tell you that? I will bear that indignity from them, but not you. It's Angelica to you. *(Coughs.)*

ROOFUS: You got a hairball or somethin'?

ANGELICA: No! I'm tense. OK? I'm tense. *Why,* you ask? Because life as we know it has been irreversibly damaged. We are in a crisis, Mr. Bowwow. Our very livelihood and food supply is in utter danger of disappearing.

ROOFUS: Since when?!

ANGELICA: Don't you remember discussing this yesterday?

ROOFUS: Um . . . *(Thinking.)* no.

ANGELICA: At dinner! When you were downing the table snacks and I was tapping out Morse code under the table with you. Remember?

ROOFUS: That was Morse code?

ANGELICA: What do you — you responded back!

ROOFUS: I don't know Morse code. I was just patting the floor with my tail because they dropped a hot dog bun.

ANGELICA: *(Beat.)* I wondered why you were so frightfully articulate.

ROOFUS: So why are we running out of food, Angelica?

ANGELICA: I repeat, life as we know it has been irreversibly damaged. Now, what are we going to do about it?

ROOFUS: Well, uh, if it's irreversible, doesn't that mean we can't do anything about it?

ANGELICA: *(Beat.)* Well . . . yes, technically, but that's just an expression! I mean, we have options. It's only irreversibly ruined by recent *additions* to our household — our family, so to speak. *(Smiling.)* Nod. Nod. Smile. The tiny fur muff is looking in our direction. We can reverse the situation by ridding ourselves of certain new feline *additions*. Do you follow?

ROOFUS: Are you talkin' about that new ottoman?

ANGELICA: No! You boob! I'm talkin' about *(Whispering.)* You. Know. Who. *(Does an imitation of the little kitty.)*

ROOFUS: *(Seems to be sinking in.)* Ohhh. *(Voice changes to sweetness.)* The cute little kitty?

ANGELICA: Shhh! There's nothing cute about her.

ROOFUS: Oh she's cute when she bats that thing around.

ANGELICA: That thing just happens to be my ear. And I assure you it's not cute. She's evil. She's very evil.

ROOFUS: She seems kinda fun. She let me play soccer with her today.

ANGELICA: Sure, soccer today, evil tomorrow. Lord knows she can't be a very good partner. She can't even reach the ball.

ROOFUS: Oh, well she *was* the ball.

ANGELICA: Oh. See now that's how it begins. First she's the ball. Later the bat.

ROOFUS: You don't use a bat with soccer.

ANGELICA: It's just an analogy! Ya know, she's been messing with your squeaky toys when you aren't looking.

ROOFUS: She has?

ANGELICA: Um-hum. She's been clawing your doggy bed too.

ROOFUS: No!

ANGELICA: Yes! The foam stuffing is all over the basement. You can go down and observe the evidence. And I'll tell you this. She has been eyeing your doggy treats all week long.

ROOFUS: Well, she, she can't have them. They're, they're . . . for dogs.

ANGELICA: Exactly. And this is just the tip of the iceberg, Roofus. It doesn't end here. Our lives are in jeopardy. And I can't believe how incredibly passive you have been about this whole thing. About this distasteful ball of fuzz entering our perfect home.

ROOFUS: Well, I've been eating these new valerian snack treats they've been giving me. They're really good, but boy do they make me sleepy. Maybe that's why I'm so passive.

ANGELICA: Exactly! They're drugging you!

ROOFUS: What?!

ANGELICA: Yes. That little doggy-snacky treat? With the valerian ingredient? It's a drug.

ROOFUS: No!

ANGELICA: Yes! They are drugging you so they can freely and easily introduce this little kitty into our home without us fighting back. And then, once the kitty settles in, that's it. That's all. No more walk in the park, buddy boy. You'll have to pee in the backyard and come straight in. No extra pat on the back. No throw-the-stick game. No jumping in the mud puddle for you, Roofyboy. No, no. We don't have time for you. We've got a little kitty now. A cute little scruffy, fluffy, back-stabbing kitty to replace you!

ROOFUS: *(Beat.)* Wow. Really? No. Really?! *(She nods.)* That's awful. I wondered why I was feelin' so good on these treats. But I read the back of the box. It said it was completely homeopathic. You know I've been tryin' to cut down on the stimulants.

ANGELICA: Yeah. Homeopathic, psychopathic. The point is that you are drugged. You feel good, right? And sleepy, right? Relaxed, right?

ROOFUS: Yeah. Yeah!

ANGELICA: They have you right where they want you. And they tried to do it to me too. A little "Cat Rescue Remedy" in my water. They thought I wouldn't notice. I was tempted once I realized. I admit that. I have had my temptation get the best of me from time to time — in the past. I have fallen for the occasional hard stuff.

ROOFUS: I remember. *(Laughs.)* Remember that time you overdid it on the catnip?

ANGELICA: Let's not bring up old indiscretions.

ROOFUS: You were rubbing up against that radiator like it was a —

ANGELICA: I said don't! I have my own ammunition, sir. Remember the Dalmatian in heat? She was too tall.

ROOFUS: OK, OK.

ANGELICA: So. The plan from now on is that you must say no to any more valerian treats.

ROOFUS: *(Disappointed.)* Oh. Any?

ANGELICA: Yes. I know it's difficult for you mutts to keep away from that stuff, but you've got to keep a clear —

ROOFUS: Mutts? Who said I was a mutt? I'm not a mutt. You're a mutt!

ANGELICA: No, darling. *(Clears throat. Laying on the thick English accent.)* I'm an English shorthair for your information.

ROOFUS: English my butt. You've been here since you were a little dust rag.

ANGELICA: That's my breed. That's what my papers say. If you want, we can pull them from the file cabinet for your examination.

ROOFUS: Well, my papers say I'm a Great Dane.

ANGELICA: *(Laughs.)* Oh come on. You're a mutt. With a little St. Bernard maybe.

ROOFUS: Well St. Bernard's are great! Not as great as a Great Dane, but still great.

ANGELICA: Yes, if you want a mound of drool hanging off your dog all day.

ROOFUS: Ack! That's gross. I thought they saved frozen people from Arctic mountains?

ANGELICA: This is Arizona. How many frozen people have you seen?

ROOFUS: Well . . . I heard that little kitty was a Persian or maybe a Maine coon.

ANGELICA: Oh come on. That can't be.

ROOFUS: They had papers when they brought her home. And now that I remember I don't think English shorthairs are all that uncommon.

ANGELICA: Are you saying I'm common? I'm not common.

ROOFUS: Well, you're not uncommon.

ANGELICA: Well . . . Look, there's no point in our arguing amongst ourselves. As much disdain as I have for the idea, we must align together against this little Maine coon monstrosity. My plan is this. Huddle down. *(He does.)* We wreak havoc on the place and make them think it's the little fuzz ball that did it.

ROOFUS: Ooh. Are you sure? She's so little to be so harsh with.

ANGELICA: Devil in sheep's clothing. Forget that. It'll confuse you. Let me just get to our plan. You know the red antique chaise lounge in the living room?

ROOFUS: The one with the silky red cushions that we can never, never touch so we scratch the hell out of the bottom of it so they won't notice —

ANGELICA: That's it! We'll pee all over it.

ROOFUS: Whoa! Whoa! That's serious. That's very serious stuff.

ANGELICA: It's all in your best interest. Then we'll scratch up the silk curtains, too. Remember this evil kitty is going to replace you.

ROOFUS: Replace me? But she's a kitten.

ANGELICA: Yes. So?

ROOFUS: Well, it just seems to me that if she's going to replace any of us, she would replace you.

ANGELICA: Well . . . sure, that sounds logical, but I —

ROOFUS: Come to think of it, that little kitty is kind of fun. At least she doesn't jump on me, claws extended, with no warning from time to time.

ANGELICA: Who does that, Roofy? *(He looks at her.)* Please. I can see what's going on here. You have some kind of crush on this little kitty, don't you? *(Beat.)* I saw you sniff her butt.

ROOFUS: Well, sure, that's what you do. I saw you sniff it too.

ANGELICA: No, I did not!

ROOFUS: Yes you did, Miss Lick-Yourself-All-Over-No-Matter-Where-You-Been. I saw you. And now that I think about it, you're the one who scratched me two days ago, not her.

ANGELICA: That was an accident, Roofy. I didn't mean for it to hurt.

ROOFUS: But it did! Who's to say if we pee on the couch that they won't think it's you — the old crotchety, can't-hold-your-pee cat? The one who is losing control? Besides, the older cat — you — definitely loses control of things when the big dumb mutt goes after her, doesn't she?

ANGELICA: You wouldn't!

ROOFUS: Why not?! I'd get in trouble at first, sure, but then they'd feel like I might need to be calmed down a bit. Do you know how many valerian treats this could get me? Ruff, ruff!

ANGELICA: Don't you dare!

ROOFUS: Ruff! *(Seeing something, distracted.)* Awww. There's the cute little kitty there.

ANGELICA: *(Taking advantage of his distraction, lunges.)* Mra-orrrrrrrrrrrrr!

HYPNEUROSIS

Janis, late twenties, has decided to go to see a hypno-
tist to get help with a problem. She is a bit suspicious
of the process, though she believes it can work. Edson,
thirties, the hypnotist whom Janis has chosen, has just
greeted her and ushered her into his office.

CHARACTERS
Janis: late 20s
Edson: 30s, hypnotist

SETTING
Edson's hypnosis office

TIME
The present

EDSON: Please, have a seat, Miss Colburn.
JANIS: *(Sitting.)* Janis. Call me Janis.
EDSON: OK, Janis.
  (Sitting. She looks suspiciously around the room.)
EDSON: Is something wrong?
JANIS: Just checking. You don't record these sessions, do you?
EDSON: Ohhh. Oh, no. What happens in this room is com-
  pletely confidential. You have nothing to worry about.
JANIS: That's what I'm worried about.
EDSON: Excuse me?
JANIS: I want other people to know what happens in this room.
  I don't mean the whole world, but perhaps a friend or two.
EDSON: *(Not quite sure what to make of this.)* Why don't we
  back up to what has brought you here today, Janis? Start
  at the beginning.
JANIS: You're not just trying to change the subject?
EDSON: Absolutely not. I'll even make a note. *(Writing.)*
  Recording sessions, friends, not the whole world. There.

Now what is it, exactly, that has brought you here to see me?

JANIS: Well, I've read that many people have had success losing weight or quitting smoking or curing insomnia through hypnosis.

EDSON: Yes, we do have a high success rate in helping people overcome the problems they have been struggling with or their fears.

JANIS: Good.

EDSON: What exactly are you looking for help with?

JANIS: My life.

EDSON: *(Beat.)* OK. Could you be a little more specific?

JANIS: Well, I would like some help losing weight.

EDSON: Good. I don't mean that it's good that you're having problems. I mean, good, we're clarifying things. Well, the way I usually work with clients with this type of problem is to —

JANIS: I'm not finished.

EDSON: Oh. Excuse me. I didn't mean to cut you off there. Go on.

JANIS: With your hypnosis you can make my mind believe that I really want to lose weight, right?

EDSON: Well . . . You do want to lose weight, don't you?

JANIS: Yes, but wanting hasn't quite done the job by itself now, has it?

EDSON: Well, think of it this way. I can help you to lessen your cravings for fatty foods and —

JANIS: Great! That's what I was hoping.

EDSON: Well, good.

JANIS: You see, I was thinking . . . if you can help me lessen my cravings for fatty foods, then you could also do some other helpful things while you're at it.

EDSON: Other helpful things?

JANIS: Yes! I'd like you to hypnotize me into thinking that I hate chocolate with a passion. And all other candy and sweets. And that my favorite food in the world is veggies — especially dark green veggies. And my second favorite food is fruit. All kinds. Oh, yes, and that I despise anything doughy, like bagels or bread or muffins or cake. And ice cream. Oh, yeah, ice cream has got to go. And that I dislike fried foods almost as much as chocolate, but not quite as much. And I was thinking that my third favorite food should probably have some protein, but not fatty protein. I think it should be beans and things that vegetarians eat that keep them alive without wilting.

EDSON: Uh, Miss Colburn —

JANIS: Janis. Now, Doctor . . . *(Looking around his office, sees his first name on his desk plaque.)* Edson Polanski. Oh, Edson. What an unusual name. I like it. So Edson, are you writing this down?

EDSON: No, Janis, I'm positive I won't forget, but you see —

JANIS: Silly me! You're a hypnotist. You've probably already stored it all somewhere in your incredible mind. So, moving on. Now, this is very important, Edson. One cannot stay thin by food alone. So, I want you to use your powers to make me believe that my favorite thing in the whole world to do is to work out.

EDSON: Well, I typically — I —

JANIS: Any type of exercise will do. Actually, it might be a good idea if you gave me a love of sports, since I've always been terrified of getting hit by balls in softball and volleyball and anything-ball really. I think that goes back to those horrid days in kindergarten, being forced to play dodgeball and being waled with those red, bouncy playground balls for no good reason at all. *(She is starting to get upset at the memory of it.)* Does it help you hypnotize me faster if you know the reason I'm screwed up?

EDSON: No, no. No. That would be therapy. Which isn't such a bad idea, Janice. You see, I can't help you to like something you don't really like or to do something you don't really want to do.

JANIS: Well, then what good are you? Huh?

EDSON: Well, I — I help people who want to help themselves.

JANIS: So now you're God, are you? And choosing to refuse my cries for help? Is this because I'm Jewish, Doctor? It's not my fault my parents birthed me and never sent me to Hebrew school.

EDSON: Janis. Stop. *(He raises his hand and does a special finger movement. She freezes but speaks somewhat robotically.)* Can you hear me?

JANIS: Yesss.

EDSON: Good. You are feeling calm. There is nothing to get worked up about. Everything is peaceful . . . serene. You feel happy and relaxed. *(He snaps and Janis comes out of the hypnosis.)*

JANIS: *(Looking around.)* This is a beautiful office, Edson. I just realized that now. It is really quite lovely.

EDSON: Thank you.

JANIS: What was I saying? I'm sorry, I think I got distracted by that gorgeous painting on the wall.

EDSON: Oh, why thank you. You were talking about dodgeball.

JANIS: *(Her mood dropping.)* Ohhh.

EDSON: And I was mentioning therapy as a possible solution.

JANIS: *(Dropping more.)* Ohhhhh.

EDSON: Have you ever tried therapy, Janis?

JANIS: Yes, once.

EDSON: Once? And what was that like?

JANIS: Hell. I talked, he nodded. I talked, he went, "Hmm." I talked, he took notes. And then I wrote him a very large check.

EDSON: Well, part of the process of therapy is to let the patient discover their own solutions.

JANIS: Well, I can do that at home with some chocolate and wine, and keep my very large check.

EDSON: Well . . .

JANIS: Anyway, why are we talking about therapy? I came here to get hypnotized. I did tell you that, right?

EDSON: Oh yes. It was just that you had so many things you wanted to change —

JANIS: Hey, look. I expected to write you a very large check to reprogram these things. But if it costs extra for you to reprogram extra things, I'm prepared to write you an extra large check.

EDSON: Well, that's very kind of you, Janis. However, as I was explaining before, I do not reprogram people's minds. Successful hypnosis depends on two key elements: a willingness to change, and a constant belief that a constructive goal will be reached.

JANIS: Well, I'm willing to have you change me, and I firmly believe if you do, the goal will be very constructive. *(Beat.)* How about two extra large checks?

EDSON: Janis —

JANIS: But I also want you to make me never want to pick my teeth, pluck my eyebrows, or pull out my eyelashes. Bad stuff. I read your pamphlet in the waiting room, Edson. It said hypnotized people experience changes in the way they think or behave in response to suggestions. So I'm merely giving you the suggestions that I want you to suggest to me. *(Edson sighs.)* OK, you win, five. Five extra large checks.

EDSON: Done!

JANIS: Done?

EDSON: Yes. Done. Finished. Fine. Finito. OK!

JANIS: Ohhh, I knew you had a kind soul!

EDSON: But one thing at a time. And I can't promise full and permanent results. You have to be willing and open.

JANIS: Yes, yes. I am open. I am so open that I think we could do more than one at once. Fix it all in one fell swoop. Oh, and speaking of open, I want to keep the door that way when we do your thing. And I'd like to videotape our session as well.

EDSON: *(Startled.)* Videotape?

JANIS: Yes. Remember the note you took?

EDSON: *(Reading.)* Recording sessions, friends, not the whole world.

JANIS: That's the one. You see, I would like to videotape the session with a friend present or just outside the door to make sure everything's safe.

EDSON: *(Panicking.)* But I don't allow videotaping. In fact, it, it makes me a bit nervous. I'm not really sure why. Look, I can assure you, Janis, my methods are completely harmless.

JANIS: Exactly. *You* can assure me. But how do *I* know, since I will be under your spell, Edson? How do I know you won't hypnotize me into stealing or killing people or watching soap operas? See my point?

EDSON: Well, if that were the case, Janis, I would have hypnotized you to do that already. I mean, why wait? I could have you out right now, killing people, stealing their money, and making it home in time for "One Life to Live"!

JANIS: *(Laughs.)* Oh my God. You're right. Silly me. *(Pinches herself.)* Oww! I'm still here. Just checking. OK, Edson, I've got about five minutes left before "Oprah." Let's do it!

EDSON: Now?! No, you see I normally schedule clients to come back after the initial consult —

JANIS: Normally, schmormally. I'm different. I'm giving you five extra large checks. Let's go.

EDSON: But what about your friend and, and the *(Winces.)* videotape?

JANIS: I come prepared. Stephanie is outside the door with a camcorder and two mirrors. *(Calling off.)* Roll 'em, Steph!

EDSON: I — this is — videotapes make me nervous. I, I — OK. Relax. Relax.

JANIS: I'm relaxed.

EDSON: Not you, me.

JANIS: Oh, sorry. Didn't mean to interrupt your process. Go ahead.

EDSON: I, I, I want you to watch my fingers. *(He starts moving them as before, in a repetitive motion.)* Very closely. You are feeling sloppy — er, sleepy. Relaxed and sleepy. When I clap my hands you will be in a state between sleeping and walking — er, waking. *(He claps. She looks controlled by him.)* Can you hear me, Janis?

JANIS: *(Robotically.)* Yesss.

EDSON: Good. Now, you are ready. You are feeling open to my suggestions. Um, uh . . . could we turn off the camera?

JANIS: Nooo.

EDSON: Please? I can't focus.

JANIS: Fiveee extraaa laaarge cheeecks.

EDSON: Right. OK. Um, yes, Janis, uh, let me think here . . . You love to play dodgeball and get hit with veggies — especially dark green veggies. *(Nervous and fumbling.)* Uh, well, that's not um, OK you have a passion for, for, for deep-fried . . . chocolate!

JANIS: Mmmmm.

EDSON: *(Peeking at the offstage video camera.)* No. No. No. From now on you will not pluck your fruit. *(Correcting himself.)* No!

JANIS: Nooo plucking fruit.

EDSON: No, Janis, that's not. Oh Jeez, um, um, OK uh when you pull out your, your checkbook, you will crave softball. *(Not completely sure where that came from.)*

JANIS: Ahh.

EDSON: Oh my God, um, um wilting eyelashes keep vegetarians healthy? No. Eating doughy food relaxes your teeth. Aah!

JANIS: Doughyyy.

EDSON: Ice cream is what you . . . pick at?

JANIS: Yesss, pick ice cream.

EDSON: No, you despise, um, what did you . . . oh, yes, you despise working out.

JANIS: Yuckyyy.

EDSON: Oh dear, oh dear, oh — oh! Your third favorite food is eyebrows!

JANIS: Yummyyy.

EDSON: *(Disgusted.)* Ehh! OK? OK. When I snap my count, you will come on — turn off — wake up. *(He snaps his fingers. Her body loosens.)* Janis?

JANIS: Yes?

EDSON: Can you please have your friend turn off that video camera?!

JANIS: Oh. *(She laughs.)* I was just making that up in case you thought you'd try anything funny.

EDSON: Making it up?! Oh, yes, funny. Ha ha. Ha, ha, ha! *(Starting to cry.)* Ha-ha-ha-ha-ha.

JANIS: *(Smiling.)* Oh, I have a friend who does that too — cries when she laughs real hard. Ya know, I feel good. Really good. I think this was successful.

EDSON: But you — I — you can't — I, I, I —

JANIS: Don't worry. I'll keep my promise. You earned your five extra large checks. Let me just grab my checkbook and — *(Robotically.)* Softball!! I must play softball! *(Sounding natural again.)* You know I have an incredible urge to play softball? *(Realizing.)* You did it! You did it! I crave softball. Here keep the whole checkbook! You deserve it — I don't care! Cause I just wanna play softball! *(Starting to leave.)* Come by for dinner, Edson, we'll celebrate. Sautéed eyelashes and we'll pick at ice cream! Bye! *(Calling off.)* Hey, anyone want to play softball?

EDSON: *(Sinking.)* Oh, dear.

STYLE WITH GRACE

Anton, forty-three, has been cutting and styling Lois's hair for many years now. She followed him from a smaller pricey shop called Maude's to a rather pretentious, outrageously pricey salon called Hair-em. Through the years the two of them have become privy to each other's personal lives. On this particular day, Lois, forty-nine, made an appointment for hair coloring. She did not, however, make an appointment to have it dried. As a result, Lois and Anton have gotten into a huge mêlée because he has scheduled an appointment right after her. There is no time to dry her wet hair. She feels this is absolutely ludicrous.

CHARACTERS
Anton: 43, hairdresser
Lois: 49, his client

SETTING
the Hair-em salon where Anton works

TIME
The present

LOIS: You can't leave me all soppy like this!!

ANTON: I have a two-thirty, Lois. I have Ms. Piro at two-thirty.

LOIS: What time is it now?

ANTON: Two-thirty.

LOIS: See? Piro's late. Finish me. You shouldn't have started me if you couldn't finish me.

ANTON: Oh I'd like to finish you all right, but you're already finished, honey.

LOIS: I am hardly finished. If this is finished, so are you, my sweet.

ANTON: No, you are, dear heart. You made an appointment for hair coloring. Is your hair colored?

LOIS: I don't know. You see, it's all wet.

ANTON: Well, it's naturally gray. Is it gray now? *(Not waiting for an answer.)* No. So you're finished. If you wanted it dried, darling, I would have been happy to do that, but you had to make an appointment to do that. That's the rule.

LOIS: What rule? Since when?

ANTON: Since four weeks ago. Raphael insists upon it.

LOIS: He's a fool, an idiot. It's ridiculous, ludicrous. *(Beat.)* Give me an appointment then.

ANTON: Certainly. For when?

LOIS: *(Puts out her hands in amazement.)* Now!

ANTON: I'm afraid that's impossible.

LOIS: Yes! You best be afraid, Anton. Be very afraid.

ANTON: I can't help it. I have Ms. Piro.

LOIS: You *can* help it, Anton. You know why? Ms. Piro is NOT HERE! She's not, not, not here!

ANTON: *(Putting his hand to his lips.)* Shh. She's a very important client.

LOIS: *(More quietly.)* She's also late!

ANTON: She's Julia you-know-who's cousin's dog companion.

LOIS: She's a *dog* walker?

ANTON: No, not just a dog walker. *The* dog walker for Julia's cousin.

LOIS: Any way you look at it, Anton, she scoops poop all day.

ANTON: Well, now, it's not —

LOIS: I know. Not just *any* poop. Julia you-know-who's cousin's pooch's poop. So what! Who cares! We live in Playda del Rey, the place is teeming with stars and their dogs' poop. Who cares?!

ANTON: *(Putting finger over his lips.)* Shhh.

LOIS: Don't shhh me!

ANTON: I don't have time. I have to tidy. I have to make fresh hazelnut coffee with a splash of vanilla for her.

LOIS: I don't care if she insists you grind the beans with your own teeth. I've been your client for more than seven years now.

ANTON: Seven years?! *(She nods.)* Oh God, Lois, I'm old. I'm old. I'm very, very, very, very —

LOIS: *(Clapping her hands.)* Shut up! Snap out of it! You're not that old. I'm older than you are.

ANTON: Yeah, I know.

LOIS: Watch it, chubby. Now, I thought we liked each other. I thought we were friends.

ANTON: We are friends! I'm just under a lot of pressure right now, Lois. I can't make good coffee, for one.

LOIS: That's because you're a hairdresser. Not a coffee maker. Do you see the difference?

ANTON: I'm not living up to their quotas, OK? I'm not bringing in enough of the right clientele. They told me this. My people aren't rich enough, OK?

LOIS: What are you talking about? I'm your people. And I'm filthy rich.

ANTON: I know, but you're not Raphael's idea of rich.

LOIS: What?! *(Anton nods.)* Screw him. I'm stinking, filthy, rotten rich! Do you know how much Noel, my first husband, made?

ANTON: Yes, I know. I know Noel. Look, *I'm* not rich, Lois. Me and Toby just barely scrape by. Raphael told me I'd better make an incredible impression on Ms. Piro or I'm out. Gone. Vamoose.

LOIS: Well, smell him. We never had a problem like this when you worked at Maude's. And where does he get off calling this place Hair-em? Do you know how demeaning that is to women? Tell him I'm disgusted. Revolted! Everyone is. It should be more fun. Curl Up and Dye. Now, that's fun.

ANTON: Don't you get it? Ms. Piro makes recommendations to Julia. Julia tells all her friends. That's a lot of business. This is the chance of a lifetime.

LOIS: From the poop picker-upper? Lovely.

ANTON: Can't you just go out with your hair wet once? It's California. Or sit under the dryer?

LOIS: You sit under the dryer. Let us rewind back to the part when I mention that I am filthy rich and you say, "But you're not Raphael's idea of rich."

ANTON: I don't mean any offense. I love having you as a customer, Lois. You make me laugh.

LOIS: Thank you. I am funny — hilarious. But you're not getting out of this so easily, Anton.

ANTON: Well, you only come in for a cut every few months. You rarely get your hair dyed. You don't get any extras — ever. No products. And, you're not exactly the best . . . well, tipper.

LOIS: What? I don't tip well?

ANTON: You never tip the shampooers. They complain.

LOIS: They do? They do not!

ANTON: Yes, they do. They don't want to work with you anymore. And let me put it this way. Your tips are pennies better than Ms. Walker's.

LOIS: Oh my God! Mitzy? But she's so, so cheap. You're not serious?

ANTON: I am.

LOIS: Oh my God! I had no idea I was that cheap. I'm cheap. Have I always been that cheap? *(Anton nods.)* Well, why didn't you say anything? You just let me be cheap all over the place.

ANTON: You had just divorced Buddy when we met. I thought you were short on cash.

LOIS: No, I had just gotten engaged to Harry, which might have been when I was divorcing Buddy. I went to you the first time at Maude's on a recommendation.

ANTON: No, you didn't even know Harry yet, so you must have just been thinking about divorcing Buddy, which makes it all the more confusing about why I didn't mention anything about the tip. But once you established that you're a bad tipper, I just expected it.

LOIS: *(Insulted, not sure what to say.)* Well!

ANTON: And you didn't come to me on a recommendation. You were a walk-in.

LOIS: Nooo! No, I don't just walk in. I've never walked in. I had an appointment.

ANTON: You didn't have an appointment. And you certainly didn't have an appointment with me. But I know for a fact that I readied your hair for your niece's graduation party. Remember? You wanted something odd. *(She doesn't quite trust him.)* The cornrows?

LOIS: *(Looking as if she bit into something horrid.)* Oh no! Don't remind me. I looked like a Jewish Raggedy Ann doll in Chanel. But I did meet Harry at that party. He liked the look. Hmm. Was that before or after Celeste had the heroin overdose and met up with Guy Swallow, the most handsome doctor on daytime television.

ANTON: Before Guy. After the heroin. During Phoebe's short-term amnesia.

LOIS: Oh. *(Beat.)* Oh. Then it hasn't been seven years.

ANTON: I knew it! *(Sign of the cross.)* Thank you God. I'm not as old.

LOIS: It's eight.

ANTON: No! It can't be. Noooo!

LOIS: Yes. Thank God we have "The Days and Nights of Passion" to help us keep track of the years. I am really losing my mind.

ANTON: Well, it's the stress, honey.

LOIS: Yes.

ANTON: The demands.

LOIS: Exactly.

ANTON: And Harry.

LOIS: Right . . . bite your tongue!

ANTON: What? You told me things had gone sour. I thought he was on his way out like the rest. I know you haven't been getting as much.

LOIS: It's not what I thought. I love him far beyond the others. Besides, he's not having an affair.

ANTON: How do you know? What did you find out?

LOIS: No dry the hair, no spill the guts.

ANTON: Fine. Get over here. The little dog-pulling name-dropper isn't showing up anyway. Just don't tell anyone I dried you without an appointment. I'd be in big trouble.

LOIS: *(Shaking her hair.)* Mum's the word. And I'll be sure to give you a good tip. *(She smiles.)* Eight percent. *(Nodding her head to him.)* That's good, isn't it?

ANTON: If I were a student loan. *(He pushes her head.)* Put your head down. Here comes my magic blow-dryer. *(Drying with a blow-dryer.)* So spill?

LOIS: Oh my, that feels nice, Anton. I was chilled. That air is nice.

ANTON: *(Not hearing above the blow-dryer.)* What?

LOIS: *(Louder.)* Nice. *(Anton nods, smiles. Talking over dryer.)* He has a physical ailment.

ANTON: What?

LOIS: *(Even louder.)* Harry's got a physical ailment!

ANTON: *(Loudly.)* I know! What ailment?

(They continue trying to talk over the hair dryer.)

LOIS: Irritable bowel.

ANTON: He's irritable?

LOIS: No, his bowel is.

ANTON: A bowel can be irritable?

LOIS: Well, apparently, his can. I never heard of it. I heard of spastic.

ANTON: Spastic what? *(He turns off the blow-dryer.)*

LOIS: *(She yells.)* Spastic bowel, you idiot! *(Looks around.)* Sorry. *(Smiles at customers.)* Spastic Cow — you know that PBS documentary on mad cow disease? *(Waves to someone else in the room.)* I had an appointment for this.

ANTON: Oh God, Lois, don't be so loud.

LOIS: Don't be so deaf. Anyway.

ANTON: Anyway, that problem keeps him less interested?

LOIS: Well, it's irritating apparently.

ANTON: Umm.

LOIS: What's umm? You don't think he's telling the truth?

ANTON: What? I never said that.

LOIS: Well, at least I have a husband, don't I?

ANTON: *I* have a husband!

LOIS: No, I've met him, honey. He's a wife.

ANTON: Whatever, Ms. Homophobia. The point is, at least, I keep him, or did.

LOIS: Did?

ANTON: Nothing. I didn't mean that.

LOIS: I love Toby. He's adorable. Where is he? What have you done to him?

ANTON: I didn't do anything to him! It's what he's done to me. He's gotten so wrapped up in this whole Buddhist deal. You know he wants to go to the San Bernardino Mountains to this place called Whispering Pines, so that he can dance at night in the wilderness.

LOIS: So?

ANTON: He wants to do it naked.

LOIS: Oh no!

ANTON: Exactly.

LOIS: The mosquitoes are terrible up there. Tell him to bring lots of *Off*.

ANTON: But he wants to go without me. We haven't been apart for fifteen years.

LOIS: Well, it's about time. He's sick of you, darling.

ANTON: Uh. That's what I'm afraid of. I've become so old, and chubby, and boring to him. He wants one of those slim, yogurt-drinking yoga boys.

LOIS: Probably. *(He gives her a look.)* That doesn't mean he's going to leave you. I had a similar stint with Harry.

ANTON: You did?

LOIS: Yes. We planned a cruise to the Bahamas. One of those ships that stop all over. Oh gosh, I remember there was this really annoying cha-cha instructor who I just wanted to smack across the ocean if she said, "Isn't it fun and easy?" just one more time.

ANTON: How, in any way, does this relate to my Toby naked on a San Bernardino mountain?

LOIS: Shhh. I'm getting there. I'm taking the scenic route. I didn't want Harry on the trip. In fact, I told him it was *my* trip. Alone. He put up a big stink, but eventually he let me go.

ANTON: And you had an awful time.

LOIS: No, I had the best time of my life. I flirted with everybody.

ANTON: But you missed Harry terribly.

LOIS: Not really.

ANTON: Lois, this is strangely not making me feel any better.

LOIS: I didn't leave him. We have a commitment. He's the best man for the job. And I love him. You see? Toby will feel the same way. I know. And he won't be a Buddhist for long. He doesn't strike me as the eternally peaceful type. He's addicted to his neuroses.

ANTON: Thank you for saying so, Lois.

LOIS: You're welcome. But it's true.

ANTON: *(Beat.)* Lois, do you ever ponder what your life is about? What it all means? What you've done in the scheme of the world?

LOIS: *(Pause.)* Oh Anton! You added a color in. You did, didn't you? I love the hint of auburn streaking through effortlessly.

ANTON: I knew you would.

LOIS: You're a genius. An absolute artist. *(Touching her hair with glee.)* I love it! *(Loudly.)* I'm giving you a two hundred dollar tip!

ANTON: *(Quietly.)* You are?

LOIS: *(Quietly.)* Not on your life, darling, but they don't have to know it. *(Loudly.)* And there's more where that came from! Several hundred more! *(Quietly.)* Just flaunt it to the snooty Raphael and tell him to shove his rotten, poorly named salon up his you-know-what. *(Beat.)* Once a job has you pondering garbage like you're pondering, you know it's time to leave. Life is about being happy, not productive. And you are *not* happy here.

ANTON: Are you serious?

LOIS: As a naked Buddhist dancing on a mountain. Did you ever fret over making coffee for a dog walker at Maude's? *(Anton's not sure what to say.)* Um-hum, I rest my case. *(She starts to leave.)*

ANTON: *(Yells out.)* Lois! Get the fu-fu drinks flowing.

LOIS: Café Milan.

LOIS and ANTON: Lance's section.

ANTON: *(Finger pulling him in.)* Oh, Raphael?

TO BE IN YOUR SHOES

Helen and Todd, mid to late thirties, have been married for ten years and have two children. Though they are opposites, they've always had a lively, vibrant relationship. Helen is a successful gynecologist, and Todd is a school counselor. Their marriage has had its ups and downs and an occasional weird moment, but nothing this weird. A week ago, while attending a neighbor's New Year's Eve party, Helen and Todd, blitzed on tequila, made a New Year's wish with the party's hired fortune-teller. Each of them wished to spend a day in the other spouse's body. Neither of them suspected that this wish would come true. However, this morning when Todd rolled out of bed and used the bathroom, he discovered that he had turned into Helen, physically, during the night. (Special note: Helen should be played by a female, though "Helen" is really Todd inside. Todd should be played by a male, though "Todd" is really Helen inside.)

CHARACTERS
Helen: 30s, the body of Helen, the spirit or soul of
    Helen's husband Todd
Todd: 30s, the body of Todd, the spirit or soul of
    Todd's wife Helen

SETTING
Helen and Todd's bedroom

TIME
The present, 5:00 AM

HELEN: *(From the bathroom.)* It can't be. I, I, I can't be. This. Can't. Be. Helen? Helen? *(Yelling.)* Heleeen!
TODD: *(Stirring, still very much asleep.)* What, what? What's going on? *(Eyes barely open.)*

HELEN: *(From the bathroom.)* Wake up, Helen. I need your help. This is crazy! I'm going crazy!

TODD: *(Turning over.)* I think I am too. Because somebody keeps yelling and yelling.

HELEN: *(Yelling from the bathroom.)* Helen, wake up!! Something is very wrong when I look in the mirror.

TODD: *(Still half-asleep.)* Oh, honey, it's not that bad. Trust me, I look at you every day.

HELEN: No, not bad. Wrong. It's wrong. It's all wrong! It's completely, utterly . . .

TODD: Wrong? You like that word, don't you? *(Looks at the clock.)* I'll tell you wrong. Small hand on five — now that's wrong. *(Looking around.)* Where are you, Todd?

HELEN: Bathroom.

TODD: Your voice sounds funny.

HELEN: Yours too. Yours too! Isn't that odd to you, Helen?

TODD: No, it's because I'm still half asleep, thanks to you. Wishing at this point to be *all* asleep.

HELEN: You don't understand. This is big. Huge.

TODD: What is? What's huge? You? Honey, you're not fat. Go to sleep. Or rather, I'll go to sleep.

HELEN: No, you don't understand. This is an emergency!

TODD: Emergency? *(Sitting up.)* Emergency?! Oh God! Are the kids OK?!

HELEN: Yes. Yes. The kids are fine.

TODD: Is the house on fire?

HELEN: No.

TODD: Did you kill someone?

HELEN: No.

TODD: Did I kill someone?

HELEN: No.

TODD: Then I'm gonna I kill you! For waking me up at this God-awful hour! So what is it?!

HELEN: I'm coming in, Helen. I'm coming in the bedroom now.

TODD: There's no reason to announce your appearance. I'm your wife. I see you every day.

HELEN: I have to warn you. I don't want you in shock. I thought I was dreaming myself.

TODD: What the hell are you talking about?

HELEN: There is no way to ease you into this. Let's just say you will be shocked.

TODD: All right. All right. I'll be shocked. What's it this time? A pimple?

HELEN: No. I have a perfect complexion — a lot like yours. Actually, exactly like yours.

TODD: Oh. Thank you, honey.

HELEN: I'm coming in now, Helen. Very slowly. Very, very slowly. I hope you're sitting.

TODD: I swear, Todd, I will never forget that you were a *drama* major. Come in.

HELEN: *(Entering.)* OK, here I am.

TODD: I swear you make a huge deal of everything! Every single, little, tiny . . . *(Looking. Gasping at first.)* Ahhh! Ohhh! *(Giving voice to it.)* Ohhh. Ahhh. Ohhh. This is . . . I . . . You. Not. That. Can't. You're. How'd you? . . . Did you? . . . Are you? . . . Listen to my voice . . . I sound . . . Very low. Oh God, Todd, you're, you're, you look like —

HELEN: Uh-huh.

TODD: And I'm afraid my . . . I'm not sure how I look . . . I'm afraid to . . . my voice is . . . I'm, I'm —

HELEN: Uh-huh.

TODD: Oh God. This is wrong. This is very wrong! This is completely, utterly —

HELEN: That's what I said! I told you it was huge.

TODD: Yes, but you didn't happen to mention that you turned into me and I turned into — I mean, that's big. You just kept going on about how flabby you look in the mirror.

HELEN: It wasn't that, Helen.

TODD: Oh my God! You think I'm flabby?

HELEN: Not at all.

TODD: So why were you upset when you looked in the mirror?

HELEN: Are you telling me you wouldn't be upset if you suddenly changed into your wife?

TODD: I don't have a wife, idiot. Or at least I didn't used to.

HELEN: I think if you look in the mirror, you'll understand why I was so upset.

TODD: I don't want to look into the mirror. I get the gist of things. I don't want to look.

HELEN: I'm that unattractive?

TODD: No. I just, I don't want to look because, because I just don't. I think we're drugged.

HELEN: What? We're not. Who would have drugged us?

TODD: I don't know. Obviously. But I'm going to have Becky run a blood test when I get into the office this morn . . . Oh no! My patients. I have patients scheduled all day today, Todd. What am I going to do? This getting drugged is incredibly inconvenient.

HELEN: Well, it's not exactly a picnic for me either. Besides, we are not drugged, Helen.

TODD: How do you know?

HELEN: Because I can tell. I know what it's like to be buzzed.

TODD: How? Do you have some drug habits I'm unaware of? Because this might not be the best time to bring it up, considering you have my body. And you better not return it with any foreign substances, buddy!

HELEN: I'm just saying there's probably a reasonable explanation for all of this.

TODD: Oh yes, I'm sure there is. I'm sure people come in with this problem every day, Todd.

HELEN: I'm just saying we need to go over things.

TODD: Oh my God. I just realized what it is. We're dead.

HELEN: We're not dead. We're talking.

TODD: What difference does that make? You think conversation ceases when you die? Those souls in hell have to be tortured by something. Why not their husbands talking at them? *(Beat.)* Oh God, we're dead.

HELEN: No. That's not it. How would we have died?

TODD: Well, I don't know. You must have kicked the bucket first, since you were the first to wake up. You should know better than me.

HELEN: *(Gasps.)* Haaaaa! Remember the fortune-teller at the Hansons? The New Year's Eve party? We wished that we were each other, remember?

TODD: Oh. And this is the reasonable explanation I suppose?

HELEN: Don't you remember her asking us to make a wish for a day?

TODD: I guess. Yes. I remember. I thought it was ludicrous.

HELEN: I thought it was kinda sweet. Me asking to be you.

TODD: It was. That's not the point, Todd! If this is true, the point is it's entirely your fault!

HELEN: Mine?! You asked to be me too!

TODD: Well! That was only after you brought it up. How would it have looked if I asked for a million bucks after you're being all sweet, wanting to understand the female experience?

HELEN: Come to think of it, a million bucks wouldn't have been a bad idea.

TODD: Oh great! *Now* you tell me. *(Remembering.)* Hey? Hey? Did she tell us how long this wish would last?

HELEN: Oh yeah. She said it would last twenty-four hours. Do you think she was right?

TODD: Well, gee, Todd, how do I know? Medical school doesn't exactly cover this kind of thing. *(Beat.)* Ooh, I'm getting hot. I wonder if this 'causes a fever. *(Touching her forehead and then her face.)* Huhh! No!

HELEN: What, what, what?! What's wrong?

TODD: *(Still touching face.)* It's so weird. It's so, so weird. I have scruff.

HELEN: Oh, Sweetie, it's not that bad. Sometimes it's even fun to shave.

TODD: Oh yeah. It's fun to wear panty hose too, hon. *(Touching her chin.)* Oh God. All those years of making fun of Aunt Millie for her chin hairs. This is the payback.

HELEN: What are we going to do? We have to think fast. I have appointments all day. We have to wake up the kids. Do you think we should tell the kids?

TODD: Are you kidding? Do you want them to be in therapy for the rest of their lives?

HELEN: What about our jobs? Should we call in sick?

TODD: I can't call in sick. I have a completely booked day.

HELEN: Maybe we should put in a call to Matt . . . maybe we can be up-front with him. He's a great doctor. He'll take us to the hospital and run a whole battery of tests.

TODD: Are you out of your mind? He will put us straight into an institution.

HELEN: He respects your work.

TODD: Yes. As a gyno. But that doesn't mean if I go to him and tell him I now have my husband's exterior, he's going to say, "Hum. Gee, Doctor, I've seen this before. Let's run a battery of tests and see how you're both doing since you became each other."

HELEN: *(Touching belly.)* Owww. God. That hurts.

TODD: Oh great. I'm getting my period. I mean, *you're* getting my period. *(Happiness.)* You're getting my period!

HELEN: No! I don't know how to . . . I can't . . . you can't expect me to . . .

TODD: Oh, I'm loving this.

HELEN: Don't you ever tell anyone this. You hear? Swear you won't.

TODD: Jeez, I swear, Todd. It's not like something that I really want to share with all my friends — you having my period. On second thought, that might be kinda fun. *(Beat.)* Ooh. I think I have to go to the bathroom.

HELEN: Oh. Well put the seat down, OK? Because I practically fell in this morning.

TODD: *(Laughing.)* You did? I know. Not funny. *(Walking.)* I'll be right out. *(Beat.)* Wow. I get to do this upright. Ya know, this is kinda fun.

HELEN: Fun? How in any way is this fun?!

TODD: It's just fascinating. Everything. I mean, I've never felt what it was like to be a man.

HELEN: What about our jobs?

TODD: *(Beat.)* I'll go to school today. It might be fun. I'd like to play you.

HELEN: But you don't know what I do.

TODD: Come on, you're a school counselor. I'd love to hear all the juicy stuff about teenagers and their parents and their love angst. It would be fun.

HELEN: That's not all it is.

TODD: I know. I know. You're very sympathetic. I know you're good. How much damage can I do in one day?

HELEN: Well, if you get to do that, then I get to go give a bunch of gynecological exams. I'm sure your assistant can help me through it.

TODD: I know what you're thinking, but it's not like that, Todd. You're imagining a bunch of twenty-year-old knockouts that you might like to see a little more fully. Trust me, my day is half full of middle-aged women with sagging everything.

HELEN: I'm not that shallow. I don't mind sagging women.

TODD: Thanks. Is that a hint?

HELEN: So do you have any twenty-year-old knockouts? *(She gives him a look.)* I'm kidding. Actually, I'm just curious how women interact with women.

TODD: So now you're curious?

HELEN: Sort of.

TODD: Well, it's too dangerous. We can't do it. However, your mother and my mother have been begging me to do a girl's day out — hang out at the museum, go to the beauty parlor. This is a perfect opportunity to see how women interact with women.

HELEN: Uuh! I don't want to do that.

TODD: *(Flirtatiously.)* On the other hand, there are plenty of interesting things we could find out right here at home. Maybe without even leaving the bedroom.

HELEN: Really? That's not a bad idea. *(Eyebrows raised.)* I always wondered what I'd be like in bed.

(They smile at each other flirtatiously.)

FLY RUDOLPH, FLY!

Tyler, thirties, has agreed to bring his wife, Alison, late twenties, on his hunting trip with a couple of friends. In the past, he has gone on these trips by himself because Alison isn't exactly the type to stay still and be quiet in the forest all day. This weekend Alison begged Tyler to take her along. She feels left out and wants him to know she can do it. She also believes that doing more activities together will bring them even closer as a couple. Tyler reluctantly agrees.

CHARACTERS
Tyler: 30s, a recreational hunter, Alice's husband
Alice: 20s, Tyler's wife

SETTING
The woods

TIME
The present

TYLER: *(Quietly.)* This looks like a good spot. What do you think, hon?

ALISON: It's all right. That was so rude. I still can't believe they made us leave.

TYLER: Yeah. Well, this is a nice spot too.

ALISON: The other was better.

TYLER: I know, I know, the caverns. The gorgeous waterfall.

ALISON: The proximity to indoor plumbing.

TYLER: I know. I know.

ALISON: Well, I just don't understand it, do you? We had a perfectly happy breakfast at the cabin. We were all happy. We were laughing —

TYLER: Yeah, but I'm not so sure Jeff thought that incident with the chipmunk and the air mattress was so funny.

ALISON: He didn't? So why did he tell it?

TYLER: He didn't. Susan did. Because you wanted an outdoorsy story.

ALISON: Well, I'm sure they have other outdoorsy stories besides the first time they slept together. I mean, they camp together every weekend. It's not my fault she chose that one.

TYLER: It's just guys get sensitive about their very first time.

ALISON: That was his first time? Ever? *(He nods.)* And the chipmunk . . . ? *(He nods.)* Oh my God! I feel terrible! That's awful. No wonder he's frightened of rodents.

TYLER: You should have seen him with the squirrel last week.

ALISON: Oh my God, that is so cute. That is so cute!

TYLER: Do me a favor. Don't tell him that.

ALISON: Anyway, it seemed like we were all having a great time. We're all admiring the gorgeous view and suddenly they were like, "Find your own spot." Out of the blue — "Find your own spot."

TYLER: Well you were dancing around quite a bit.

ALISON: So! I was happy. I felt like, like Laura in *Little House on the Prairie* but more slutty. *(Realizing.)* Hey, you don't think it was *me*, do you? *(Tyler shrugs, not sure what to say.)* You do?! Why?! I was just kidding around.

TYLER: Because you're too loud.

ALISON: Loud?! I'm not loud! *(He looks at her. Getting much softer.)* I'm not. All the time.

TYLER: Oh and singing a jazzed-up version of *(Sings.)* "The hill's are alive . . . " is quiet?

ALISON: Well, I wouldn't call it especially loud. Especially retarded, maybe, but not loud.

TYLER: Well, I'm sure banging "We Will, We Will Rock You" on a Tupperware container didn't help either.

ALISON: Umm. Well, they don't seem to usually mind my "loudness." In fact, we've always had a great and sometimes "loud" time together. Jeff and Susan are usually so fun and sociable.

TYLER: You don't want to be sociable when you're hunting, Alison.

ALISON: You don't?

TYLER: No! I keep telling you that.

ALISON: Well that doesn't seem very vacation-like. If I wanted to be antisocial, I'd sit in our den in the dark with the TV on eating candy all day. Molding away like some weirdo with a lisp.

TYLER: What are you talking about?

ALISON: I know what you think. "What's her problem? Susan can hunt. She doesn't have a problem with not being loud." Great! Maybe you should have married Susan.

TYLER: I didn't want to marry Susan. I didn't even know Susan. Again, what are you talking about?

ALISON: You know, my loudness is very convenient sometimes. When you wanted to call out to a college buddy in the stadium, who did that for you? What got his attention? Who?!

TYLER: You did, honey. I just don't know what the hell you are talking about right now.

ALISON: How you're ruining my vacation. How you want me to be all different than I am.

TYLER: I don't want you to be all different. I just want you to be part different. *(Beat.)* Well why did you come then?! Because I warned you about this, this quiet thing with hunting.

ALISON: No, no, don't start up again with that. We decided! I want to come with you and share in your little hobby with you. It shows love and devotion. I mean, you hate shopping. You hate big parties and amusement parks. But that doesn't stop me from dragging you along. Why should you stop me from being miserable with the things you like?

TYLER: I know we've been married awhile because that somehow made sense.

ALISON: Of course. I just don't understand all the insider rules yet. I have to get acclimated to this hunting thing. Like I have to remind you over and over not to rush the shopping experience. You, apparently, have to remind me not to talk too loud when we're hunting. OK? I'll just, I'll just talk quiet. I know how to whisper. And if it was so bad for all of you "experienced hunters," why didn't someone tell me straight out?

TYLER: I did!

ALISON: Well, not *you*! You always say I talk too much.

TYLER: Well, *they* aren't going to tell you to shut up. Whether they want to or not.

ALISON: Why not?

TYLER: Because they're our friends. What are they going to say? "This is so great. Having a great time. You know what? Shut up, Alison!"

ALISON: Well, that's what friends are for. It's better than, "Isn't this a great spot — get out!"

TYLER: OK, OK. Technically, I don't know exactly why they told us to find our own spot. The point is, Alison, ideally you don't want to be talking. At all.

ALISON: *(A bit wounded.)* OK! Fine!

TYLER: Sometimes it's even *fun* not to be talking.

ALISON: In what way?

TYLER: In a non-talking-fun way. I don't know. I can't explain it. It just is. Trust me.

ALISON: OK. OK. Fine. I'll try. OK?

TYLER: OK, honey, I'm sorry this is so hard. I don't have any desire to change who you are.

ALISON: It's not hard for me not to talk. It's just hard for me to understand why that's fun.

TYLER: *(Patting her back.)* OK, OK.

ALISON: *(Pulling away.)* Just get our gun thingies. Let me stand here for a second. I'll lean against this tree.

TYLER: OK. That's a good spot.

(Tyler goes to get the guns. Beat.)

ALISON: And I have never been, in my whole life, accused of being loud. *(Tyler looks at her.)* Oh. OK. Once. But that was because Miriam asked me to sing for the wedding. I told her I wasn't a professional.

TYLER: Nope, not a professional — a professional probably

wouldn't have shouted the S-word in the middle of the ceremony at the top of her lungs.

ALISON: I can't believe you're bringing this up now. I've told you before it just came out when the organist shot me a dirty look for forgetting to come in. And all I could think of was like "oh sh . . ." — S-word. I didn't mean to have that echo throughout the chapel in stereophonic. And I certainly didn't know she videotaped it for posterity and plays it over and over. *(Beat.)* You know some people think that was the best part of the whole damn wedding.

TYLER: I know. *(Chuckles.)* It really was. It had a complete sincerity that other parts of the wedding sorely lacked.

ALISON: Well, I don't say my S-word willy-nilly, honey.

TYLER: I know you don't, honey. *(Kisses her.)* I love the way you say your S-word.

ALISON: Thanks. *(Beat.)* OK, I'm going to be quiet now. You won't hear a sound. Not a peep.

TYLER: Good. You'll see how fun it can be. We'll just watch for deer and you'll notice how peaceful it all is.

ALISON: Shh. *(Putting her finger to her lips.)* Be quiet now.

(They are silent for a few seconds. She clears her throat.)

ALISON: *(Quietly.)* Phlegm. *(Silence.)* It's cold, huh?

TYLER: *(Quiet back.)* Well, we are north.

ALISON: I can see my breath. *(Blowing out her breath.)* Haa. Haa. See?

TYLER: Yes. *(Putting his hand to his lips. She rolls her eyes and complies.)*

ALISON: I'm cold, Tylie. Maybe we should go to the clearing down there. There seem to be less trees.

TYLER: Alison, where there are less trees, there are also less animals.

ALISON: I'm sure there are some animals there.

TYLER: Not many.

ALISON: Well so? How many do you need? There's probably smarter animals there who perhaps prefer the sun. Know how to get out of the cold. Smarter is more of a challenge.

TYLER: I'm not looking for smarter animals or more of a challenge.

ALISON: You have something against smarter animals?

TYLER: No! It's just there's more deer in the inner forest here and I told you you might get cold. Why didn't you bring my fleece like I told you?

ALISON: It's plaid.

TYLER: So?

ALISON: Well, I — it makes me look fat.

TYLER: Who cares? No one is going to see you out here anyway?!

ALISON: *(Singsongy.)* Look who's being the loud one now? Let's all take note. *(Pause. He gives her a look.)* Well, I didn't know it was going to be like this exactly. I thought there might be fellow hunters on the road milling about. OK? I wanted to look all cute — my best for you, honey. Now that I know it's all unsocial, yet "fun," I'll wear the ugly plaid fleece, but for right now —

TYLER: OK, OK, we'll move up toward the clearing where all the *smart* animals are in a few minutes so you can warm up. But please, for a moment, for five minutes let's be completely quiet. And see what happens. *(Angry as hell.)* It'll be very fun to see what happens! We'll wait patiently and have fun!

ALISON: Are you OK? Your forehead is doing that crinkly thing it does when you get all tense.

TYLER: *(Shushing with vigor.)* Shhhhhhh!

ALISON: OK. *(Under her breath.)* In amusement parks you don't have to *wait* for fun, it just is. *(He looks at her.)* All right. You like waiting.

(They are silent. Tyler watches in a fixed position. Alison stretches out her hands quietly. She cracks her knuckles. Then she stares out with him. Suddenly she takes a deep long breath, like a sigh. He looks at her.)

ALISON: *(Quietly)* What? What? What's with the look? I'm breathing. I can't breathe?

TYLER: *(Quietly.)* No. *(She shrugs. Silence. Suddenly, Tyler sits up straight like he's seen something.)* Look. *(He points.)* *(Alison gasps and looks lovingly at the thing.)*

TYLER: *(Whispers.)* I can't believe it. We were so loud and . . . it's a deer.

(Alison looks at Tyler and her mouth drops open mouthing "He's so cute.")

TYLER: *(Whispers.)* We'll both aim.

(Alison shakes her head no fiercely.)

TYLER: We've got a great shot?

ALISON: *(Whispers.)* Look at his nose. *(Sounding all sweet.)* Look at his big cute nose.

TYLER: *(Whispers.)* So he has a big nose.

ALISON: It's Rudolph. I think it's kinda like he's Rudolph.

TYLER: *(Whispers.)* No, no, he's definitely not Rudolph. He's a yucky deer. Cruel to his fawn.

ALISON: How do you know?

TYLER: He just is! Besides, he's a deer, not a reindeer.

ALISON: Oh. Is there a difference?

TYLER: Yes. *(Lifting his gun.)* He's not going to be celebrating Christmas! *(Alison's pushes his gun down.)* Alison! There's a surplus of deer in the United States and they'll only suffer if they all live. *(Alison gives him a boo-boo look.)* Don't do that look. Stop with the look. Would you rather he get hit by a car or starve to death? *(He aims his gun.)*

ALISON: *(Suddenly yelling.)* Fly! Fly Rudolph — fly!

TYLER: What are you doing?!!

ALISON: You can't kill Rudolph! Even if he isn't . . . Rudolph. His eyes were all big and sad-like and he was saying, "I'm Bambi's best friend. Bambi needs me even if I'm not Rudolph."

TYLER: You are a crazy person! You are insane! Bambi? Bambi?! What has Bambi got to do with Rudolph?! Bambi is Disney! Rudolph is . . . Santa! And this is not a cartoon! We're hunting. We're hunters. We're merciless. We're fierce. We're strong.

ALISON: We're cold. *(He looks at her.)* But we're hunting. We are. You want to shoot something. We will. It's all good. I'm sure some ugly rat or something will wander by eventually, why don't you shoot that instead?

TYLER: I have a better idea. *(He raises his gun.)*

ALISON: *(She giggles and pushes his gun down.)* You're funny. You know, I'm really hungry anyway. Why don't we go back to the cabin and have a hot mug of cider and something yummy to eat? We can refuel. Come back here and have more fun after we shop in town a while. I'm sure they'll be some mean-looking nasty deer out here later.

TYLER: Alison, I am going to kill something before we leave today.

ALISON: Sure you will, honey, but no Bambis, Rudolphs, or Easter Bunnies. Or any of their friends. Anyway, I'm so glad you invited me along. I really understand why you like this so much. It's peaceful out here. All these cute animals around. I like hunting. I'm going to come with you as much as I can. Isn't that great?

TYLER: *(Beat.)* Run!

ALISON: *(Beat.)* Umm . . . OK, race you there. *(Running, singing.)* "The hills are alive with the sound . . . "

HOUSING TO SHARE

Dorrine, late twenties, and Cal, early twenties, have both gone to a roommate agency to find their perfect match. Dorrine is trying to find a roommate to fit her present apartment. The only problem is that she has control issues, which have driven three roommates away in the past year. Cal is laid-back, but a bit irresponsible. He is trying to find a place where he won't be shot at again and where the roommate is willing to, at least, pay rent regularly. Today, they are explaining their potential wants to Cheryl at the agency. At the beginning of the scene, they are speaking to the offstage agent, not to each other.

CHARACTERS
Dorrine: late 20s, in search of a roommate
Cal: early 20s, potential roommate

SETTING
Dorrine's apartment

TIME
The present

DORRINE: *(To audience.)* I jotted down a few notes to help you help me, Cheryl. Let's start with age. I'm looking for a female roommate who is approximately twenty-six to thirty-two years —

CAL: *(To audience.)* I got a couple of IDs here that'll say I'm anywhere from twenty-one to twenty-five.

DORRINE: I think new-to-the-city, sociable, but not too sociable. Female. Definitely female.

CAL: Sex? *(Grin.)* Well, I uh . . . *(Realizes.)* Oh? You mean like male or female?

DORRINE: Well educated is important.

CAL: Hey, I was gonna finish college, but it was, like, a lot of work.

DORRINE: No excess drinkers, partyers, and *definitely* not a smoker.

CAL: I'm real picky on that. On smoking. I want my roommate to use an ashtray. Ya really got to, ya know? Because I almost burned my place down once. *(Beat.)* What? Not recently!

DORRINE: I'm looking for a real professional, making mid-thirties or so.

CAL: Employment? Yeah, I've got a couple jobs.

DORRINE: And I will accept the occasional vegetarian if there are no curry smells that turn my place into an Ethiopian armpit.

CAL: I always cook with loads of garlic and curry. But that's not a good thing to do if you're tired, and hungover, and without a lid. I found that out.

DORRINE: Also, Cheryl, I prefer no bike messengers, aerobics instructors, dog walkers, or gothic magicians. Don't ask. I don't want to go into it. Oh, and absolutely no actors!

CAL: Yeah, I'm an actor.

DORRINE: Someone who can carry on an intelligent conversation, well-read, and well-traveled.

CAL: Yeah, uh, someone who pays rent is probably good.

DORRINE: I find it's best if they have no car, no pets, and no boyfriend.

CAL: I mean, they don't have to pay it on the first, but it probably would be good if it's like within the first week or so. I mean, believe me, I've been late with rent. Who isn't? *(Beat.)* Not *real* late. What are you writing down?

DORRINE: And uses coasters. Can't anyone use a coaster when they're right there and available?

CAL: And not paying rent, that's . . . that's like bad.

DORRINE: Oh. And finally, they should love my cat, Modesty Blaze. *(Beat.)* Yes, I said no pets. But that's no pets for them.

I have an existing pet in our home. So therefore, they should love Modesty if they want to live here.

CAL: Oh, yeah, Cher, and I majorly love cats. I really, really dig 'em.

Scene change: Dorrine and Cal are now in Dorrine's apartment. Dorrinne is interviewing Cal as a potential — and potentially disastrous — roommate.

DORRINE: *(Turns to Cal.)* Cats?

CAL: *(To Dorrine.)* Yeah. Cheryl at the agency said you had cats. Where are they?

DORRINE: I think there's been some sort of a mix-up here, Cal. I don't have cats. I have *a* cat.

CAL: Oh. OK. Well, where's the cat then?

DORRINE: Let's wait on that. She not friendly at first anyway. Besides, we've got a problem.

CAL: Problem? Is she OK? What are you feeding her these days?

DORRINE: It's not my cat. The problem is that you're not a female. I requested a female.

CAL: Oh gee, well if you're gonna be picky.

DORRINE: I don't know how this happened. Cheryl is wasting our time.

CAL: No. I don't mind that you're a woman. In fact, I like it. And I love your doorbell, Dorrine, and this room. I have a good feeling about the walls. Ya know when that happens, it happens. You can't force these things.

DORRINE: Yes, but this is a real problem *for me*. You not being a female.

CAL: Well, there was that short period where I liked shaving my legs. I could complain about my weigh periodically, would that help?

DORRINE: *(Beat.)* I'm gonna go ahead and call Cheryl.

CAL: Now wait. I was kidding. Hold up. I'm a very cool guy. Don't you want to know more about me?

DORRINE: *(Beat.)* No.

CAL: I love animals. I work at the shelter on Mack.

DORRINE: See. Now that's another thing. I explicitly said that I didn't want a dog walker.

CAL: Dog walker? Who said anything about a dog walker? I'm not a dog walker. I'm an animal caretaker. See? There's a difference. *(Beat.)* Besides, I thought you wanted someone who liked your cat — who liked animals?

DORRINE: Of course. But I don't want them bringing home fleas and other sick diseases to my little Modesty Blaze.

CAL: Modesty Blaze? What a cool name. I bet she's a little, cutie, scrunchy, sweetie cat.

DORRINE: Oh, yeah, she is. She's a snuggly wuggly baby cat. *(Beat.)* Now about your wrong job.

CAL: That's just part-time really. And I always wash. I have a real job. I'm an actor.

DORRINE: An actor?! You're an actor?

CAL: Yeah, but I'm not big-headed or anything. I just do a couple of steady gigs as an actor that bring in the cash.

DORRINE: Cash? Actor? Same sentence? Something's wrong.

CAL: Yeah, I play Banana Man and Bob the Bear for a balloon delivery service. I'm considered their best — their top. Can you believe it? Get this. I never even had one acting class. Never. *(Beat.)* You got a cig on ya?

DORRINE: Oh God, you smoke too?!

CAL: Hey, you too? Cool! But listen, you have to use an ashtray. I'm picky about that.

DORRINE: No, no you misunderstand me. I don't smoke. At all!

CAL: Oh. So why did you say you did? Honesty's the best policy.

DORRINE: I didn't say I did! In fact, I don't allow smoking in my place under any circumstance!

CAL: Ohhh, quit recently, huh? Yeah, I've done that a couple of times. Gets ya cranky. But I can see why you don't like people smokin' here. The walls are so white, no cracks or peeling like my last place. Don't get me wrong. I loved my last place. Really big. Loved my roommate. I woulda stayed there forever if he hadn't shot at me.

DORRINE: *(Beat.)* Shot at you? With a gun?

CAL: Yeeahh. *(Her face is full of fear.)* Oh no, it's cool. He didn't mean to or anything. I was just breaking in the window and he mistook me for a burglar. No biggie.

DORRINE: Ya know, it's getting kinda late.

CAL: I forgot my keys. That's why I was breaking in. And he fired — the gun. It woulda been totally cool. 'Cause he didn't hit me, but he did kinda shatter the neighbors' stained glass window, so the neighbor sued. And Robby was kinda weird about me ever after, which is cool because I didn't like the mice there anyway.

DORRINE: Mice?

CAL: Yeah, one night I woke up and one of them was running across my face. That was it. They have diseases, ya know? Yeah, that's exactly why it's good we'll have a cat here.

DORRINE: We'll?

CAL: This is going to be much better. How are the roaches here?

DORRINE: Oh — kay. You are not moving in here. I mean — no offense, but — we — there is no *we* here.

CAL: But I thought Cheryl said we were a match.

DORRINE: I don't care what Cheryl said. Cheryl is an imbecile. Cheryl could die for all I care!

CAL: Wow! That's sorta harsh. You having a bad day, huh?

DORRINE: A bad day? Try a bad year. I've gone through three roommates.

CAL: Yeah, me too — totally kicked out! *(Beat.)* Not that I didn't want to leave.

DORRINE: I haven't been difficult. I haven't. But my therapist thinks that —

CAL: Hey, don't worry. Relax. I lived with crazy people before.

DORRINE: I'm not crazy! I'm not saying I'm crazy!

CAL: Yeah, uh-huh, that's what all crazy people say. What drugs are you on?

DORRINE: I . . . uh . . . I — I — can't believe this! All I was saying was that my therapist —

CAL: I think therapy's good. So what drugs *are* you on?

DORRINE: I am not on drugs! I'm on — medication! There's a difference. I'm a nervous person. And nervous people need quiet roommates. I want someone calm and quiet this time.

CAL: Well, I'm quiet. And jeez, the band would only play once or twice a week.

DORRINE: *(Beat. Face drops.)* The band?

CAL: Oh, didn't Cheryl mention it? We're the Cool Cats. Heard of us?

DORRINE: *(Beat.)* My therapist has advised me that it's OK that I have some control issues. Some people have control issues and are, therefore, very particular about some things. One of those things, for me, is roommates. And you would not be good.

CAL: Aww, I just saw your little baby peek her little head around the corner. She's long-haired? *(He coaxes the kitty from the hiding place. Whispering to the kitty.)*

DORRINE: Yes. She is. *(She watches. He still coos at the cat.)* That's odd. She usually hisses at new people. *(Looking. Excited.)* Aww, she's looking at you! Look at her little, teeny — *(Stops.)* Wait a minute. Stop trying to distract me. I was making a point. The point is my therapist says I obviously need control.

CAL: Well, humm, as Dr. Phil says — lost three roomies. How has that been working for you?

DORRINE: Uh, ya know, I don't like you. And beyond that, you are not what I requested. You are not female. You're an actor. You smoke. You're in a band. You were shot at. And small rodents crawl across your face at night.

CAL: Well, is that my fault?!

DORRINE: *(Yelling.)* My point is that you are not calm!!!! *(Breathes heavily to relax.)*

CAL: You know what I think? *(She shakes her head no.)* I think the universe brings certain energies together. Sometimes in a way that doesn't make complete sense to anyone. But these different kinds of energies benefit from bouncing off one another . . . and they blend together to form like this positive . . . blended thing — like those yummy blended frozen fruity drinks that create . . . *(Waving arms to think of word.)* energy. Don't you think?

DORRINE: No, I think someone f'd up at the agency. Maybe they spilled a fruity drink on our applications and they stuck together. That's about the closest this has anything to do with yummy blended frozen fruity drinks. And I refuse to pay that roommate service fee because you are the antithesis of what I asked for!

CAL: The antithesis?! Really? Wow! *(Beat.)* What does that mean exactly?

DORRINE: The opposite! You're the opposite of what I want!!

CAL: Well, um that's a good thing. You know uh . . . Yin and Yang. Peanut butter and jelly. Fred and Barney. *(Looks at her.)* Wilma. Fred and Wilma. *(Beat.)* The point is what's so wrong with me, huh? Besides being an actor, smoker, band person who was shot at? I'm a nice guy, right?

DORRINE: Well . . . well I know for a fact that you wouldn't do a revolving chore wheel with me.

CAL: A what?

DORRINE: A revolving chore wheel. It's color coded? It revolves around revealing certain chores around the apartment. Each person is assigned a different color chore in a month cycle. I know you would refuse.

CAL: *(Sincerely interested.)* Oh wow! Cool! Very organized. I like it!

DORRINE: *(Beat.)* You do? It's driven others away. They think it's anal.

CAL: I don't. I love things that are color coded and alphabetical. You think the chore wheel is anal? I had a roommate who organized the cupboard according to food groups. Isn't that completely nuts?

DORRINE: Nuts? Yes, well, I think *nuts* is a very strong word for that.

CAL: Oh wow, you do that? I love that!

DORRINE: But you just said that was completely —

CAL: Shhh. *(Puts his fingers over his lips.)* Look. *(Points to cat.)* She's so friendly.

DORRINE: Oh my God. She's never done that with anyone. *(Shocked.)* Modesty Blaze? Behave yourself.

CAL: I think she likes me, huh?

DORRINE: Well, she certainly seems to like your . . . your muscular leg.

CAL: I didn't say this but I think organizing according to food groups is sexy in a way.

DORRINE: You do?

CAL: Shhh!

DORRINE: *(Whispering.)* So you don't really think it's nuts?

CAL: *(Whispers.)* No, I think it's totally nuts — but in a sexy way. *(Looking down.)* You're kitty seems to like me, isn't that something?

DORRINE: Yes, I, I noticed that, but, but what about my control issues and your rodent problem?

CAL: So you have control issues? Works for me. I'm all about lack of control. You're so tense, Dorrine. Let me help you. *(Massaging her shoulders.)*

DORRINE: Mmmmm. *(Pointing to her shoulder.)* Right there, will ya? *(He moves to that spot.)* Ooh. Ahh. Mmm. Uh — Oooh — that's good.

CAL: You were saying?

DORRINE: *(Moving her shoulder up.)* What? *(Laughs.)* Ha, ha, ha. *(Beat.)* Um, when do you move in?

THE PINNACLE

Liz, thirty, and Lincoln, twenty-eight, have been dating for two years now. They met right after law school when they both got jobs working for the Justice Department. The two lawyers are opposites in some respects: Liz is casual, unabashed, and free-spoken; Lincoln is formal, humble, and reserved. Lincoln has planned a lovely getaway to Italy for the two of them. They are currently staying in a hotel in Tuscany. For several months, Lincoln has been planning to ask Liz to marry him, but he wanted a proper setting in which to ask. The only problem is that Lincoln has lost the engagement ring. He suspects the hotel maid of stealing it, so he's been complaining to the management and obsessed with trying to locate this maid. Liz, not knowing his plan, is feeling hurt and fiercely angry because Lincoln has been ignoring her throughout the entire vacation. He is constantly talking to his friends in the nearby villa and acting like an idiot. In this scene, Lincoln has taken Liz to a romantic Italian restaurant to pop the question. Liz wants to break up with him.

CHARACTERS
Liz: 30
Lincoln: 28, Liz's boyfriend

SETTING
A restaurant in Italy

TIME
The present

LINCOLN: He said he gave away our reservation because we were late. I'm really sorry, Liz.
LIZ: Great. Fine. Let's go someplace else then.

LINCOLN: No, he said he would have a place for us in ten to twenty minutes.

LIZ: Well is it ten minutes or twenty minutes?

LINCOLN: I think it's probably fifteen. *(Beat.)* Or less.

LIZ: Let's go. There was a street café right around the corner.

LINCOLN: Wait. I researched this restaurant for weeks. I chose it. It's a special place, Liz.

LIZ: I researched the café just now. It's special too. It has food. I'm starving. Let's go.

LINCOLN: No! Now, *this* has one of the finest chefs in Lucca and a glorious view.

LIZ: Whoop-dee-do. I've already had great food for days now. That's all we've had is great food. I haven't had one bad meal since we arrived in Italy.

LINCOLN: You sound disappointed.

LIZ: I'm just being realistic. We *will* have one bad meal while we're here. It's statistics. So why don't we plan it?

LINCOLN: Please? Why don't you sit?

LIZ: I don't want to sit.

LINCOLN: Here's a bench. Why don't you sit here and rest?

LIZ: I said I don't want to sit.

LINCOLN: You look beautiful, you know?

(Liz is slightly annoyed, turns and stars at him with disgust.)

LINCOLN: That's a remarkable fresco. They have a violinist here as well. Interesting fact: This restaurant has a tradition of being a place where local men often propose marriage.

LIZ: Interesting fact: I'm starving. *(Pointing.)* Café! Café!

LINCOLN: Look, I planned this. I orchestrated this as best I . . . and then — things . . . I chose an incredibly romantic and intimate place to be with you. That café has a boisterous atmosphere. I don't think we'd be able to talk.

LIZ: Talk? Suddenly you want to talk to me now?

LINCOLN: Yes, I do. I told you today. I have wanted to the whole . . . I just . . . things got all . . . here. I know I've seemed a bit preoccupied, Liz. If you only knew.

LIZ: A bit? You spend half the time hanging around with your friends in the villa from undergrad who obviously aren't the least bit interested in getting to know me.

LINCOLN: No, that's not true. They really, really want to get to know you. Really.

LIZ: They *really really* have a strange way of showing it. Really. They avoid me every time they see us.

LINCOLN: That's because they're afraid. Not of you. I mean, they think I'm going to want to . . .

LIZ: What?

LINCOLN: Talk to you . . . about . . . things — and stuff.

LIZ: Oh. *(Confusion.)* Uh-huh. *(Beat.)* What took you so long at the hotel anyway? We wouldn't have been late. What were you talking to the manager about for all that time?

LINCOLN: Nothing. I just wanted to check on the maid service.

LIZ: Again? That's the fifth time in two days.

LINCOLN: I'm unhappy with their service.

LIZ: The room looks fine. When did you suddenly become obsessed with cleanliness?

LINCOLN: I'm not obsessed. Things were just not to my satisfaction.

LIZ: Not to your satisfaction? We've dated for two years. I've known you for three. I don't think I've ever seen the carpet in your bedroom. In fact, honey, that's what endeared you to me in the first place. This is the one area where you drop the whole pretense thing, the whole formal thing, and act somewhat normal or even flawed. That's why I fell for you, ya know?

LINCOLN: I'm still a messy person, Liz. Really! I am.

LIZ: I'm glad. I'm glad because I don't know who this person is who came with me on this vacation. And the messy guy, that's you, he's the one I want to be with.

LINCOLN: He's still here. He is. And I'm sorry talking to the manager took so long and made us late for dinner. This was supposed to be — well, *will be* a very special night. I hope.

The manager was just having difficulty understanding my Italian. And I was trying to locate the maid from yesterday.

LIZ: The one I saw you talking to in the lobby this morning?

LINCOLN: We weren't talking. She doesn't really understand English.

LIZ: Well, you seemed to be in passionate discussion.

LINCOLN: Because she couldn't understand me.

LIZ: *(Beat.)* Right. Why do you need to talk to her in the first place?

LINCOLN: Well, I —

LIZ: Let's not talk about it. It's pissing me off. Talk about something else.

LINCOLN: OK. *(Thinks. Pause.)* Well, I, I think you look beautiful.

LIZ: You already said that. Are you nervous or something?

LINCOLN: No. I just, I, I've been considering a great many things over the past month, Liz.

LIZ: Have you? OK. Good. *(Beat.)* And?

LINCOLN: I've reached a pinnacle. A pinnacle in my life. I've completed law school, moved on to a position at the justice department. I'm glancing down at the mountain I've scaled and staring up at the ascent ahead. I'm, I'm in a province, a province of change, of transition, of sorts. Waving good-bye to past aspiration and expectations, especially if they are not a foothold to the next plateau. I need to forgo my routine safety and forge forth. Cut loose the excess weight drawing me down and grab for the rope of the future.

LIZ: What are you talking about?

LINCOLN: My, our, my future?

LIZ: Does this mean you want to quit your job?

LINCOLN: I don't know. Maybe, but I was starting to —

LIZ: I know there are a lot of weirdos in the justice department, but it beats corporate hours. You want to quit, hon, quit. No biggie. I'm keeping my cushy situation because I still have delusions I can occasionally do good somewhere. I swear you should have been born in the eighteenth century. What was that all about?

LINCOLN: I don't know. I was trying to explain . . . launching into . . . Did it sound too lofty?

LIZ: You have to ask? "I've reached a pinnacle in my life. A province of change."

(Lincoln looks embarrassed.)

LIZ: Aww. I have too, hon. I've reached a province of change too. I'm changing to decaf. Caffeine gives me the shakes. *(Joking.)* Don't want to be falling off my pinnacle. I'm sorry. Go ahead.

LINCOLN: No, you're right. I do always do that. I'm sorry. I want to say — ask something important, but I think maybe I should wait till after we sit. I'm feeling dizzy. I guess I'm hungry too.

LIZ: Me too. *(Noticing.)* My God that looks good. *(Points to the waiter.)* You flirt with the waiter and distract him. I'll grab the plate.

LINCOLN: Why do *I* have to be the one to flirt?

LIZ: Trust me. He'll like you better. Smile at him. *(Looks at him and then at the waiter.)* You're not going to follow through?!

LINCOLN: I reread the brochure on Lucca.

LIZ: I know you're not gay. But that's the point of being a couple. Tag-team food stealing.

LINCOLN: It looks like we've done almost everything. We should visit the Villa Garzoni gardens tomorrow and then head over to the Duomo di San Martino.

LIZ: What's that?

LINCOLN: It's the Cathedral of Saint Martin. It's supposed to have, uh, uh, elaborate exterior sculptures and inlaid marble scenes and the Volto Santo — the holy face.

LIZ: We've seen a ton of inlaid marble and sculpted crap, Lincoln.

LINCOLN: It's supposed to be exquisite.

LIZ: I have no doubt it's exquisite. I just don't know how much culture and beauty a person can take. I don't know how many amazing sculptures, and carvings and frescos a person can look at day after day before you say, "OK, enough! Let me veg with the tube and some cheese balls." I mean, I'm not complaining, honey, believe me. The Sistine Chapel was undeniably the most incredible thing I've ever seen in my entire life. And I'm glad we did it together. I just want to spend a day doing nothing. That's it. Nothing.

LINCOLN: Sure. Maybe we could take a long walk. Follow the rampart promenade making a complete circuit of the city. Parts of Lucca face out toward the rolling hills and vineyards. Other parts are supposed to give really intimate views of backyard verandas.

LIZ: There's only one intimate view I'm really interested in tomorrow. *(She smiles.)*

LINCOLN: *(Smiles. Takes that in and then continues.)* But the Villa Garzoni garden has this cascading water staircase that's supposed to be spec —

LIZ: So does the First National Bank building around the corner from work. Did you not hear me?

LINCOLN: Yes. Of course I heard you. And I love that idea. I just thought we could then get up and walk the circuit of the city.

LIZ: Didn't I just go into a long explanation as to why I don't feel like going all over the place tomorrow?

LINCOLN: I know. You didn't want to go to the Cathedral of Saint Martin. So we won't.

LIZ: Wow. That is all you heard.
(He looks at her.)

LINCOLN: Yeah, and the . . . making love part.

LIZ: Look, honey, no lush hills, no gorgeous gardens, just sleep and whatever else comes to us. We get up whenever we want. Maybe we'll go some place, maybe we won't, but we're not making any plans! Understand?

LINCOLN: Sure. *(Puppy-dog.)* Sure.

LIZ: Oh God. Don't do that.

LINCOLN: What? I'm not doing anything.

LIZ: Yes, you are. You're doing that puppy face of yours.

LINCOLN: It's just . . . we only have two more days.

LIZ: Yes, we have two days. And none of the days did I decide what we do. Besides which, I think this running here and there is just a means to avoid me.

LINCOLN: What? That's not true. No, you don't understand what's been —

LIZ: I'm serious. We go to museums or cathedrals, and you're completely silent. I'm oohing and ahhing, and talking about opera, even singing arias and telling you how I want to be Sophia Loren and you, you're not there. I have to pull you back from whatever planet you've been visiting these last few days.

LINCOLN: *(Looking toward the tables.)* Liz, I think those people are getting up.

LIZ: You're not even listening to me!! Do you realize you aren't listening to me? I'm leaving.

LINCOLN: No! Wait. I love you. I mean, I'm totally listening. I'm just — I know you're hungry.

LIZ: Well, I'm suggesting lying in bed, meaning being together all day until we're exhausted and you, you want to go every place else on the planet! So how is that supposed to make me feel?

LINCOLN: No, I want to be with you. I do. Definitely.

LIZ: So why so interested in the first maid then, huh?

LINCOLN: I, I thought — I mean, she —

LIZ: Why, huh? What's going on with her?

LINCOLN: Honestly, it's because I think she may have, this is unethical to say without real knowledge, I think she might have taken something.

LIZ: Did she steal some money from you? *(Beat.)* Wait a minute, I thought you did mostly traveler's checks?

LINCOLN: I did. No, it's not money. It's . . . something. I can't say.

LIZ: What?

LINCOLN: I, I can't say. It's something I was going to talk to you about tonight.

LIZ: Wow. Wow, you really caught me off guard, Lincoln. So how long have you known her?

LINCOLN: What? Who?

LIZ: I wondered why you were spending all those hours on the Internet.

LINCOLN: No! No, you've got the wrong idea.

LIZ: And all those times pretending you were some cool, feminist-interested kind of guy. Impressing my mother by quoting Gloria last Thanksgiving.

LINCOLN: Wait, wait. This is not. You have it all wrong.

LIZ: You didn't want a strong woman after all. You just wanted some little thing who barely speaks your language.

LINCOLN: I'm not seeing the maid, Liz!

LIZ: Have you slept with her?

LINCOLN: No! No! Not at all!

LIZ: Now the whole thing with your friends feeling awkward and the, the pinnacle speech make sense now! I'm the weight you wanted to cut loose!

LINCOLN: No, no you're not the weight! Not the weight! You're the rope! The rope!

LIZ: Right. So what was the weight-thing then, hum?

LINCOLN: My record album collection.

LIZ: Why don't we just break up now, Lincoln? I was going to break up with you when we got home anyway.

LINCOLN: You what? You were? But, but I was going to ask you to marry me tonight.

LIZ: Ha. My God, that is the lowest! I mean, talk about try-ing to get out of confrontation. We've had a disastrous time all week. You've barely even spoken to me. I know things aren't working. I don't know if it's this maid or what. I know things are bad. And I'm sad, and miserable about it all too, but how dare you try to get out of our breakup by saying you were going to ask me to marry you! That's pathetic!!

LINCOLN: No, no. I was nervous. I was really nervous and going over and over it in my head — my speech. I was really going to ask me to marry you tonight. Urgh, you to marry me. That's why I was picky about the restaurant. That's why my friends weren't talking to you. They were nervous. They were nervous for me. Didn't know how I was going to ask. See, I kept changing how I was going to ask you, finding better, more beautiful sites. And then the whole ring thing. Who knew that would happen? Her stealing the ring. And then everybody said just ask her tonight — ring or not! And then we're late! God, I love you. *(Sighs.)* That's all I wanted to say. It seems easy. I love you. Will you marry me?

LIZ: Don't play games with me, Lincoln. Don't tread on my heart.

LINCOLN: I don't want to tread on your heart, Liz. I want to take care of it. Protect it forever.

LIZ: Oh, I think I'm gonna cry here. You. *(Beat.)* That witch stole my ring?

LINCOLN: I don't know. But I'll get you another immediately if you say yes.

LIZ: Aren't you supposed to be on your knees?

LINCOLN: Oh. God . . . *(He starts to kneel down.)* I just thought you would think that was too —

LIZ: *(Reaching for him.)* I do. I mean, I do think that's too sappy. *(He starts to stand.)* Kneel. I just need a minute to think about this, Lincoln. You've had a lot of time with this.

LINCOLN: Yeah, sure. Take your time.

LIZ: *(Pause.)* Lincoln, where did you have the ring?

LINCOLN: In a bag in the bottom of my suitcase.

LIZ: Oh. *(Pause.)* Not a Payless shoe bag?

LINCOLN: It was white with — yeah! It was in a box. I put it in that bag to disguise it.

LIZ: Really? Umm. The maid didn't steal the ring then. I never saw it, but I think it's still properly cushioned in the bag, probably stuffed between my dirty underwear and a smelly sock. In the pocket of my suitcase. I used your bag as a dirty laundry thingy.

LINCOLN: You're kidding?!

LIZ: Sorry.

LINCOLN: That's good. I'm mean, I'm glad it wasn't lost or stolen. Really glad. *(Beat.)* So . . . I guess you need a couple of days to think about it then?

LIZ: No.

LINCOLN: No?

LIZ: Yes.

LINCOLN: Yes?

LIZ: Yes!

LINCOLN: Really?

LIZ: Yes!

LINCOLN: *(She nods.)* You just made me the happiest guy in all the world.

(They kiss.)

LIZ: *(She smiles.)* So what are we doing tomorrow?

LINCOLN: *(Smiling slyly.)* Nothing. *(Beat.)* I love you, Liz.

LIZ: I love you too.

FYI

Cheryl, twenties, has applied for a new position in a dif-
ferent section of her company. The director of this area,
Donald, thirties, has called her in for an interview today.
Cheryl has been incredibly nervous all morning. This is
exactly the kind of promotion she wants. Donald, whose
father owns the entire business, tends to act defensively
when asking people about their qualifications because
he is less than qualified. To make up for his lack of ed-
ucation and experience, he has made a habit of creat-
ing new work-related acronyms in an effort to confound
his underlings.

CHARACTERS
Cheryl: 20s, a job applicant
Donald: 30s, the potential employer

SETTING
Donald's chic office

TIME
The present

DONALD: I'm sorry my office is a mess. Messes breed creativity
for me. I'm certainly breeding something in here, right?
(Laughs. Gestures.) Take a seat wherever you'd like, Cheryl.
Any where you'd like! *(Stops her with high pitch.)* Oop. Ex-
cept there. *(She goes to sit again.)* Oop, or there. *(Points.)*
Hup — now, that's my favorite chair.
CHERYL: Sorry.
DONALD: *(He goes to move it.)* No problem. Isn't that goofy?
I have a favorite. The fabric's so soft. *(Points to a chair.)*
Why don't you sit right there?
CHERYL: Thanks. *(She sits.)*
DONALD: *(He sits, touching the chair.)* I like the pattern too.
A lot. *(Abruptly interrupting chair obsession.)* Well now, as

I mentioned a moment ago, I'm the RDM. here, so every-one — the RAs, the RCs, the ARs, the CRAs, as well as the RCAs — they all report to me. That's how I like it. I like to crack the whip. I may look sweet, but I'm a CTW kinda guy when it comes down to it. *(Chuckles.)* Kidding. So what about you, Cheryl?

CHERYL: Huh? Well, I, uh — I'm here for the new position.

DONALD: No. I mean, well yes. I know. But what *are* you ex-actly? *(Beat, as Cheryl looks confused.)* Your current posi-tion? Marla told me you work in one of our other areas.

CHERYL: Oh God! *(Hitting her head.)* I'm sorry. *(He nods.)* I get it. I'm doing this esoteric thing in my head like, "What *are* you?" I'm thinking, hmm . . . I'm a human, I'm a phi-losophy grad, I do yoga, I love pretzels. Sorry, I get very nervous for interviews. Actually, I'm a Research Assistant in the NIHP area here.

DONALD: RA?! *(She nods.)* RA, huh? In NIHP? *(She nods.)* Well, I'll be darned.

CHERYL: That's right. *(He nods.)* Do you need a copy of my résumé? I have several extra here.

DONALD: Save it. Marla has a copy. I prefer to look at peo-ple without seeing all their past education. I mean, who cares in the end? Who cares! So you got a master's from Brown.

CHERYL: Ph.D.

DONALD: Just a bunch of letters. You don't think I have an education? You don't think I earned this? Just because my father owns this place, you think I just got a free ride? *(Cheryl shakes her head no furiously. Donald sighs. Shakes her head no.)* OK, I did, but that's not the point. Sure, you may know how to program this or that. Sure, you may know how to read three languages. But la-de-dah. Compe-tence is overrated. Who said that's all I wanted? In the end, what matters is how *symbiotic* you are with us, right? Dif-ficult questions must be answered. Will you be part of our team? Will you bring something to the table? Will you spon-taneously bring in Crispy Kremes? Just kidding. Now really. Will you be in harmony with our symphony or will you simply suck — in other words, OOTN? *(Nodding.)* Right? You see? *(Beat.) This* is what matters. OOTN. Do you understand what I'm saying?

CHERYL: Sure. Sure. Absolutely! OOTN, right. That's important. That's the new software, right?

DONALD: Out-of-tune nincompoop, Cheryl. Out-of-tune nincompoop. I'll say it again. Out-of-tune nincompoop. *That's* what matters. *(Nodding.)* See?

CHERYL: *(As if this idea is causing her to rethink her entire life.)* Ohhhh.

DONALD: You can't get that from a résumé. I want to see *you* — the *real* you, the undocumented you, the unrevised, unedited, unaltered, bare-naked you!

CHERYL: Should that be unrevised or nonrevised?

DONALD: Don't get OOTN on me already. The question is, will you reveal yourself today?

CHERYL: Well, I, I think maybe —

DONALD: OK then! I'll let you see the bare-naked me too.

CHERYL: *(Uneasy.)* Well, that's, that's not entirely necessary.

DONALD: RA, huh? *(Takes a breath, sighs.)* So. RA? *(She nods.)* Good ole RA *(Shakes his head.)* You are . . . an RA Sure, an RA today, but who knows where your future lies? Could be an RC tomorrow, and tomorrow after that, a CR, CRA, and then, who knows, the sky's the limit — RDM, RCA, DVD, whatever. You never know what can happen if you're ambitious, Cheryl. I know because that was my destiny, my path. That was me!

CHERYL: Really?

DONALD: *(Nods. Beat.)* Yep. And it hasn't taken that long. Not long at all. Just a moment. Just a blink of the eye. I'm glad you could come in today. *(He nods.)*

CHERYL: Thanks.

DONALD: Now, before I start, Cheryl. I think it's important to say that this interview is for you as much as it is for me. Sure, I want to learn about your abilities. Sure, I want to learn your interests. Sure, I want to learn about your capabilities, but I also want *you* to learn all you can about the position and the atmosphere here. In the end, we just want to be HP, right?

CHERYL: Right.

DONALD: Sure it's good to be FS. But HP — that's our aim here. That's the focus. That's how you get to be FS. Right?

CHERYL: Right.

DONALD: In some ways, HP is far better than FS. Actually HP is the ultimate be all and end all. Am I right?

CHERYL: *(Hoping to God that he won't ask her what* HP *means.)* Absolutely.

DONALD: Good. We're on the same SP So would you say you were H.P. in your current position then, Cher?

CHERYL: I . . . uh, yeah, I think I'm uh, pretty darn HP. Pretty HP, I'd say.

DONALD: Good. Good. Anyway, let me go forth with the job description, so we can MO. Coming from the NIHP section here will give you an LUO, if you know what I mean. You'll come with some foundation for what we do and the QC we expect. In this section of the company, our focus is entirely on PS., which is different. PST is absolutely a totally new way of designing things for us. And, in fact, I developed it. I bet you heard about PST in NIHP, didn't you?

CHERYL: Um . . . I, I uh —

DONALD: You should have. It went out in memo 45982C-ZIT. Anyway, in our area, our main goal is to develop new proposals — complete S.R. — which become W.S. or written solutions for many of the manufacturers we work with. You know, I was written up in our monthly newsletter, MMMP, two consecutive months in a row for PST. That was partially based on memo 45982C-ZIT. Are you sure you didn't hear about PST?

CHERYL: Um . . . yeah . . . I'm sure I did. PST? Yeah, that does sound very familiar. It's just been so busy in our area.

DONALD: It was on the front page.

CHERYL: Oh yeah. I'm sure I did. I think I thought the idea was incredible.

DONALD: Thank you. It was, wasn't it? One of our biggest customers in this area is Clean Feet — foot powder and soles mostly. They loved it too. I tell folks here we deal with souls each and every day. Ha ha. Anyway, we use data mining and PSD, and PST theories to show them which segment to GB *(Making little joke.)* It's kinda like which stinky feet to go after first if you know what I mean.

CHERYL: *(Chuckles.)* Yeah, like getting a *foothold* on the market so as to be a *shoo*-in.

DONALD: Yes, but we don't joke about our business here.

CHERYL: No, of course not. Sorry.

DONALD: Our goal is always WP or WPNS or sometimes WPNS . . . S! But our real value is our people. People-people. That's it for us. PP. Their spontaneous ideas, their thoughts, their contribution. PP. Do you follow? *(She starts to say something.)* PP . . . I love saying that. In the research center position, sometimes you would be working very directly with a client and sometimes you'd be working directly with me who would be working directly with a client. And sometimes you'd be working for someone else who would be working directly with a client and sometimes you and I would be doing absolutely nothing. *(Laughs.)* Just kidding. We're hands-on, but not too HO, we want the client to give us a clear HO incentive to be really HO or Ho as we like to call it. Do you think you're Ho, Cheryl?

CHERYL: Oh, I'm Ho. I'm all about Ho.

DONALD: Hold that thought for later. I want you to say PP for me?

CHERYL: Excuse me?

DONALD: You heard me — say PP, Charleen. Say it for me.

CHERYL: Cheryl.

DONALD: No, PP. Not your name.

CHERYL: No, I meant that's not my name. My name's not —

DONALD: I'm asking you kindly to say PP.

CHERYL: OK, PP.

DONALD: No, Charleen. Say it like you mean it! Not with hesitancy. Don't be afraid.

CHERYL: *(Matter-of-fact, nodding her head to show she believes it.)* PP.

DONALD: That was very weak. I don't want shrinking violets here. You've got to mean things here. We look for meaning here. Feel it, shout it, live it — we are all people-people — PP!

CHERYL: *(Shouting incredibly loudly.)* PP!

DONALD: *(Wiping her spit out of his eyes.)* Good . . . my . . . very nice. *(Turning to Marla.)* No, Marla, everything's just fine. We're all HP in here. *(Turns to Cheryl.)* So, Charleen, what do you think so far?

CHERYL: Well, I think it's just fantastic, but —

DONALD: No, no. I haven't heard one word about you yet. Are you trying to keep your talents a secret?

CHERYL: No, no I was trying to find out about the data —

DONALD: And don't you have any questions? You can jump right in.

CHERYL: Oh definitely. I would love to know about the systems you —

DONALD: Not that I'm really finished with the total job description. I like to be thorough. I like our PPs to know what they're getting into. But you should speak up or I'll think you're a little OOTN as I like to say.

CHERYL: *(Quickly.)* Do you use CMS data modules or SPSS?

DONALD: Excuse me?

CHERYL: *(Speaking quickly to get in.)* Well, I'm very familiar with both. I just wondered if you used CMS data modules or SPSS for WPs?

DONALD: *(Beat.)* What?

CHERYL: I recently downloaded CMS and EDU.I and felt that they really helped throw charts together a lot more efficiently than SPSS. Unless you have SPSS for Windows. Now that works really well. But I heard that EDI version 6.0 might have a Window's platform too, so that might be a lot easier with the variables. I have a heavy-duty background in C +++ that really makes all these programs feel like a walk in the park. Don't you agree?

DONALD: *(Beat.)* Are you trying to show off? You making this up?

CHERYL: *(Stunned.)* What?

DONALD: Trying to get all fancy with CMS and EDU and C+, +, -, +, =. You making up a bunch of fancy-dancy little programs that don't exist to threaten my intelligence now, Charleen? To put the ole interviewer in his ole place? I don't know what program we use for our WP or our WPNS or our WPNS . . . S! What do you think of that? Huh?!

CHERYL: It was only a question. I wasn't trying to threaten your intelligence, Donald.

DONALD: *(Standing up.)* Oh-ho, trying to get all personal now, are we? Spouting your fancy terms. Using all those initials — those holograms —

CHERYL: Acronyms?

DONALD: *(Staring at her sternly.)* Listen, little Miss Know-It-All. You think you're smart, don't you? *(She shakes her head no.)* You do. You don't even care about PP. It's all you, you! Well, you know what I think? PU!

CHERYL: I was just trying to help.

DONALD: Oh please! Just because you fancy-termed your way into being an RA when most people are RC — or worse, BO — doesn't mean you are going to dictionary your way to the top here. You better clip those wings and ground your, your, your — something. 'Cause you don't just come in here and inherit this job. *(Realizing he did.)* You have to earn those wings, bumblebee! We are stinging a different tune, Miss Bzzz, Bzzz. Pretending like you didn't know about PST. You Bzzzzzt! You think you're too good for this job?

CHERYL: No, please, please, I really would —

DONALD: Wouldn't we all! Well, you know what? Ha!! Ha.

Ha. Ha . . . Ha! You are going to work here! You got that?
You are going to be a PP whether you, you like it or not!

CHERYL: What did you say?!

DONALD: You heard me. You're hired indefinitely! Ha!

CHERYL: Oh my God! I can't believe it. I thought you were
going to say . . . never mind. I, uh, this is such an honor. I
won't let you down. I'll read up on PST first thing. This is
really a, well, I think an HP moment. And for the record,
I really am PP. I'm Ho too. Really Ho. And no offense? But
FYI? My name is Cheryl.

DONALD: Details. Be here tomorrow. Eight AM. And no BS!

CUDDLES AND WACKY AND
THE LITTLE CAR

Cuddles and Wacky, late forties, a married couple and both veteran clowns in the Topsy Turvy Circus, have had another act screwup again tonight. Wacky keeps missing cues and seems to be lacking the usual "oomph" in his performance. Cuddles doesn't know what's wrong with him. As it turns out, it's a case of midlife clown crisis. Wacky's sick of the tiny car act and the screaming kids and the makeup. He wonders what it's all about. As the scene begins, Cuddles is reminding him of his missed cue.

CHARACTERS
Wacky: 40s, a clown
Cuddles: 40s, his clown wife

SETTING
A dressing room at the Topsy Turvy Circus

TIME
The present, after this evening's performance

CUDDLES: Hey, did you forget something out there or what? *(Wacky looks at her.)*
WACKY: *(Really upset.)* Oh no! The rolling pin?
CUDDLES: What's the matter with you?
WACKY: *(Quickly.)* I don't know. I don't know. I don't know. I don't — *(She hits him like he's a skipping record.)* Ow!
CUDDLES: Sorry. Yesterday it was the fire-hose fiasco. The day before it was a juggling ball right in the eye. Today it's the rolling pin. What is up with you?
WACKY: Hey, yesterday was not my fault, Cuddles. I told you Loonie was early.
CUDDLES: No, she wasn't. She was right on cue. The fire music was playing. Jello brought the fire engine around right on

cue — axe in hand and no you. And I had to be on fire for like . . . I don't know . . . a long time.

WACKY: You're good at that, Cuddles. You keep it fresh.

CUDDLES: Don't sweeten me up. I'm pissed. Burning for a long time is not funny. Short burning — funny. Long burning — not — at all — funny!

WACKY: *(Getting impatient.)* OK!

CUDDLES: It's all about timing. And you've been blowing it for all of us. Kids aren't laughing. I saw one little girl screamin' her head off in the front row.

WACKY: Well, let her scream! *(Cuddles' mouth drops.)* So what? It's good for her.

CUDDLES: Good for her?

WACKY: Life is hard. Life is tragic. Empty, difficult, and . . . blah-zie.

CUDDLES: Have you been reading *Catcher in the Rye* again?

WACKY: Yeah. Besides, they always scream their heads off. The little ones are the only ones with any sense. Parents beat them out of it. We do look scary. Florescent hair, abnormally large features, really tacky clothes. I feel scary, not at all funny. I feel surreal.

CUDDLES: You don't look surreal. You look real. Good. Better than ever. All that weight you lost. You've been eating great! Cholesterol down.

WACKY: I'm sick of the act. It's too much of the same, same. And there's absolutely no depth to it!

CUDDLES: It's a clown act, Wacky. It's about running around pratfalling and slapsticking and things flying out of the hose and your nose and your hair flying off you head. This is not subtle humor we're talking about. You turning up all black and burnt to a crisp with your shoes smoldering. Now, that's funny. Look, the fire engine act has gotten laughs for sixteen years. You don't argue with consistency.

WACKY: Yeah?

CUDDLES: Yeah! I'm a very funny burner. You're a very funny incompetent fireman.

WACKY: So what's so funny about it? We end up all black and burned. The house burns. It's tragic. I'm a complete loser. And you're homeless.

CUDDLES: And that's funny. Don't start thinking on me now.

WACKY: Why not?

CUDDLES: Thinking is going to ruin your career. 'Member Howie? *(Nods. Beat.)* Humm?

WACKY: That's different. He was crazy.

CUDDLES: He started thinking. *(Gives him the knowing look.)*

WACKY: Yeah, that he was an alien. I'm just thinking maybe I want something more than clowning in my life.

CUDDLES: More than clowning? We're the stars of Topsy Turvy!

WACKY: Oh yeah? And what would you call The Flying Zippola brothers?

CUDDLES: Oh. *(Beat.)* Stinky. Unkempt. Icky comes to mind. *(Beat.)* Do they understand that deodorant is not an optional hygiene product?

WACKY: Yeah, well they are all over the posters and making salaries about five times ours.

CUDDLES: No?! *(He nods.)* Inbreds! So they can do a triple somersault. So what?! Can they produce a flower bouquet from their butt? Hum? They couldn't make a balloon animal to save their lives.

WACKY: Maybe my lack of timing has to do with distraction. Bigger things keep coming into my head.

CUDDLES: Oh? These *big* things wouldn't happen to be in ring three would they?

WACKY: What are you talking about?

CUDDLES: *(Obviously referring to something.)* Nothing!

WACKY: Oh no! You're not thinking . . .

CUDDLES: I've seen how you've been eyeing old iron throat and her rather large —

WACKY: What are you talking about? She's half my age!

CUDDLES: Exactly! *(Doing her accent.)* "Katova. Katrina Katova. Katova. Va. Vvv. I swallow svords, vords, and husbands. Vvv." She flirted with you over coffee this morning. *(Doing an imitation.)* "Do you vant sugar or are you sveet enough?"

WACKY: Well, you got to admit that she's got a pretty good act.

CUDDLES: Oh come on! You've seen one sword-eater, you've seen them all. They all do the same thing. It's not like you can do anything unique with the act. You pick up the sword. You show them the sword. Oooh, ahhh, and then down the hatch. Real special. Oh boy, she's going to swallow a *different* sword for an encore. Whoopee!

WACKY: I know but she does have a flare.

CUDDLES: Yes, she does. She's seventeen and wears tassels. Only tassels. Very flarish.

WACKY: Oh Cuddles, you know I love you. So my eye sways over to one tassel or another every once in a while. That doesn't mean I care for anyone else but you, sweetie.

CUDDLES: Oh yeah? What about Feona and her pooches in ring two?

WACKY: What?!

CUDDLES: Don't lie to me. You want to jump through her hoops — I see things.

WACKY: That is completely ridiculous! Yes, I have noticed both acts.

CUDDLES: Ahh-ha!

WACKY: Professionally. From a professional standpoint. You see, they both seem to love their work.

CUDDLES: So!

WACKY: So . . . so I don't.

CUDDLES: *(Angered and insistent.)* Yes you do!

WACKY: No, I don't.

CUDDLES: You don't?

WACKY: I don't! My whole life is a vast desert of death and failure.

CUDDLES: *(Thinking to herself.)* That's what I am to you? A vast desert? I mean, I may be vast, but a desert? *(Looking at herself.)* I guess I could use a nighttime moisturizer.

WACKY: What? No! You're not hearing me. I love you. No matter what you look like. That I'm sure of. I'm just saying I feel dissatisfied with me. With what I've accomplished.

CUDDLES: Oh, well then that's not so bad. *(Beat.)* Wait a minute. I do the same thing you do!

WACKY: Yes, but that's different. You like it. And it fits you.

CUDDLES: OK. Clarify. If the vast desert of death and failure is the job, and that *fits* me, what exactly are you saying?

WACKY: I'm just saying that . . . I don't know what I'm saying. I was thinking maybe about getting an office job. Something quiet.

CUDDLES: Quiet?! Quiet?! How boring! Who wants to be quiet?! I was not made to be quiet!

WACKY: Obviously. It's just every day feels like the same thing over and over.

CUDDLES: Well . . . so! Try stilt-walking again, talk to Sigmond about throwing fiery batons around, but don't stoop to an office. What do you think's going to happen in an office?

WACKY: Nothing. But at least it will be different for a while for me. Now, it's the same tent. It's the same costume. It's the same little car we cram into every day. It's the same —

CUDDLES: I get the idea. And that's not entirely true. We got a new car in ninety-nine. It's much, much roomier!

WACKY: In the little car. In the little car. In the little car. Every night. Jello's on my head. Twinkee's armpit in my eye. Boo Boo's butt in my face.

CUDDLES: I thought you liked those people!

WACKY: People yes, it's the little *car* I can't stand!! Maybe we need a new act.

CUDDLES: A new act?! But people look for the little car. Just like they look for the fire engine bit.

WACKY: Well, maybe you just think that. Maybe they hate the fire engine bit. Maybe they want to throw up when they see the stupid little car. Talk about lack of surprises there!

They just *think* they like them because they were told to laugh over and over and over when they saw these things as children. Now they're brainwashed and unhappy as hell so they make their own children suffer through them as well, telling them to laugh — Always to laugh over and over and the whole sick cycle continues until we perish! Ha ha ha ha ha! Brainwashing one child after another until oblivion! And we'll never know until some brave child someday stands up and plants a little bomb in the little car and we'll all literally explode all over the place! And won't that be funny!

CUDDLES: *(Beat.)* You really don't like the car bit, do you?

WACKY: I'm just thinking out loud there.

CUDDLES: Don't do that.

WACKY: Maybe we need a tragic leading character, someone who lost a family member.

CUDDLES: We aren't doing *Hamlet* here, Wacky! You're a clown! You have polka-dots on your pants! You're wearing a nose that goes "honk, honk"!

WACKY: Yes, but *Hamlet* has some funny parts.

CUDDLES: Which part — when his girlfriend drowns or when he ponders suicide?

WACKY: When you put it like that, it does sound rather unfunny. I guess it's just a regular ole midlife crisis — this. Nothing feels right. The smell of the elephants, the roar of the lion, the screams of terror from the children, it just doesn't have the same umph!

CUDDLES: *(Rubbing his head.)* I understand, Baby. I know how you feel. You wake up one day and you're putting on your ole butt pads and you realize, you don't need as much padding as you once did. Your putting on your red nose and your start to notice your real nose is not all that attractive. It's just been hidden for all these years. You wonder . . . What have I done with my life? Where has it all gone? How have I contributed to the world at large? My God, I'm getting depressed. *(Hits him.)* You have a lot of nerve! I wasn't thinking about this stuff.

WACKY: *(Suddenly excited.)* Why don't we run away? We could do it? We could run away tomorrow when we hit Chicago. I could work in an office. You could do freelance for kids' birthday parties. We could find a little apartment. Settle down.

CUDDLES: In a big city? But there's all kinds of weirdos in a big city like Chicago.

WACKY: We sleep in a train car next to Loonie, Jello, and a guy who sticks his head inside a lion's mouth on a regular basis and you're worried about weirdos?

CUDDLES: You'd have to learn how to type and use a PC for an office job.

WACKY: So! I learn fast.

CUDDLES: And you'd have to buy some dress-up clothes.

WACKY: Well. I dress up all the time — every day.

CUDDLES: Not those kind of dress-up clothes.

WACKY: *(A little less sure.)* Oh. Yeah. Well, . . . I could do that.

CUDDLES: We'd have to really adjust our schedule.

WACKY: You'd consider this? Honestly?

CUDDLES: Hell! If you're willing to get up at seven every morning, I can certainly give it a try!

WACKY: That's great! I — Seven? Did you say seven?

CUDDLES: Yep.

WACKY: AM?

CUDDLES: Uh-huh.

WACKY: In the morning seven?

CUDDLES: Yes.

WACKY: *(Beat.)* You know, I think you're right. The little car has been seeming a lot roomier.

EATING FOR TWO

Hal, early twenties, has been talking to Nicole, twenty-six, online for the last few weeks. They've been spending hours and hours in private chat rooms and sending e-mails to each other. In the past week, they have begun talking on the phone. Today, they discuss plans to meet face-to-face.

CHARACTERS
Nicole: 26, pregnant
Hal: late 20s

SETTING
Nicole's and Hal's apartments; later a suburban
    Denny's restaurant

TIME
The present

NICOLE: *(On phone.)* OK, axe murderer check. What about strange collections? Candle-dripped bottles? Skulls? Hello Kitty paraphernalia?

HAL: No, no, and *no!*

NICOLE: Well, you sound healthy. But the thing is, I don't know. You could be a serial killer.

HAL: Oh come on! I still watch cartoons on Saturday morning.

NICOLE: See! Exposed to a lot of violence. All I'm saying is that knowing someone online is a lot different than meeting them in person.

HAL: How profound. Look, my butt is sore. Isn't that even more profound? These late nights online and on the phone are killing me. If we don't stop this behavior, I might be permanently damaged. Even my mother seemed to notice it's lost its shape.

NICOLE: OK, leaving yourself wide open on the mother thing.

Won't touch that. And I apologize to your butt. But I feel I need to get to know you better.

HAL: My God, you already know my deepest secret.

NICOLE: I do? Oh. Yeah. Right. I do.

HAL: Oh my God! You don't remember, do you?!

NICOLE: No, no. I remember!

HAL: You do? What was it then?

NICOLE: Umm. *(Beat.)* Could I get a little hint?

HAL: About the closet? The remote-control fire engine?

NICOLE: Oh, oh, yeah! That girl's graduation party thing.

HAL: Exactly. We were playing ten minutes in the closet and I rolled over onto the remote and it sent the fire engine right toward her . . .

NICOLE: Oh yes. I remember.

HAL: See? We have memories already, and you know my deepest secret. You can use it against me. Cruelly. See, I'm honest. And sweet. Completely meetable.

NICOLE: No offense, but that's not much of a dirty, dark secret. In fact it's sort of cute.

HAL: Fine, unman me why don't you?

NICOLE: In fact, I bet to this day, Becky Johnson still looks at fire engines and gets all hot and bothered.

HAL: You don't know Becky Johnson. Bothered maybe. Hot — not a chance.

NICOLE: Oh God. I must be getting hard up. Somehow ten minutes in the closet doesn't sound half-bad to me. It's been a long time.

HAL: I know what you mean. Now, let's meet. In person. Some place real public if you don't feel comfortable. A very public restaurant. Not too far from campus. *(Beat.)* You know so much about me already. You know I work at the TV station. You know my dreams, my aspirations, even my shoe size.

NICOLE: See. That's the thing. Maybe we know too much.

HAL: But do you know my ATM PIN number? Huh, huh?

NICOLE: Sixty-five. Thirty-four.

HAL: Holy . . . ! I told you my PIN number?!! Jeez, I must've been drunk.

NICOLE: You were. *(Beat.)* It's just weird. Ya know when someone knows weird, specific things about you? Ya know, bizarre things about you . . . like some sweaty guy who tongued you when you were thirteen or some strange habit you have of sucking the salt off of pretzels and spitting them out? It's scary. We share things because we feel connected, but if we don't have that same connection offline, it's just weird. And then you can't be friends online again, because you're too disappointed by how bad offline was. It's like . . . it's like it's all ruined.

HAL: You mean, like, you aren't attracted?

NICOLE: Yeah.

HAL: Well, you saw my pic. You said you liked it. And I *loved* your pic and your profile. You didn't lie about anything, did you?

NICOLE: No! Of course not. Did you?

HAL: No.

NICOLE: You're sure about my profile?

HAL: I told you that from the start. You sound great!

NICOLE: You know, you really are pretty cool too — as far as guys go.

HAL: I am. In person as well as online. So you'll meet me then?

NICOLE: *(Beat.)* Denny's. Tomorrow. 6:30 PM. I'll wear a black jacket. You won't be able to miss me, trust me.

HAL: Cool!! I'll be in a brown leather jacket. OK. See ya there.

NICOLE: Wait, Hal, have you ever done this before? Met other women?

HAL: No. *(Beat.)* Have you met men?

(Cut to Hal and Nicole in their cars.)

NICOLE: No. *(To audience, miming driving.)* Of course I'm lying. I met at least fourteen guys before I got pregnant. But Hal would be the first one since. So I don't feel I'm totally lying because, since I got pregnant, I've become a totally new person. *(Beat.)* It was number thirteen, Hashbrown Sixty-nine, who caused my condition. I dated him for a month. Jerk! And total liar. Hal's different. He doesn't mind that I'm pregnant. Maybe he even likes it. Never even asked me about it after he read my profile. Saying "Hal" is weird. I've called him Camaro for two months now. That's his online name. He's really into Camaros. He owns two.

HAL: *(To audience, miming driving.)* God, I just keep sweating and sweating. Thank God I have my leather jacket. I won't take it off when I get to Denny's. If I ever find Denny's. It's so cool that she picked a breakfast-food place for our first meeting. Most women choose overpriced bars with silly names like — Neo or Anti. Oh, I have met women before. Only eighteen or so times, but I didn't feel I was lying because it's never worked out. Besides, it's different with Superwoman. We are simpatico. After hours of amazing conversations, from existentialism to steakburgers, I'm finally going to meet her. Nicole's incredibly intelligent, has a great sense of humor, has her life together. I'm really thinking this may be the one! *(Beat.)* I think I'll play it cool though. I mean, she could be a lot uglier than her picture. Right?

NICOLE and HAL: *(Simultaneously.)* Oh God. We really should have been more specific.

HAL: Carry a red rose?

NICOLE: Meet in front of the revolving refrigerated cake display?

HAL: Wear signs that say, "Losers."

HAL and NICOLE: Denny's is packed!

NICOLE: *(To a Denny's patron.)* Hi! Hal? I'm — *(Beat.)* Oh. *(Laughs uncomfortably.)* Oops.

HAL: *(To Denny's patron.)* Hi! Nicole? *(Beat.)* Oh! I thought you were my friend. Haven't seen her in a while. Had facial surgery.

NICOLE: *(To Denny's patron.)* No, no. I'm waiting for a friend. *(Beat.)* He's got brown hair and brown eyes. About 160 pounds. Brown leather jacket. *(To audience.)* Do you know how many friggin' guys fit that description?

HAL: *(To Denny's patron.)* I am not trying to steal your wife, sir! I just simply thought she looked like . . . No, no, I don't want to step outside.

NICOLE: No, God, I'm not interested! Uck!

HAL: *(Not turning to see her yet.)* Nicole?

NICOLE: *(Seeing him.)* Hal?

HAL: *(Turns.)* Oh my God, I've been looking all — *(Seeing she's pregnant.)* Oh my gosh!

NICOLE: What? *(Looking down.)* Oh. Bigger than what you expected, huh?

HAL: No, no, I, uh, wow, uh . . . Hi!

NICOLE: Hi. What? Don't I look like my picture?

HAL: Well, I, well, your face is, is, but —

NICOLE: I know, it was taken a few months before I started showing. Normally, I'm a medium. When I'm not pregnant, you know.

HAL: Right!

NICOLE: But you knew that. From my profile. Right?

HAL: No. I don't think I did. Did you — did I — did we discuss — that? 'Cause I'm thinking I'd remember that discussion if we discussed that.

NICOLE: Well, sure we did. Several times. I asked you the first time you instant messaged me if you were OK with my profile.

HAL: Yeah. I remember that.

NICOLE: Well, it states clearly on my profile that I am eating for two.

HAL: Ohhhh. Ohhh, I thought that meant that you liked to eat a lot or that you were a little chubby. And I like women who are a little chubby. So when I read that, I just thought you were a little —

NICOLE: Chubby?! News flash. Women don't like the word — *chubby*. So are you saying you never knew I was pregnant?!

HAL: *(Beat.)* That's what I'm saying.

NICOLE: Well then, you weren't listening.

HAL: Not listening? Not listening to what? You never mentioned that you were pregnant.

NICOLE: Look, I asked you if you read my whole profile. You said you did and that you loved it. It's not my fault you skimmed.

HAL: I didn't skim! I read it. I just misunderstood.

NICOLE: Who *mis*understands, "I'm eating for two"? It's a classic American line.

HAL: So is, "I'm pregnant." Now, that's really clear!

NICOLE: So obviously you have a problem with this?

HAL: *(Beat.)* No . . . it's not like, well, I just —

NICOLE: Fine! *(Crying and whimpering.)* "You know my deepest darkest secret, Nicole. I never told this to anyone, Nicole. Please meet me, Nicole."

HAL: *(Comforting her.)* Hey, hey, . . . hey, I think we got a table.

NICOLE: Well, go sit at it. *(Sniffs.)* And eat for two, chubby!

HAL: Hey now. Look, I'm just surprised. I'm not . . . I'd like to get to know you still. Let's sit. *(Beat.)* Please? *(Nicole nods. They sit.)* So how far along are you?

NICOLE: Well, I met Hashbrown Sixty-nine last May, and it's been about seven months.

HAL: Hashbrown Sixty-nine? *(She nods.)* He sounds nice. So he's the father? *(They nod.)* Hey, I thought you never met anyone before?

NICOLE: Well! What about you? You're going to tell me that I'm the first person you met for real?

HAL: Well, the first one on MSN.

NICOLE: You online Ho!

HAL: I'm not a Ho. I'm not even a hhh. Trust me.

NICOLE: Why not? I mean, you're not exactly bad looking.

HAL: Thanks, I think. I guess I'm just really picky.

NICOLE: *(Beat.)* Couldn't get any?

HAL: Nada. *(Pause.)* Do you know if it's gonna be a boy or a girl?

NICOLE: A boy. I'm naming him Cody.

HAL: Cody? Did you say Cody? I love that name! I had a gold-fish named Cody.

NICOLE: Really? Did you take good care of him?

HAL: Of course! Until Lee got him. My cat.

NICOLE: No way! That's what I picked for his middle name. Cody Lee.

HAL: Freaky! Don't tell me your last name is Spot?

NICOLE: How did you . . . ? *(She smiles.)* Rosedale actually.

HAL: That's very pretty. It suits you.

NICOLE: So . . . have you ever dated a pregnant girl before?

HAL: Not that I'm aware of.

NICOLE: What if you *were* aware?

HAL: Well, that could be interesting.

NICOLE: Yeah?

HAL: As long as you stay away from the hashbrowns!

NICOLE: Deal. *(Smiles.)* Oops. Don't look now, but there's a kid with a remote-controlled fire engine.

HAL: I know. But guess who pinched the remote? *(He wiggles his eyebrows suggestively.)*

PERSONALLY SPEAKING

Dan and Bess, twenties, are best friends on a quest to find their perfect mates. Every week they meet for brunch to discuss the "personals" dates they went on the weekend before. Today, they meet to discuss their disastrous dates.

CHARACTERS
Dan: 20s, gay
Bess: 20s, Dan's best friend

SETTING
An International House of Pancakes

TIME
The present, Sunday breakfast

DAN: Hey, it wasn't my fault! Two trains passed me by. I was waiting for like twenty minutes. I started at nine fifteen. Right when I called you. I really did, Bess.

BESS: Um-hum.

DAN: And I had a crazy person try to rip me off on Thorndale! I'm fine. I didn't get hurt or anything. He was one of those drunks from the rehab around the corner. Had awful teeth. I could have been killed. It was really scary! *(Beat. She pats his shoulder.)* You don't believe a word of this, do you? *(She looks at him.)* Oh my God! You honestly don't believe me at all?!

BESS: You left at nine-forty-five, didn't you?

DAN: I can't believe you! *(Beat.)* Ten to.

BESS: Figures. I ordered you coffee. Cream?

DAN: You ordered me coffee? You're sweet. You're understanding.

BESS: You're buying.

DAN: I'm broke.

BESS: Yes, and I'm on time. And I don't lie incessantly.

DAN: OK. Good point.

BESS: And I might have bought it if you didn't leave your cell phone on after you called me.

DAN: Oh my God! What did I say? Did I talk? Out loud?

BESS: *(Baby voice.)* "I love you little puddie, little kitty, my squishy, little Holleroo."

DAN: Oh no!

BESS: *(Continuing.)* "I'm very late and Bessie is going to be a total and complete witch!"

DAN: I didn't say that.

BESS: *(Bess nods.)* Then you threw on the shower and started to sing the theme song to *Titanic*, which you *said* you hated by the way.

DAN: Yes, but was I on key?

BESS: No. Finally, you let loose with a mouthful of rather colorful language. I guess you must have noticed the time. Running to catch the train, panting, heavily — more colorful language.

DAN: Well, at least I'm colorful.

BESS: *(She laughs.)* True.

DAN: I'm hungry. Let's order.

BESS: I already did.

DAN: You ordered food for me too?

BESS: Of course. *(He looks disappointed.)* You're upset? You always get the same thing.

DAN: No, I don't.

BESS: OK, there was that one time you got the Mexican omelet. You didn't like it.

DAN: No! I got the waffles once. That was different.

BESS: No you didn't. You *debated* getting the waffles once, but you talked yourself out of them.

DAN: Well!

BESS: Face it, Dan. Steady and dependable with a dollop of sour cream on the side is how you like everything. So cut to the chase. And get to the heart of it. How was it?

DAN: I told you on the phone. *(Beat.)* Blah.

BESS: Yeah, but what kind of "blah"?

DAN: What do you mean by "what kind"? Are there several kinds?

BESS: Well, was it just blah-blah or was it OK and then end blah?

DAN: *(Thinking.)* Blah sporadically with an explosion of blah at the end.

BESS: Oh no. Details?

DAN: Fine. He was kinda cute when he came to my door. I definitely thought . . . "He's cute." So I showed him around my apartment, which he thought was great. And very manly. He said that — manly.

BESS: Was that when he was looking at your honey-colored Martha Stewart comforter and matching pillow set or when he was perusing your Judy Garland doll collection?

DAN: Shut up! So we decided to go to eat at Mario's and there were moments of uncomfortable silence when we were eating and I thought, "He has no personality at all. Here he gets to listen to people's problems all day long and he has nothing to say for himself. Has he no life? No interests? The least he could do is dish up some dirt about some old client whose confidentiality agreement has expired or something. But nooooo . . . he'd rather sit there in silence eating ravioli and listening to me gag on my meatball." Then I realize that the whole time I was thinking this thought, *I* was probably looking like *I'm* the one who appears to have no personality because I'm sitting here *thinking*. Then I thought, "Oh God, now I'm thinking this thought about thinking I have no personality, which is perpetuating this continued silence at the table. I've got to stop thinking thoughts and talk." So I took a sip of wine and said, "Do you like pigs?"

BESS: What?!

DAN: I didn't know what to say. It was the first thing that came into my head.

BESS: Right. Of course.

DAN: I just thought it would open up the conversation.

BESS: To what? The subject of your insanity?

DAN: Well, it turns out, little smarty-pants, he loves pigs. Ever since seeing *Charlotte's Web*. In fact, he went to a pig-racing thing recently.

BESS: He did not!

DAN: He did! And . . . he's got a Porky Pig thing. He also thinks Miss Piggy might be Porky "in drag."

BESS: What?! What do you mean he's got a Porky Pig thing? *(Beat.)* What kind of thing?!

DAN: I don't know. He likes him. Anyway, it all lead to a game with us asking, "Do you like — dot, dot, dot?" I tried things like . . . do you like squash, do you like nuns, do you like hammers, do you like me?

BESS: What did he say to all that?

DAN: Yes, if prepared with brown sugar. Nuns, if they sing in choirs and act like Whoopee, and need you ask?

BESS: Oh my God! Wait? Was the "need you ask" the hammer or you?

DAN: Me! *(Brief beat.)* I think.

BESS: That's great! This is blah?!

DAN: Then it came.

BESS: What?!

DAN: The knee thing — the tap.

BESS: A tap on the knee?

DAN: That's right. The ole knee . . . *tap*.

BESS: As opposed to what? The knee smack, the knee shake, the knee bend?

DAN: The knee rub.

BESS: Ohhhh. *(Beat.)* Are you sure it wasn't a tap with a little rub? Because that would be something, right?

DAN: That would. But nope, straight tap. Just your regular knee *tap*.

BESS: Awwww. Well, that's just . . . Maybe in time the tap will be converted to a rub.

DAN: No, no. Not this time. Not next time. No time. It was a two-tap knee-tap with a vocal. "You seem great."

BESS: Ohhh. That's almost insulting. So it wasn't really "blah-blah," it was just blah because . . .

DAN: He rejected me! Friends. He wants to be friends. Like I need another friend!

BESS: Well, if it makes you feel any better, my date sucked too.

DAN: It doesn't. At all. *(Beat.)* So what was wrong with Mr. Convertible?

BESS: He was so not convertible. He was such a "top up" kinda guy. All the fantasies of us on a mountaintop out West — me in my head scarf, him in his leather went to hell when he pulled up in his SUV. He had the voice of a guy with a convertible, but the truth was he was a gas-guzzling jerk with no awareness of the SUV turnover problem.

DAN: SUVs have a turnover problem? *(Beat.)* What's a turnover problem?

BESS: What's wrong with you? They flip. They roll. They turn upside down and kill people.

DAN: Ohhh. That's not good.

BESS: People have been dying right and left in SUVs since the early eighties due to the turnover problem. There's a height-width ratio problem that somebody didn't want to fix — Republicans — because it would cost the auto industry too much. And they didn't want to compete with Japan's much better, nonturnover cars. Didn't you see "Frontline's" feature on the SUV turnover problem?!

DAN: No, but I saw "The View's" feature on pizza turnovers.

BESS: *(Throwing up her hands.)* Uhhh.

DAN: You didn't say that to him, did you?!

BESS: Of course I did.

DAN: You know, hon, sometimes guys don't particularly like it when you bring up faulty aspects about their cars. Their car is kind of like their . . . their, an extension of their . . .

BESS: Ewww. I get it! Well, his "extension" is an accident waiting to happen. Somebody needs to shrink his extension or make it disappear all together.

DAN: Umm. Sounds like you might have done that already. So it didn't go well?

BESS: No, we had a good time. At the pool hall. I won and he didn't bellyache.

DAN: Well, good. This is sounding good.

BESS: Yeah, I think things would have been fine if he didn't have to be hospitalized.

DAN: Whoa! Missed that. Back it up there.

BESS: It wasn't my fault. He insisted on watching my technique up close.

DAN: I'm sure.

BESS: Stop. *(Pointing to her eye.)* I backed the cue stick into his eye. By accident.

DAN: Well, I should hope.

BESS: And then his eye started gushing blood!

DAN: *(Mortified and disgusted, contorted in vogue-style poses.)* Uck. Ckk. Uhh. Nnn.

BESS: What a crybaby he was. It was just a little blood.

DAN: Eww. Very eww. Stop.

BESS: But that's not the worst of it.

DAN: *(New pose of disgust out of fear of what's to come.)* No?

BESS: As I was changing his gauze, he told me he had a great time — the best ever — and wanted to see me again this weekend.

DAN: With what? His one remaining eye! Eww.

BESS: He really did. He was so sincere.

DAN: *(Still somewhat disgusted, but positive.)* That's so cute and puppy dog. Awww.

BESS: Right.

DAN: And he sounds very "nice guy"?

BESS: Um-hmm.

DAN: Has a kind of decency.

BESS: Exactly!

DAN: Yeah, that's never been for you. This is the kind of guy you shove, and maim, and beat, not the kind you actually date.

BESS: Right, but God, now that you say that I sound kind of terrible.

DAN: Well . . .

BESS: I love that about me. *(She opens the paper.)* I think we ought to dive right in again and give it another shot with someone new. Have you seen any good prospects for me?

DAN: I don't know, Bess. I saw a massage therapist with a thing for hot air ballooning and yogurt.

BESS: Umm, nice but too Mary Poppins. I think I found a good one for you. Shall I read? *(He shrugs.)* "Cultured painter with professional day job" —

DAN: Oh God. He has no money.

BESS: Now wait . . . "Attractive, emotionally secure, stable" —

DAN: A stable painter? You can't fool me. I saw *Pollock*.

BESS: "Looking for someone who's cute, cuddly, and sweet."

DAN: Sounds like he wants a Cabbage Patch doll.

BESS: *(Reading more.)* "A good sense of humor." Huh? Huh? *(Quickly since this part doesn't describe him.)* "With a complex, intense worldview."

DAN: That doesn't sound like me.

BESS: Well . . . you have cable? *(Continues reading.)* "A guy who likes to go out for brunch" . . . Huh, huh? "Who enjoys good talks." Huh, huh?

DAN: Who's going to smack you, huh, huh?!

BESS: Fine. *(Quickly again because he doesn't look Italian.)* "Italian looks a plus."

DAN: OK. So let's review. We both like breakfast. We're both broke. And I'm as Italian as Meryl Streep.

BESS: You kinda look sorta Italian. Anyway, that was just his plus thing.

DAN: Oh, oooey for extra points. Look, Bess, I think this personal ad thing is getting a little old.

BESS: But we've only just begun.

DAN: I've met twenty-nine guys! And I haven't had more than one date with any of them.

BESS: OK, OK, I admit things haven't been perfect.

DAN: Not perfect? Try disastrous for both of us.

BESS: I think you're overstating this.

DAN: I never overstate! Your third date almost drove you off a cliff.

BESS: It was a hill, and it wasn't on purpose. His glasses fogged.

DAN: Oh, sure, fine, as long as it wasn't an SUV with a turnover problem.

BESS: Oh shush!

DAN: My fourth date wanted me to meet his mother.

BESS: OK, so he was a little too ready for wedlock. That's just part of the search.

DAN: The twenty-third took me to a folk-music-slash-poetry-slam.

BESS: OK. That was unforgivable. But, but, we . . . All right, things haven't been great, uh . . . Maybe you're right. Maybe this personals thing is not the way to go.

DAN: Definitely. It's too spotty. You can't know what you're going to get by reading a list of random attributes. "Barbra Streisand fan, enjoys yoga." He could mean that he heard a Barbra song once or that he plasters life-size posters of her all over his bedroom while saluting her sun. *(Sun salutation yoga posture.)* Besides, these "dates" create false expectations, more pressure, and attract more weirdos. I think sometimes the old-fashioned meet-the-guy-at-the-bar-or-gym is the best way to go.

BESS: Yeah, you're right. You're right. Gym?

DAN: Well bar. The point is that the personals set up a false, uncomfortable situation — a fabrication through words. You need to meet in person.

BESS: Yes. I agree. Better to go much more natural.

DAN: Exactly!

BESS: *(She nods.)* Open the paper. Where's the next singles three-minute dating thing? *(He looks at her.)* That's natural. You talk for three minutes. You meet. You dump. Just like in the bar. You don't read about each other. It's more bang for your buck. Twenty-five dates in seventy-five minutes. You just churn those rejects out. You can't lose!

DAN: Are you insane?! *(Pause.)* Page twenty-seven. There's one at five tonight! *(Gasps.)* I've got to go shower and change. *(He starts to leave in an excited fluster.)*

BESS: Well, call me when you're ready! But do me a favor. Kill the cell phone in the shower. Judy you are not.

CAREER MATCH

Dennis, thirties, works as a career counselor. Today he is meeting with a new client, Sally, late twenties. At the beginning of each session, Dennis likes to conduct exercises in order to discover what careers would best suit his client's personality. As the scene opens, a rather sad and angry Sally tries to maintain a positive attitude toward this process.

CHARACTERS
Dennis: 30s, a career counselor
Sally: 20s, a client

SETTING
Dennis's office

TIME
The present

DENNIS: It's very nice to meet you, Sally.

SALLY: Thank you. You too, uh . . .

DENNIS: Dennis. It's Dennis. Well . . . I always think it's best to just jump right in.

SALLY: Jumping is good. Let's do it.

DENNIS: OK. Now in order to find the perfect career match for you, I need to know a bit about your personality. So, I'd like to do a little exercise with you.

SALLY: OK.

DENNIS: It's very simple. I am going to say a word and I want you to respond with the first thing that pops into your mind.

SALLY: Like word association?

DENNIS: Exactly.

SALLY: OK. Shoot.

DENNIS: Money.

SALLY: None.

DENNIS: Sales.

SALLY: Fifty percent off.

DENNIS: Coworkers.

SALLY: Annoying.

DENNIS: Black.

SALLY: My life.

DENNIS: Interesting. Sorrow.

SALLY: Anger.

DENNIS: Anger.

SALLY: Yes.

DENNIS: Yes?

SALLY: Yes!

DENNIS: Oh-kay. Happiness.

SALLY: Not a chance.

DENNIS: *(Beat.)* Why don't we stop there. I'd like to ask you a few questions.

SALLY: Go ahead.

DENNIS: Do you consider yourself to be a positive person?

SALLY: Yeah. Absolutely! Just because I'm angry that I'm sad because I'm out of work, and I have no money, and I can't pay my bills doesn't mean I'm not a positive person!

DENNIS: OK. Good. Just checking. Um, next question. Where do you see yourself in five years?

SALLY: At the rate we're going, homeless.

DENNIS: Please understand, Sally, that this is a very important part of the process.

SALLY: At a hundred bucks an hour, I'm sure it is.

DENNIS: Think of it as an investment. An investment that comes back to you many times over. Like playing the stock market.

SALLY: I lost fifteen thousand dollars in the stock market.

DENNIS: Forget that. More like a boomerang. You, you send it . . . you give . . . you let it *fly* and it comes back to you with added vigor.

SALLY: No kidding, I got smacked in the face with one of those suckers! Twenty-three stitches and a reoccurring tick. *(She twitches.)*

DENNIS: Forget the boomerang. Bad example. All I'm saying is that this is an initial investment in your financial future.

SALLY: Then let's get to the financial part.

DENNIS: Fine. I'm flexible. We can skip ahead. I must warn you though that the less information I gather at the beginning, the harder —

SALLY: Skip!

DENNIS: Skipping. OK . . . what type of jobs or industries do you find appealing?

SALLY: Ones that give me money.

DENNIS: Good. Good. Anything else?

SALLY: A job where I don't have to wake up early.

DENNIS: Right. I remember you said that makes you negative.

SALLY: Actually it makes me kill people.

DENNIS: *(Beat.)* Then we won't do that. We'll think second- or third-shift jobs.

SALLY: But those hours are for crap.

DENNIS: I'm sorry, I — what hours are you looking for?

SALLY: Nothing too early. And not too late 'cause I like to watch my must-see TV shows. And not too long 'cause I get tired and bored.

DENNIS: *(Realizing.)* So you want a part-time job. Great! Now we're making progress.

SALLY: Yeah. But it has to pay like full time or I'll never afford my bills.

DENNIS: How about sales? Sometimes they offer good commissions and you can work less hours.

SALLY: Yeah, but then you have to suck up to people. I don't do sucking up very well.

DENNIS: I can see that about you.

SALLY: That's why I don't like bosses.

DENNIS: No bosses . . . ?

SALLY: No. Can't deal with them. Always looking over my shoulder. Telling me what to do.

DENNIS: Well. We're definitely narrowing things down. How about education?

SALLY: Not too bad. Uh, middle of my class.

DENNIS: No, no. I meant teaching. Shorter hours. Being the boss of your own classroom.

SALLY: Hey, they even get summers off!

DENNIS: Well, there you go!

SALLY: Except that I had a really mean teacher in high school that scared me to death. Now I mostly think teachers are evil.

DENNIS: I'm sorry to hear that. But if you were the teacher, that would change the situation. You wouldn't be evil to your students.

SALLY: Are you kidding me? Those brats would drive me up the wall!

DENNIS: *(Beat.)* Sally? Do you want to work?

SALLY: Who *wants* to work? Nobody I know. What I want is money. As quickly and easily as I can get it.

DENNIS: Have you considered robbery? *(He laughs. She stares at him.)* That was a joke.

SALLY: Well, maybe I should because it seems to be working for *you*! Look, I came here for your help. You're supposed to be an expert at helping people like me find the right job.

DENNIS: People, yes. People like you, no.

SALLY: What is that supposed to mean?

DENNIS: You don't want to do anything, so how am I supposed to help you, huh?!

SALLY: *(Tearfully.)* That is not true!

DENNIS: Oh no? You won't work nine to five.

SALLY: No, but —

DENNIS: You won't work full-time hours.

SALLY: Yes, but I said —

DENNIS: But you want full-time pay.

SALLY: I don't see what's wrong —

DENNIS: You can't deal with a boss.

SALLY: Not every job —

DENNIS: You want money without working!

SALLY: I didn't say without working. I said as quickly and easily as possible.

DENNIS: OK then. Sales!

SALLY: Sucking up.

DENNIS: Customer service.

SALLY: Bothersome.

DENNIS: Marketing.

SALLY: Slavery.

DENNIS: Telemarketing?

SALLY: Phone slavery.

DENNIS: Florist.

SALLY: Allergies.

DENNIS: Waitress.

SALLY: Sucking up again.

DENNIS: Bank teller.

SALLY: Too tempting.

DENNIS: Receptionist.

SALLY: Dressing up.

DENNIS: Editor.

SALLY: Spelling.

DENNIS: Cook.

SALLY: Bugs.

DENNIS: Plumber.

SALLY: Toilets.

DENNIS: Finance, computers, inventory?!

SALLY: Numbers, typing, counting!

DENNIS: I give up! I give up! You are impossible! There is no job out there for you!! All you can see is what's wrong with every single blasted possibility!

SALLY: Jeez. You're really getting worked up, huh? That's not good for your blood pressure. Maybe this isn't the best job for you. Have you thought about that?

DENNIS: No, no, I love this job! I love it to pieces! To itsy, bitsy, torn up, ragged little pieces!

SALLY: That's a lot of pieces. Hey, maybe I can help you. I'm good at puzzles. I think they're kinda fun. Maybe I can help ya put the pieces back together. Look at the bigger picture.

DENNIS: It's no use.

SALLY: Come on, now. Don't be so negative. Ya got a nice office here. Lots of people to give advice to. You make a killing.

DENNIS: It's just not worth it. And I'm sick of giving advice. Giving, giving, giving.

SALLY: Well maybe you should think that you're telling, not giving. And taking, taking, taking lots of money.

DENNIS: You seem so positive about it. Why don't you take it? Huh? You think my job's so easy — take it!

SALLY: OK. I will. I think I'd like to do this job. Make my own hours, be my own boss, tell people what to do, make lots of money. *(Beat. Realizing.)* Wow, I'm really glad I came to see you. You are very good. To tell you the truth I didn't really think you'd find me anything. But look, ya did. Just goes to show you, the world isn't quite so black. And you were right. Ya gotta make that initial investment. *(Beat.)* So, Dennis, in order to find the perfect career match, I'd like to do a little exercise with you . . .

BACK TO SCHOOL

Greg and Tess, late twenties, are married and have been living together for several years. Tess has gotten into the habit of spending large sums of money at Office World and other office supply stores. Things have gotten worse ever since Greg's hours at work have increased. Crisis point hit when they realized she had maxed out several credit cards. Greg has been understanding and has even gone with Tess to Shopaholics Anonymous meetings, but he has now reached his limit. Tess, therefore, has made a promise not to buy anything from Office World without Greg's approval. Tonight, he has found some suspicious new-looking paper products. Tess is just arriving home as the scene begins.

CHARACTERS
Greg: 20s, Tess's husband
Tess: 20s, Greg's wife

SETTING
Greg and Tess's apartment

TIME
The present

TESS: *(Entering. Surprised by seeing Greg.)* Oh! *(Waves.)* Hi!! Greg! Wow! I didn't expect you to be — here.

GREG: I got off early. I finished writing my story early.

TESS: Oh. Yeah. *(Looking at her watch.)* It's early. My gosh. It's real early for you.

GREG: Yes! We covered that. Now, where were *you?*

TESS: What? Well, I was out. I was out. I went out.

GREG: Out? Oh. Where'd you go?

TESS: Food. I was out with dinner. I mean — *for* dinner. Out with Tanya and Joe for dinner. They called me last minute at work.

GREG: Uh-huh. How are Joe and Tanya doing then?

TESS: Great, great — wonderful — really great — They're great!

GREG: I heard they both got laid off yesterday.

TESS: Ohhh! *(Laughs.)* Right. Wow. Yeah. Wow. I forgot that. Yeah, yeah, that sucked, huh? But besides that, they're great. We had a great time. *(Sweetsie voice.)* I wish I knew my Little Honey-Bunny was going to be home. I would have grabbed you to come with us.

GREG: Yeah?

TESS: Yeah, of course. I missed my Little Honey-Bunny.

GREG: Don't Honey-Bunny me.

TESS: What is that supposed to mean?

GREG: Just as it sounded.

TESS: Well, it sounded like Honey-Bunny is getting a little Poopsy-Whoopsy for no reason at all. Every night *I* come home to an empty apartment. And now suddenly, I'm not at home *one* night and out pops Poopsy-Whoopsy.

GREG: Myyy aren't we defensive? Isn't that interesting?

TESS: Defensive? I'm not defensive! I just don't like your accusations!

GREG: *(Calmly.)* Accusations? Did I make accusations? No. I think we're acting a mite guilty.

TESS: *(Feeling guilty.)* Why would I be feeling guilty?

GREG: You tell me, Tess? Why would you?

TESS: I wouldn't. I shouldn't. I don't. I asked you first.

GREG: I know where you've been tonight, Tess.

TESS: Ohhh. Oh, I see. I see now. Well, you couldn't know where I was, Greg. Unless, of course, you followed me which you promised me that you'd never, never, never do unless someone hung you by your toenails!

GREG: I saw the desk organizers, Tess.

TESS: *(Pause.)* Yeah. So? *(Beat.)* So! Tanya gave them to me for your information. Ha! Did you think I would just leave them out if there was anything suspicious about them?

GREG: And the new manila folders in the file cabinet?

TESS: *(Can't look him in the eye.)* Oh, well . . . She gave me those too.

GREG: Oh come on! Since when does Tanya bring you office supplies?

TESS: Well, she did. She dropped them by last week sometime, Mr. Accusations. One of those nights when you were at the paper until some god-awful hour. Do you want to do an all out investigation? *(Lifting up her arms.)* Search me for paper clips and staples if you'd like.

GREG: Doesn't Tanya know about our little problem?

TESS: Yes, she knows about our little problem. But I don't think it's part of our little problem if I'm not purchasing the things . . . if I'm given the things. It's not part of the little problem. No one's presents were part of the little problem. I don't think a couple of desk organizers and a few piddily-widdily folders are a problem. Do you?

GREG: That's all she gave you?

TESS: Of course.

GREG: Ah-hah! See! Then explain the pink stinky notes.

TESS: Stinky notes?

GREG: Sticky notes! Don't distract me. You know what I mean. Those sticky notes are brand new.

TESS: I knew you were going to bring those up. I knew it! They were in the back of our office closet. I cleaned up that closet this week. I didn't buy them. I found them.

GREG: Wait a minute. The ones I remember having brand new were yellow.

TESS: *(Beat.)* Maybe you remembered wrong. Pink sticky notes, yellow sticky notes. What do you know about any sticky notes anyway? The only kinds of notes you write are on little pieces of scrap envelopes spread out throughout the apartment.

GREG: Come on. You went there, didn't you?

TESS: Like a post office gone wrong —

GREG: You've been back there, Tess, haven't you?

TESS: Birthday card envelopes, phone bill envelopes, work envelopes —

GREG: Admit it! Haven't you?

TESS: Every which way like a tornado sucked the mailman into our apartment and slammed him through the paper shredder!!

GREG: Tess!!

TESS: So I went! Big deal! It was just one time. And that's not where I got the pink stinky notes — we had them.

GREG: I knew it! I knew it!

TESS: I didn't buy anything — I just looked.

GREG: What will Michelle say? And the rest of the SAA group?

TESS: Nothing. Because you aren't going to tell them. Right, sweetheart?

GREG: Tess, you went to Office World unaccompanied, without phoning for help first, and of your own free will — despite your promises to me, to Shopaholics Anonymous, and to yourself.

TESS: But . . . but I didn't buy anything. I just . . . browsed.

GREG: For you, there is no such thing as browsing. One peek at some pretty pens, one touch of a corkboard, one whiff of a freshly opened notebook and wham! You're sunk. *(Beat.)* How bad was it?

TESS: Gregggg. *(Silence.)* One plastic portfolio pocket. *(He waits.)* And a six-pack of Scotch tape — it was on sale. And some stuff.

GREG: How much?

TESS: Just a few things.

GREG: How much?!

TESS: Two hundred and seventy-four dollars and thirty-three cents.

GREG: What?!

TESS: It was a bargain!

GREG: For who? How do you spend two hundred and seventy-four dollars at an office supply store?

TESS: It's really easy. I can show you.

GREG: *(Crazed.)* I don't want you to show me!! I want you to stop!!

TESS: I didn't buy the postal scale with the print-your-own stamps option.

GREG: Well, isn't that good news considering the post office is in the building!

TESS: You're getting a little excited! We aren't supposed to get excited at me!

GREG: I'm just feeling the need to express myself. Of which I am allowed!

TESS: Excited!

GREG: I'm not excited! I'm broke!

TESS: *(Panicked.)* Word! Word!

GREG: OK. Heard. Heard. I think we should stop and have a meeting right now.

TESS: But the meeting isn't until Wednesday night.

GREG: I know, but this is a special meeting. It's a keep-a-roof-over-our-heads-until-Wednesday meeting. Just the two of us. Of course all S.A.A. rules will remain intact so there is no cross talk. Now. Who wants to start? OK, I will.

TESS: But —

GREG: No cross talk please. *(Takes a long deep breath.)* I put up with converting our living room into an office. I even bought you the connecting file cabinets and the revolving computer stand. Even though you don't have a home business. I know you like to be organized but there has to be a limit. I have been going to the Shopaholic meetings with you every Wednesday. I listen to you. I support you. But now I want to kill you.

TESS: Hi, I'm Tess. *(Looking at him.)* I'm just trying to stick to the rules. Today I'm feeling a little annoyed because my husband has been getting a little excited. Repeatedly. We're not supposed to be getting excited. That's a rule. I only had one little splurge. It wasn't anywhere near as bad as that time at the seventy-two-hour sale at Paper Max. Although, I admit, I did break a few promises —

GREG: A few?!

TESS: *(Points, warning.)* Cross talk. *(He hushes.)* I must say that I did refrain from some difficult bargains which included a fabulous make-your-own stamps electronic postal scale. Anyway, the point is . . . I had a breakthrough today. You see, I was burrowing through boxes of binders that hadn't been on display yet. I picked up one with Winnie the Pooh on the front, and I remembered when I was a little girl how exciting it was at "back to school" time. I got to go shopping. And my mom would buy me all kinds of brand new folders and notebooks and pencils and stuff. It was a time to start a new adventure . . . a new beginning each year. And it all started with those school supplies. God, how I loved them!

GREG: I never knew that.

TESS: How could you? *I* just remembered. So, my big breakthrough today is that I realized that I have been addicted to supplies since I was a child.

GREG: Tess?

TESS: Well, that's all for today. Thank you for listening. *(Beat.)* Yes?

GREG: Do you think that maybe you want to go back to school?

TESS: Well, I . . . I hadn't really thought about it. I do feel kind of lonely and bored when you're at the paper. I know I could get an office job, but that's so . . . grown up-and yucky. *(She giggles.)* Can you imagine me starting school all over again? Going to classes? Doing homework? God, that sounds exciting!

GREG: It does?

TESS: It does.

GREG: Really?

TESS: Really-really-really!

GREG: Tess, I think we just solved our little problem!

TESS: Yes! If I went back to school, I'd actually have a reason to buy all those supplies!

GREG: No, no, no — you have enough to last you from freshman to Ph.D.

TESS: Did I say buy? I meant that I'd have a reason to *need* them.

GREG: Need still sounds a little . . . needy.

TESS: Use! To *use* them, Greg. That's what I meant to say. *(They kiss.)*

TESS: God, college. How exciting! So many choices. *(Beat.)* Honey, do you think I should get a backpack or a tote bag?

GREG: Aaaaahhhhh!

HONEYMOON HEIST

Kevin and Rachel, early twenties, are planning to get married and go to Hawaii for their honeymoon. Unfortunately, they don't have any money. So, they decide to break into a rich friend's father's house to steal money from his safe. As the scene begins, they have just crawled through the living-room window.

CHARACTERS
Kevin: 20s
Rachel: 20s, Kevin's fiancée, pregnant

SETTING
A beautiful colonial home owned by Kevin's wealthy friend's father

TIME
The present, evening.

KEVIN: *(Motions for Rachel to come closer.)* The coast is clear.

RACHEL: Thank God! And I'm not going back out that way. I could have hurt the baby — I was practically stuck.

KEVIN: Rachel, you're fine. The baby's fine. We're in. No one's home. Everything's fine.

RACHEL: That's comforting. I feel comforted. I'm all about the comfort you're giving me.

KEVIN: Trust me. I know what I'm doing.

RACHEL: Me too. I'm going to jail. I'm going to give birth to our baby in a stinking, rotting cell.

KEVIN: Rach, we are not going to jail. I'm doing this for you, baby. For us. So we can be happy. You want to be happy, right?

RACHEL: Yeah.

KEVIN: You want to get married, right?

RACHEL: Yeah.

KEVIN: You want me to take you to Hawaii for our honey-moon, right?

RACHEL: Oh, yeah.

KEVIN: Then shut up and let's get to work here.

RACHEL: Kevin!

KEVIN: What?

RACHEL: Shhh! *(Whispering.)* Did you hear something?

KEVIN: *(Listening.)* No.

RACHEL: *(Whispering.)* I definitely heard something.

KEVIN: *(Whispering.)* You just imagined it. You're nervous. I scoped it out. No one is home. Besides, Darren told me over and over no one was going to be home this weekend. He went to his cousin's and his father went to New York for a getaway.

RACHEL: *(Whispering.)* There! Did you hear that?!

KEVIN: *(Whispering.)* No, I told you — that? Ohhh, I think I heard that.

RACHEL: I knew it. God's punishing me for wanting to go to Hawaii.

KEVIN: *(Whispering.)* Shhh! What is that?

RACHEL: The police obviously.

KEVIN: Would you calm down! It's not the police. It's thumping.

RACHEL: So the police can't thump? They thump all the time. They thump their shoes. They thump people on the streets. They thump with those sticks. They're all about thumping. I'm sorry God. Please forgive me. I don't want to give birth in a cell.

KEVIN: Rachel, stop. I'm going to see what that is.

RACHEL: No! Stay here. We'll go back out the window.

KEVIN: Calm down.

RACHEL: I'm calm.

KEVIN: Calm down.

RACHEL: I'm calm!!

KEVIN: Good!! *(Beat.)* Don't move from this spot.

RACHEL: I'm coming with you.

KEVIN: No. *(She grabs onto him hard, nails digging in.)* Oww! OK. But be very quiet. *(They inch together over toward the sound. Whispering.)* It's in there. *(She nods.)* On the count of three we push the door open. *(She nods no.)* OK, I push the door open. *(She nods yes.)* Thanks. A lot. One, two, three! *(Kevin pushes the door open and Rachel screams. Beat.)*

RACHEL: Kevin? Are you alive?

KEVIN: Yep.

RACHEL: What's going on in there?

KEVIN: Oh, I'd say, the dryer.

RACHEL: *(Peeking in.)* Oh, thank God! Laundry. I love laundry. Laundry is good. Are you OK?

KEVIN: You mean aside from losing hearing in one ear and being threatened by a Clingfree sheet? *(Beat.)* I forgot. Darren did say the maid would be in and out.

RACHEL: You forgot?! Are you crazy? You mean the maid might still be here?

KEVIN: Well, what is she going to do? Blast us with her Pine Sol?

RACHEL: This is not funny. She could be a witness. Oh God, I'm going to be a convict!

KEVIN: Trust me, she's left.

RACHEL: How do you know?

KEVIN: I saw her leave half an hour ago. I have been scoping the place, you know?

RACHEL: So how do you know she won't come back?

KEVIN: Because she's a maid. They don't work long when no one's home.

RACHEL: This is not instilling confidence. This is an assumption. This is not certitude.

KEVIN: What? It's human nature. When your mom's not home for the weekend and you're home during the summer and she asks you to do the dishes, do you finish the dishes on Friday?

RACHEL: We have a dishwasher. And my mother doesn't go away on weekends. Besides, my brother does the dishes.

KEVIN: OK, forget it. Just trust me. She is *not* coming back.

RACHEL: How did you talk me into this? I don't think it's right. I don't think it's fair. I don't think it's nice.

KEVIN: Would you rather go to Cleveland?

RACHEL: Where's the safe?

KEVIN: He's not even going to miss the few thou we take. Darren told me. He has too much to handle. And you, you're going to look beautiful in Hawaii when I give you the ring, and fantastic with a coconut drink in your hand and your toes in the sand.

RACHEL: Aww, you're so sweet, Baby. Now cut the bull and open the safe.

KEVIN: OK. *(He reaches in his pocket. Then checks another.)*

RACHEL: Is something wrong?

KEVIN: Nooo. Nothing's wrong. Not a thing. What would be wrong?

RACHEL: When you do that something's wrong.

KEVIN: Do what? What do I do? I didn't do anything.

RACHEL: That. That stuttery-repeating-hyper-question thing.

KEVIN: What thing? A stuttery thing? I — I don't, I — a hyper thing?

RACHEL: That would be it. You did it when you told me you failed your driver's test and gave that guy a mild heart attack. You did it when you ran over Mrs. Brundo's cat.

KEVIN: I didn't run him over. I bumped him. It's a driving thing. I get nervous when I drive.

RACHEL: You did it the first time we made love.

KEVIN: What? That's ridiculous.

RACHEL: "Do you wanna? Should I just? Could I? I wanna. Do you" —

KEVIN: OK! Excuse me for having manners and not simply attacking you.

RACHEL: No, I appreciate that. You were nervous. But that's not the point. The point is you forgot the condom. Something was wrong. That's the point. You do that thingy when something is wrong. Man has heart attack, cat is squashed, condom is missing —

KEVIN: Safe combination is not in pocket.

RACHEL: What?! I thought you said it was something obvious. Something you didn't have to write down.

KEVIN: Well, it is, but you know I have that memory problem thing when I get nervous. So I wrote it down and put it in my pocket, but . . .

RACHEL: You are not serious about this? Tell me you're kidding?

KEVIN: My mother still washes my jeans when I come home for breaks.

RACHEL: And you didn't check?

KEVIN: Oh, I'm sure she washed them. They feel really snug.

RACHEL: I mean for the combination!!

KEVIN: I know! I know what you mean! I knew what you meant. I did. It was there. Right in my pocket where I put it.

RACHEL: Well what are we supposed to do now, Sherlock?

KEVIN: Just calm down. I'll remember it.

RACHEL: Think. Think hard. Think before I kill you.

KEVIN: Shh. I'm trying to think.

RACHEL: Think. Think something obvious for Darren and his father.

KEVIN: OK. Rich. Wealthy. Golf stuff. BMW-like.

RACHEL: Good. Move it along. Back it up. Rewind to when he told ya. Replay.

KEVIN: We were up late shootin' the bull and he said . . . "God, my father has so much money he doesn't know what to do with it. He barely works anymore. My father is filthy rich, but he is so dumb. Do you know what my father's safe combination is?"

RACHEL: Good, good, go on.

KEVIN: Oh yeah, then Darren kinda got sick and I took him up to the bathroom. That was gross.

RACHEL: Kevin, the combination! I know the story.

KEVIN: This is how detectives do it. They go over all the details.

RACHEL: OK, but do it faster!

KEVIN: Lying on the tile . . . laughing. He said the combo was . . . ? Said . . . said . . .

RACHEL: Yesss??

KEVIN: *(Straining.)* I can't remember.

RACHEL: No, no Kevin. You can. You will. You better!!

KEVIN: I think . . . I think . . . I think, we're screwed.

RACHEL: I refuse to be screwed! *(Beat.)* OK, look, in the movies they always have these scenes where the F.B.I. is trying to break a code and they always check things like nicknames, birthdays of their kids —

KEVIN: I don't know. I don't know. I can't handle this pressure.

RACHEL: Well, at least try! I'm not the one who let Mommy wash away our ticket to Hawaii.

KEVIN: Leave my mommy out of this! I mean, Mom.

RACHEL: What about Darren? That's six letters?

KEVIN: But isn't that *too* obvious?

RACHEL: To most people — yes. But you didn't think of it. *(He shrugs.)* What are the numbers? *(They both start singing the alphabet out loud and counting on their fingers.)*

RACHEL and KEVIN: *(Singing.)* A, B, C, D —

KEVIN: OK that's four.

RACHEL: Then A is one.

RACHEL and KEVIN: *(Singing again, mumbled.)* A, B, C, D, E, F, G, H, I, J, K, L, M, N, O, P, Q, R —

RACHEL: Eighteen!

KEVIN: Twice.

RACHEL: Then E is five. So that's 4, 1, 18, 18, 5 . . .

RACHEL and KEVIN: *(Singing again, faster.)* A, B, C, D, E, F, G, H, I, J, K, L, M, N —

KEVIN: Fourteen!

RACHEL: That's it. Try it. Try it.

KEVIN: *(Turning the safe lock.)* 4, 1, 18, 18 . . .

RACHEL: Five.

KEVIN: Fourteen. *(He tries to open it.)* Come on, baby. *(It won't open.)* Well, there goes that idea, Ms. Obvious! This is ridiculous. What are we gonna do, just keep spelling relatives all night? God, I hate my mom! I hate Darren! Mr. Suthers is a jerk!

RACHEL: There goes our marriage! There goes our honeymoon!

KEVIN: An uncaring, selfish, mean, rotten jerk!

RACHEL: There goes Hawaii!!

KEVIN: Who doesn't care about anyone but himself! And that damn Chow Wow that died —

RACHEL and KEVIN: *(Beat. Realizing.)* Muffin!!!

RACHEL: *(Singing alphabet quickly.)* A, B, C, D, E, F, G, H, I, J, K, L, M — thirteen!

KEVIN: *(Continuing.)* N, O, P, Q, R, S, T, U — 21!

RACHEL: F is six. M was thirteen so N is fourteen.

KEVIN: *(Trying safe lock again.)* 13, 21, 6, 6, 14. *(He pulls and it opens.)* Yes! Yes!!

RACHEL: Ahhhhhhhhh!! *(Kevin holds his damaged ear.)* Sorry. *(Beat.)* Wait!

KEVIN: What?!

RACHEL: We can't do this. I can't do this. I know Mr. Suthers and Darren have more money than God. I know Darren practically begged us to take it by telling us every detail about his alarm system. I know both of them are stingy, and spoiled and braggy, but it's still stealing, Kevin. It's still morally wrong. It's bad karma for us. For the baby. For our lives. I couldn't live with myself. I just couldn't live if I stole this money.

KEVIN: You're right. You're right. What if *I* take it?

RACHEL: OK.

KEVIN: *(He stares in the safe with disbelief.)* Oh, my God! Oh, my God! Oh, my God!

RACHEL: What, my God? Is there that much? Why don't you just take a couple thou — maybe five or ten or so. And you'll pay it back as soon as you're able, right Kevy?

KEVIN: No. My God. *(He gestures for her to look into the safe.)* Look. My God.

RACHEL: *(Peering into the safe with shared disgust.)* What is that?!

KEVIN: It's Muffin. Stuffed. And a note. "April Fools. Love ya, Darren." Uhhhhhh!

RACHEL: *(Beat.)* Well . . . look on the bright side. At least we won't go to jail for robbery.

(There is the sound of a key at the front door.)

KEVIN and RACHEL: *(Turning suddenly, gasping.)* Oh no! *(Simultaneously pointing.)* Window!

QUIET MISTY MEADOWS

Bart, twenties, has come to Quiet Misty Meadows Cemetery to make arrangements for his recently deceased pet fish, Moo Moo. Annette, thirties, the director of Quiet Misty, has just had all four wisdom teeth removed and has taken some heavy-duty medication to ease the pain. As the scene begins, Annette is beginning to explain the ceremonial options to Bart.

CHARACTERS
Annette: 30s, director of Quiet Misty Meadows
  Cemetery
Bart: 20s, a client

SETTING
A pet cemetery

TIME
The present

ANNETTE: *(Holding her cheek, trying not to move it.)* Hello. My name is Annette Hope and I'm the director here. On behalf of Quiet Misty Meadows, I want to extend our deepest sympathies for your loss, Mr. Martin.
BART: Thank you. Are you OK?
ANNETTE: Oh, I'm fine. I'm fine. *(Cries out a little.)* Ahh! No problem. I just, I just moved my cheek is all. I had a little oral *(Sucks in air in severe pain.)* surgery today. They just yanked all my wisdom teeth, but I'm fine. *(Cries.)* Ah-hah! Just moved things wrong again. But I'm fine. I'm fine. I took some heavy-duty medication right before you came in. I'm sure it'll kick in any minute. Now, Mr. Martin, the real question is, *(Looking meaningfully at him.)* how are you?
BART: I'm OK. As best as can be expected for —
ANNETTE: *(Cries out.)* Ahhhh! *(Trying to be at ease.)* Go on.
BART: For someone who lost my very best —

ANNETTE: *(Yells.)* Yahh! *(Beat.)* I'm sure that little Vicadin pill should be kicking in any minute now. Excuse me.

BART: No problem.

ANNETTE: *(Holding her cheek.)* Now, do you require pick up at your home?

BART: No, I brought her in myself. I gave her to one of your staff persons.

ANNETTE: *(She nods.)* OK. I want to assure you that we have a very careful group here. We've been providing lasting memorials for the last thirty-four years, so we have a great deal of experience. And we do our best to care for your loved one in a respectful manner. Gosh, I seem to have a pool of blood gathering in here. *(Tongue touching her cheek.)*

BART: Oh.

ANNETTE: No worry. No worry. You're just not supposed to spit. *(She swallows. She makes a disgusted face.)* Uhh. *(Beat.)* Now, why don't you take a seat? There are several things we should discuss. *(He sits.)* When we spoke on the phone, you told me that she passed away last night, correct?

BART: Well, it's hard to tell. *(She looks a bit surprised.)* You see, I wasn't home. I was in Milwaukee for vacation and my idiot brother who was watching her said she turned all brownish-blue at some point and started flopping about on her stomach and this stuff —

ANNETTE: I see no reason to replay those painful moments. *(Touching her tummy.)* Feelin' queasy anyway. We'll just say it occurred last night for the paperwork, OK? *(She writes.)* Uh, firstly, what was your dear pet's name?

BART: Moo Moo.

ANNETTE: *(Taking in.)* Moo Moo. Umm. *(He nods.)* What a unique name.

BART: It was because of how she opened her little lips toward me.

ANNETTE: Uh-huh.

BART: *(Does imitation.)* She'd look right at me and her lips seemed to be saying, "Moo moo. Moo moo." She was just my Little Minnie Moo Moo.

ANNETTE: Would you like Little Minnie included on the headstone, plaque, and memory table?

BART: No, no. We'd want to be formal.

ANNETTE: Yes, of course. So then that would read Ms. Moo Moo Martin then?

BART: No, um, Moo Moo *Mary* Martin. Mary was her middle name.

ANNETTE: OK. *(She writes.)* And Moo Moo is spelled M-O-O and then again M-O-O, as in a cow saying moo moo.

BART: Are you making fun of this?

ANNETTE: No. No, Mr. Martin. I have to get this correct for the paperwork so that we can talk about the services available for your dear . . . pet.

BART: *(Tearful.)* I'm sorry. It's just . . . my Moo Moo was so wonderful to me in every way.

ANNETTE: I bet she was. I bet she was a lulu of a Moo Moo, wasn't she?

BART: Yes. And my stupid friend Susie said I was like this big goofball for making such a fuss.

ANNETTE: *(Gasps, opening her mouth too wide causing pain.)* Ahh! *(Beat.)* No. Well, sometimes friends are insensitive because they don't understand the bond that forms between people and their pets. Maybe your friend has never known that bond or is incapable of any kind of bond, Mr. Martin, which is really sad. Really, really sad! *(Bart nods.)* Maybe Susie's a big pathetic, rotten loser who no one even likes! Ever think of that?

BART: Well, I, I think that might be over —

ANNETTE: I'm sorry. I don't know where that came from. These drugs sometimes make one a little . . . woo-ooh — exaggerated. I'm sorry. Obviously, we're talking about you and Moo Moo here. Look, my point is that we know how you feel at Quiet Misty Meadows. We know it well. This is a very difficult time for you.

BART: Umm-hmm. It is.

ANNETTE: So we try to make you feel at ease. We even have a bereavement counselor available to help you through this. For another small fee. Everything costs money these days. You're sad, they bilk ya for all ya got. Anyway, there's nothing unusual about how you feel, and this I can assure you. I can pass your name onto the bilking, I mean, bereavement counselor and she can call you later today if you'd like. Would you like?

BART: *(He nods.)* Yeah. Moo Moo was so smart. She loved me so much. She was cute and good.

ANNETTE: I know. I know she was. I too have lost several pets that I loved through the years. Misty was the reason I started Quiet Misty. I also have Bandit, Fluffy, and Lead Belly buried here.

BART: My gosh, you've had so much loss.

ANNETTE: Yeah, well Fluffy and Lead Belly I was kinda getting sick of anyway. I mean, they were kinda sick. I mean . . . never mind. I'm just saying that I understand your pain, Mr. Mootin.

BART: Martin.

ANNETTE: Right.

BART: It's so great that you offer this service. I mean, even my mother laughed at how emotional I got over my little fish.

ANNETTE: I know that's *terrible* that even family members — fish?

BART: Yes, I know Mom didn't mean to laugh. She apologized right after.

ANNETTE: *(Beat.)* We're talking about Moo Moo, the fish?

BART: Yeah. Why?

ANNETTE: *(High-pitched.)* No reason.

BART: And she wasn't just a *fish*. She was a *zebra* fish.

ANNETTE: Riiiight. Which explains why you named her Moo Moo then.

BART: What do you mean?

ANNETTE: Nothing. I just think it's a very unique and clever name.

BART: Is this a problem that Moo Moo's a fish?

ANNETTE: No, no. Of course not.

BART: Haven't you ever had a fish here before?

ANNETTE: Well, I wouldn't — I don't have all the records but — look, I admit that we more frequently deal with the loss of cats and dogs, but we have dealt with countless different types of pets. We're professionals here even if we do sleep around with each other. *(Shocked at herself.)* My God where did that come from?

BART: You haven't had one fish?!

ANNETTE: We've had rabbits, hamsters, guinea pigs —

BART: But those aren't fish?!

ANNETTE: *(Angry.)* Well, duh! I realize that Mr. Martin! OK? But we've had a penguin, an octopus, a turtle, a tarantula —

BART: You had a turtle?

ANNETTE: Yes! Yes, we did! We did have a turtle. Todd. Todd the ugliest turtle we'd ever — I mean, the mug on that thing, only a mother — *(Realizing.)* we loved Todd like a mother . . . in a very sweet way.

BART: You're acting very strangely, Ms. Hope.

ANNETTE: Well, well, well and you're Mr. Normal with the kissy-lips-moo-moo thing? Who's calling the fishy striped, huh? *(Snapping out of it. Pausing in horror.)* Oh, dear God, I'm sorry.

BART: Well, if this is how people who are mourning get treated here at Quiet Misty Meadows, I am appalled! I am taking my little Moo Moo and going somewhere —

ANNETTE: *(Grabbing his arm.)* I'm sorry, I'm sorry, Mr. Martin, this is highly unusual. I don't know what's come — it must be this medicine. I assure you I'm a professional. And I don't think you had any weird thing with your little Moo Moo Zebra fish even if it sounded fishy. *(Laughs.)* Forget that. I know that you loved her very much, and we, the only

pet cemetery in a seventy-mile radius, want your moola —
Moo Moo, I mean we want to take your Moo Moo to her
resting place. So please, please, I'm sorry. Take a seat, buddy,
please.

BART: All right.

ANNETTE: Thank you. Now, why don't we discuss the kinds
of services we have here at Quiet Misty Meadows. We offer
several options for the lasting memorial of Moo Moo. We
have a cremation service, with a full line of urns —

BART: No, no, I couldn't just put her in an urn.

ANNETTE: OK, well, your pet's remains may be entombed in
our mausoleum instead or we could bury her.

BART: I'd like to bury her.

ANNETTE: OK. We have several options in a private burial
service with a nondenominational ceremony held here in the
At Peace Room.

BART: Oh, that sounds nice. Is it nice?

ANNETTE: Nice? It's so nice. Okey-dokey-smokey. Whew. Isn't
this fun? What we would like to do then is hold the ceremony and then do a short procession up to the Hilltop
Gazebo for a final blessing.

BART: Final? Final sounds so . . . final, you know?

ANNETTE: *(Rubbing his arm, doing baby voice.)* Aww, well
we can call it the semifinal then. Hell, we can call it the plop-
her-in-the-ground thingy. Whatever you'd like. The point is
she's gone, dead, vamoose. Headin' to the big fishbowl in
the sky!

BART: No!

ANNETTE: Could be worse. She could be swirling down the
toilet bowl in your brother's john.

BART: I don't think this is funny in the least.

ANNETTE: Who's joking?

BART: Would we be able to view her before we take her to her
final resting place?

ANNETTE: You want to embalm Moo Moo?

BART: Could we?

ANNETTE: Oh, sure, we could embalm her, we could stuff her, we could freeze-dry her and put her on a pizza. Whatever you want, Mr. Marmoo. Whatever you can pay for. You come first. You, you, you. Whatever your wishes are, we will do for you, Moo Moo.

BART: I would love to have an open casket, but she's so disfigured and *(Tearful.)* it's all my fault. I let my stupid brother watch her and he has cats. I told him to keep her away from them, I told him, but those nasty little beasts pulled her out of the tank and started to —

ANNETTE: That's all righty, let's movey onie.

BART: But it's my fault that she's, that she's . . .

ANNETTE: Oh, Mr. Martin, we always blame ourselves at times like these even when it's totally, completely our fault.

BART: I know, I know I shouldn't . . . *(Realizing.)* What did you say?

ANNETTE: Me? I didn't say. What do *you* say? We've been told not to say. *(She's in utter confusion.)*

BART: I'm having second thoughts about the burial. I don't think it's natural for her.

ANNETTE: We could plop her into the serenity pond. Let nature take its course. *(Dancing.)* Free Moo Moo — free!

BART: And let her rot out in the open?

ANNETTE: You're right. You're right. We could sink her? We could get fin-size cement blocks? What do you think about that?

BART: I think it's sick! I think you're sick!! I think this whole place is sick!!!

ANNETTE: Wow! You've got a theme going there. Look, Bud, she was a fish! Got it? A smelly, rotten fish, not a lover or something!!

BART: She was exotic!!

ANNETTE: Whoa! So are the dancers on Fifth and Green. That doesn't mean I want them in my living room.

BART: *(Angry.)* Can't you understand?! You evil witch! *(Breaks down in tears.)* It was terrible to die like that. Those cruel monsters tore her from my bosom. And now I have to live and go on without her. I have to return home to her things. To her little treasure chest and her little snorkle guy and her little seahorsey and . . . her little . . . net. I loved her, Ms. Hope. We had a connection. And every time I walk past her fish flakes, I think of us. She won't nibble or moo moo anymore! Do you understand that? And the question remains, what will I do with all the little pebbles at the bottom of the tank? I can't just throw them out. What will I do with them?

ANNETTE: You know, Barty, I don't think that's a good question to ask me. *(She snaps her fingers.)* 'Cause I'll tell ya. I know, I haven't been right to you, Mr. Moo Flakes. I can tell you're really hurting. The thing is, the thing is, Mr. Martin . . . I don't care. And you know what? Neither would you. Neither would you if you just had your wisdom teeth yanked out today. Ripped right out from your gums, just like the cats ripped your little Moo Moo to shreds. But you know what? Now, I'm feelin' good. You know, gooooood! *(She holds out her hand.)* So what I suggest, is this. You take one of these. Here. Take it. *(She hands him a pill.)* Take this little Vicadin pill and forget about the damn fish. You'll feel a whole hell of a lot better. Trust me.

BART: You are the most disgusting, deranged funeral home director I have ever come across.

ANNETTE: *(Sexy.)* Oooh. I like your alliteration! You're not so bad yourself, Barty. *(Pulls him into her and kisses him hard.)* Let's go make peace in the At Peace Room!
(She drags off the speechless, shocked Barty.)

ASKING TOO MUCH

Jess and David met in their twenties. They became good friends, and eventually roommates. They fell for each other right from the start, but as Mother Nature would have it, David is gay. Finally, the two of them decided to join forces in having a baby together. This scene tells the tale of their life together with direct addresses to the audience.

CHARACTERS
Jess: 20s
David 20s, Jess's best friend

SETTING
Various locations and Jess and David's apartment

TIME
The present

JESS: *(To audience.)* I met David twelve years ago while I was in law school. He was cute, had a sweet face. Poor guy was stuck talking to this freaky woman while I watched. I'm not good at parties. She was this performance artist named Nelina.

DAVID: That was her name. Nelina! I was making guacamole. She was telling me about the people she knew at this theater group. Apparently, the group's claim to fame was throwing green goop at a spinning record player center stage for a full two hours. Now, it's a little too Blue Man Group gone green to me, but back then I just thought — weird — really weird. Nelina wanted to talk all night. I saw Jess smirking a bit as she hung by the cheese mound. I mouthed "help!"
(Going into the scene.)

DAVID: Oh God! Hi! I didn't know you were coming, hon!
(David hugs Jess. She smiles and hugs him back.)

JESS: *(To David.)* Me either. It's great to see you, darling. What a surprise!

DAVID: You look wonderful! I could eat you up. *(Whispers to Jess.)* Uh . . . ?

JESS: *(Whispers to David.)* Jess. *(Out loud.)* I'm so happy to see you too, uh . . . *(He whispers in her ear.)* David. I'm here for your nibbling pleasure.

DAVID: *(To audience.)* She gave an Oscar-winning performance. Nelina left the room when Jess started sucking loudly on my ear. After Nelina left, she said . . .

JESS: *(To David. Joking.)* So were we very much in love, David?

DAVID: Desperately. I hated to do that but nothing was working. I rue the day I lent that woman my gummy eraser. She's in the art program with me at Emerson.

JESS: Art program, huh? I thought you were in law school like the rest of us.

DAVID: You're one of them, huh? Is that how you know Brian? From law school?

JESS: No, my roommate knows everyone from everywhere. I go to B.C. actually.

DAVID: Oh good. Boston College. Can't drop the H-bomb then.

JESS: H-bomb?

DAVID: Harvard bomb. One drops every five seconds of conversation here. It's so dramatic. Pause, pause for applause. That's what impressed me most about Brian. I didn't learn that he went there until the third time I met him.

JESS: Are you roommates?

DAVID: No, no. Um, friends.

JESS: *(Looking around.)* I hate parties.

DAVID: *(He laughs.)* Was it something I said?

JESS: No, no. I feel stupid. You have to make small talk and act like you actually care.

DAVID: I hate 'em too. People across the room look like they're having such a good time.

JESS: I know. And then people pretend they're talking to you but their eyes are always darting behind or around you like they're looking for someone more interesting.

DAVID: *(Pretending to be looking about the room.)* Huh? I was looking over . . .

(She hits him in the arm.)

DAVID: Oww. Touchy.

JESS: *(To audience.)* The next time we met, for brunch a few days later, I rushed in . . . popped the big question. *(To David.)* So are you gay, David, or what?

DAVID: *(Reacts.)* Wow. That's quite a segue. No idle chitchat about hash browns. Straight for the G drop. Does it make a difference?

JESS: Yes. Of course it does. It puts you in the correct category. Available, unavailable. Sugar Daddy —

DAVID: Sugar plum fairy. I don't hold it against you that you're straight.

JESS: Oh thank you. Very kind. I'm glad this is all clear now so we can move on. Do you have a dog?

DAVID: Yes, but you can't categorize him. He's fixed. And bi- from what I can gather in terms of his sniffing preference.

JESS: *(To audience.)* After ten years, many failed attempts at long-term relationships, and twenty pounds of weight gain between us, things were looking doomy. *(To David.)* I hate men.

DAVID: So do I.

JESS: *(Toasting.)* To Alan and Lewis. *(To audience.)* Our cheating boyfriends.

DAVID: May they rot in hell!

JESS: *(Clinks glass.)* Or end up with each other.

DAVID: *(To audience.)* Each time we got back in the saddle again. Or sort of.

JESS: Have I seen this date in our living room before? Is he a repeat?

DAVID: No. But he looks like a couple of the other ones. I think it's love this time.

JESS: I think you're high on turpentine. Now, shut up and listen. I met the most terrific guy in the elevator. He asked to borrow my blow-dryer, just so he could return it later.

DAVID: Exciting. When he asks for your styling gel, you'll know it's love.

JESS: *(To audience.)* Each time, each relationship ended disastrously. *(To David.)* He's a jerk. Every time I let him into my bed, he leaves by dawn. Why can't he just dump me or at least have the decency to say, "You know, I'm so busy, I couldn't possibly get involved right now"? He promised me last night he wouldn't leave again.

DAVID: I don't know what his problem is, Jess. So stop asking me. He's just a jerk!

JESS: So where was the boyfriend last night? You have a new one every night lately.

DAVID: I think you're misdirecting your anger.

JESS: I'm not misdirecting anything. I'm asking you about this habit of yours.

DAVID: How can you put up with this guy? He leaves you every night. It's humiliating.

JESS: Humiliating? Who's up every night drinking and watching videos? Who can't connect to anyone unless it's totally meaningless? You're still hung up on Brian, and you know it. It's been years and years since Brian left. Now that's humiliating!

DAVID: Are you finished?

JESS: Yes! No! I didn't mean . . . Am I a bad person, David? Am I that ugly and undesirable? *(She reaches her arms out to him.)* I liked him so much. I thought he was the one. I didn't mean what I said.

DAVID: Sure you did. It *is* time for me to get over him. And you're none of those things.

JESS: I love you, David.

DAVID: You should. I hate you, by the way. You want to have my baby?

JESS: Absolutely. *(To audience.)* That became our pet phrase whenever expressing our solidarity. We'd just ask the other if they wanted to have our baby. I'm not really sure when the phrase changed from being just a phrase. Maybe after my breakup . . .

DAVID: Why don't we go out and build a snow dog, Pooky? *(Jess shakes her head no.)*

JESS: Maybe we could make some popcorn in the microwave? We'll watch it pop as it goes round. And you can have my baby.

DAVID: OK.

JESS: When do you want to do it?

DAVID: Tonight is as good as any.

JESS: No, I'm serious. We talk about it all the time.

DAVID: We're joking all the time, Jess. It's a joke.

JESS: Is it? Neither of us is getting any younger.

DAVID: Yeah, but some of us are getting really crazy.

JESS: Why? I want a baby and you do too. You've told me a million times. I can't do it without a man and you can't do it without a woman.

DAVID: I can't do it *with* a women either. That's the problem.

JESS: Have you ever tried?

DAVID: Well, no. Not exactly. *(Beat.)* And what if one of us gets involved down the line?

JESS: The more the merrier.

DAVID: Right. That's realistic. What if you get married and want to live in a house?

JESS: You can live in a section of it.

DAVID: What if I get involved?

JESS: You can get an apartment nearby.

DAVID: What if it's with your husband?

JESS: We'll move to San Francisco.

DAVID: *(To audience.)* I don't know how, but somehow this conversation started to convince me.

JESS: I've been looking into surgical fertilization, it's sort of expensive.

DAVID: Why not bear down and just do it?

JESS: David? Really?

DAVID: Quick, clean, and generically.

JESS: *(To audience.)* It's so sexy when he talks like that.

DAVID: *(To audience.)* How hard could it be? *(Beat.)* Hard.

JESS: Want me to do something butch to start off? Arm wrestle?

DAVID: Don't make fun. Do you want me to kiss you to get things rolling?

JESS: That might be good, but hey . . . I don't want to cramp your style. *(Beat.)* Relax, David. Enjoy the novelty. *(She goes to kiss him.)*

DAVID: What are you doing?

JESS: Lie back and think of England. *(To audience.)* Some way or other . . . he managed to pull it off.

DAVID: I did it. I did it! *(Throws up his hands.)* I did it! *(Sings.)* I am strong. I am invincible.

JESS: David, that's "I Am Woman."

DAVID: Oh yeah.

JESS: *(To audience.)* It did work. Quite surprisingly. And we quickly took to playing the roles. *(To David.)* I thought that was the point of being pregnant. To eat.

DAVID: Healthy.

JESS: Whatever you want!

DAVID: *(David puts his ear to her stomach.)* Hum? You'd like some prune juice and a nice salad, topped off with a fig? Sure.

JESS: Grab me the chocolate fudge ice cream cookies with carmel before I ram this cart back and forth over your body. I've a baby inside me who has mistaken my bladder for a trampoline and nothing is funny ever again. Ever, ever again!

DAVID: *(To audience.)* As you can see, everything would have been pure bliss, perfect, but I met someone. A nice someone named Tom. *(Jess sticks her tongue out.)* He wanted us to get together — all three of us. He understood. It was complicated, but he was interested. Maybe we'd go to a concert, a play, but Jess always said no. *(To Jess.)* You had to stay home for this? *The Fly* is your favorite movie?!

JESS: My favorite with an insect for the lead.

DAVID: This timing with Tom has been all wrong. Maybe I should call it off — end it.

JESS: Lamaze class was awful. Everyone thought I should divorce you.

DAVID: But we're not married.

JESS: I think I should divorce you, David.

DAVID: I didn't say good night to the baby. *(He kisses Jess's stomach and rubs it gently.)*

JESS: I'm serious. I don't think I can do this, David. *(He looks at her.)* I wanted to look over during class tonight and have you magically appear. I wanted to kill Tom for taking you on a date. I've gotten myself too attached. To you.

DAVID: Jess? I'll marry you if you'd like. For real. Please. I'll be a good husband. Won't cheat with other women. I don't even mind that you're knocked up.

JESS: I'm not joking this time, David.

DAVID: Neither am I.

JESS: It's not fair. To either of us. It means we give up the hope of ever really being in love. *(Pause.)* Will you leave tomorrow?

DAVID: *(To audience.)* And that was it. The end of our marriage. No big fireworks. No divorce papers. Just a big D drop. Plain and simple. I left the next day. We weren't hopeless.

JESS: We still had Samantha.

DAVID: Seven pounds five ounces. All parts in good working order. She's quite a girl. It's lucky that we didn't give up. We found "someones." They're quite a lot better than what we had hoped for.

JESS: I won't say it isn't complicated. But life's complicated, isn't it?

DAVID: Yes. Complicated . . . and wonderful. *(Beat.)* Were we very much in love, Jess?

JESS: *(Beat, thinks.)* Desperately.

PU PU SURPRISE

Beth, twenty-five, and Tom, twenty-six, are planning a wedding in the next eight months. This evening, they are celebrating their third anniversary of dating. Tom is fifty-four minutes late to their romantic dinner, making it not at all romantic. Beth is angry, worried, and suspicious all at the same time. Tom was supposed to be checking out a new property inspector so that they can buy a home or condo before the big day. Unfortunately, Tom got caught up in certain details. He arrives at Ming Wong to find Beth rather cool — but seething.

CHARACTERS
Beth: 25
Tom: 26, Beth's fiancé

SETTING
Ming Wong restaurant

TIME
The present, evening

TOM: Hey sweetie. You look absolutely beautiful. I'm sorry I'm a bit late. This looks great. I told someone today we were going to Ming Wong for our anniversary, and they said it was just great. I'm afraid to take off my shoes though, Beth, because, because well, *(Whispers.)* that fungal problem last August. Are you OK, Beth? You look pale.

BETH: *(Composed.)* A bit? A bit late? You think you are a *bit* late?

TOM: Well . . . maybe it's a bit more than a bit.

BETH: Try fifty-four minutes late, Thomas.

TOM: No? That late? It can't be. *(Looks at watch.)* Oop. Well, time flies sometimes.

BETH: *(Still feigning calmness.)* So does flatware. And chopsticks. Hell, I bet this table will fly if I give it a college-girl try.

TOM: Well, it's a long story, honey.

BETH: That includes ambulances and emergency care I trust.

TOM: Right. *(To waiter.)* I'll have a shot of —

BETH: Nothing. He'll wait. *(To waiter.)* Give us a few minutes.

TOM: I was meeting with the property inspector like you told me to, Beth.

BETH: That was at three o'clock. I was doing laundry at three o'clock. But do I now have bleach in hand? No. *(She shakes her head.)* Because between three o'clock and eight o'clock, there are five hours. *(Holding her hand up.)* Five. After washing *your* disgusting laundry —

TOM: I told you not to do my workout stuff.

BETH: I promise it'll never happen again. *(Continuing from earlier.)* I called your mother because I was worried about you. By the way, she hadn't heard one word from you.

TOM: Teaming up on the guilt trip now?

BETH: I visited three reception halls and environments and made a down payment on one.

TOM: You did? Which hall?

BETH: Environment. The Hanson Gardens. We can do the ceremony and the reception there. It's gorgeous and the food is out of this world.

TOM: You got free samples? I told you I *love* free samples. Like the cake place?

BETH: Don't distract me. Besides, I tried to call your cell phone to see if you wanted to meet me and *have* free samples. No answer. I left a message. Waited for an hour. Nothing. I came home. Balanced my checkbook. Showered, dressed, perfumed. I assumed you'd be doing similarly since it is our anniversary. I drove here. De-shoed and settled. Sat crossed-legged ready to eat a Pu Pu Platter for our special occasion. But guess what? Guess what?

TOM: They don't have a Pu Pu?

BETH: No. You were the Pu Pu! Because you weren't here! Not

only were you not here, you were not here for the next fifty-four minutes. You may wonder what went through my mind.

TOM: No. I think I have a pretty good idea.

BETH: He's dead! He's lost. He's hurt. He's dead! I'm alone. I'll kill him!

TOM: *(Trying to comfort her.)* Oh honey.

BETH: *(She smacks him.)* Don't touch me! *(He pulls back.)* I thought, he better be dead.

TOM: I was just trying to figure out if this property inspector had the right credentials to be deciding where we live. This may be the biggest investment of my — our life.

BETH: Are you telling me that you spent five hours with him?

TOM: Her.

BETH: Her? Ohhh. Her. So what property were you inspecting?

TOM: Chris Thomas is a her. Who knew? She's really great.

BETH: Um-hum.

TOM: Now, honey, wait. Don't be ridiculous. It's not like that. I visited a few houses and condos with her and a friend. She has a friend, Lydia, who's a real estate agent.

BETH: Without me? You went without me? You went with Lydia, and the property slut?

TOM: Well you put a down payment on a hall without me.

BETH: Environment, environment. That's what they call it.

TOM: The point is that you got free samples.

BETH: And they were *really* good.

TOM: *(Whiney noise.)* I was simply trying to scope out a place you might love.

BETH: I told you what I love. The cute, little, green-and-white-trimmed house with the rose garden. But nooooo —

TOM: It looked like it was sinking on its foundation.

BETH: Well so do you, Pudgeball. You wouldn't even call the realty company to have them show it to us.

TOM: That's because I thought it looked too expensive. And big. And it is big. And nice.

BETH: How do you know? *(Realizing.)* Ohhh. Did you go see it with those icky people?

TOM: Well . . . I . . .

BETH: You did? *(Angrily.)* You did!

TOM: Well, I wanted to see what Chris thought.

BETH: Naturally. And what did she think?

TOM: She said it was sinking on its foundation. But it's two hundred years old and houses that old do that. Besides, the slanted attic might be great for kids. It's perfect for race cars. Chris and I thought that was cool!

BETH: Did you?

TOM: It's big. It has four bedrooms.

BETH: Great. That'll give you plenty of rooms to sulk in alone. *(Whining.)* I drank two and a half pots of green tea waiting for you.

TOM: I'm sorry, honey. But I'm here now. Let's just celebrate.

BETH: Celebrate?! I had to pee like twenty-four times. Do you know how embarrassing that is? And the host kept looking to see that I had no date, no date at all. He looked at me all pathetic-like.

TOM: Oh baby. I didn't mean to be running so far behind schedule.

BETH: And do we have no forms of communication to communicate such lateness?

TOM: Well, I didn't have your cell phone number on me.

BETH: What? You don't know it? We're getting married and you don't know it?

TOM: I sort of know it.

BETH: No, no! You either know it or you don't.

TOM: I never call it. I programmed it into my cell phone.

BETH: Well. Where was your cell phone?

TOM: Home.

BETH: Great. So why didn't you leave me a message at my place? So I wouldn't worry? *(He shrugs sheepishly.)* I had this fantasy that you were late because you were buying me a gift — a big gift — a fifty-four-minute-type gift.

TOM: Gift? What kind of gift?

BETH: Well, duh. An anniversary gift.

TOM: I understand. But you told me no gifts. You said that the other day. Tuesday. You said no to gifts. You said we should save up for the house and the wedding plans.

BETH: I didn't say no gifts. I said no *big* gifts.

TOM: No, no. I know you said no gifts. On Tuesday morning when we were in bed naked.

BETH: No, I said no *big* gifts.

TOM: No. Time out. Unfair. Untrue.

BETH: Well, I don't know what I said. But just because I *said* that doesn't mean . . .

TOM: Oh God. Was this one of those times when you say something that means the opposite?

BETH: I thought you knew that.

TOM: But how could I . . . I was going to . . . But you said no. You said no —

BETH: I bought *you* a gift.

TOM: Oh no! No. No. I don't want it. Take it back.

BETH: It's at home. It's that CD player you wanted.

TOM: Oh God. Well, I'll get you something this week. Whatever you want.

BETH: No, I don't want anything. The whole anniversary thing is ruined. We're late, and I'm beyond starving. And I seem all mean now. And you like the, the property slut. And I just wanted everything to be romantic, and perfect and Chinese. And I love you.

TOM: Oh honey. I love you too.

BETH: You don't act like it.

TOM: I love you. I so love you. And I wasn't flirting with anyone. I was thinking the whole time of you. Lost in what it would be like for us to live together finally.

BETH: Aww, Tommy. Really?

TOM: Really. I was looking at places you liked the best. And I never thought the psychic was going to take so long.

BETH: Um. Tommy? What psychic?

TOM: I didn't mention her?

BETH: No, no. You didn't happen to. You stopped to see a psychic?

TOM: No. I didn't stop. She was just there. Actually, strangely, she lived in the green house with the white trim.

BETH: Oh-kay. So you thought you'd chat with ole . . . ?

TOM: Rosa.

BETH: Rosa. The psychic. So how much did you drop on Rosa, while bringing zippo to your fiancée on her anniversary?

TOM: It was fascinating. She even analyzes handwriting too.

BETH: I repeat. How much?

TOM: OK, twenty bucks. But she did a complete analysis of that note you gave me with all the questions to the inspector. She was right on the money. She didn't charge me, but I felt obligated to give her a tip. *(Realizing.)* Oh, now that's kind of a gift I could give you. *(He pulls it out to hand it to her.)*

BETH: My note to you on the side of a ripped envelope is a gift?

TOM: No, well her perception of your personality is sort of interesting in a sort of very pregift kinda — more like door-prize-kinda way. I'm never getting out of this, am I?

BETH: No. Well, what's the next gift? A piece of priorly chewed gum?

TOM: Actually, I talked to Rosa so long because I thought she was the type I could endear myself to. Actually, I genuinely liked her. *(Beth gives him a look.)* Not like that! The house had a good feeling to it. Rosa loves it, but all her kids moved out. It's too big. She seemed like the type to come down on the price if she liked me . . . *us*. Do you want to see her analysis?

BETH: I'll give you an analysis. You seduced a crazy old psychic and gave her my note.

TOM: She analyzed you and assessed how we'd be together as a couple.

BETH: You actually asked her to do that? How dare you —

TOM: She said we were very well suited.

BETH: That's not the point — She did?

TOM: But opposites. I was gentle, calm, and spontaneous.

BETH: Oh great. And I'm fierce, bitchy, and rigid, right?

TOM: She put it as strong, intense, and organized actually. *(Holds out the note.)* See?

BETH: *(Grabs the note out of his hand.)* Let me see that! Ridiculous bull! *(Reading.)* "The considerable difference in length of upper T's and P's portrays the writer's never-resting ambition, passion, and goals." *(She looks up.)* Well, she's got that right. *(Reading.)* The higher form level, angularity, and regularity in arrangement and pressure of the letters reveals that the writer possesses good intelligence and hardworking qualities. *(She looks up.)* Aww. That is sweet. I'm liking this present more and more, Tom.

TOM: *(Grabs it away.)* That's a good representation. I forgot. I don't think she gets this next part right at all.

BETH: *(She pulls it back.)* No, it's my gift. I'll read it. *(Reading.)* "The compressed quality of the writing, together with the largely missing or down-reaching counterstrokes reveals the writer is selfish and whiney. And the ink-filled ovals suggest a violent temper, quick to judge." Selfish, huh? Whiney, huh? Violent temper, huh? *(She looks up from the envelope, saying nothing. Pause.)*

TOM: See. She's way off there. Totally wrong on everything. I'm sorry. I'm really sorry, Beth. She's just a psychic. *(Beat.)* Beth? Beth? Why don't you speak? *(He looks closer.)* Beth? Beth, I think you are quiet and sweet. None of this is true.

BETH: *(Whining.)* Yes it is, Tom. *(He shakes his head. Furious.)* Yes, it is!! It just proves we'll be in an unhappy marriage. We are not meant to be. You'll always be late and carefree, and I'll always be organized and hungry. I'll buy presents for you professing my love and you'll buy me nothing. It'll never work.

TOM: Beth, I think you're overreacting. If you only knew the whole reason I was late.

BETH: Well, tell me already! I haven't heard one good explanation.

TOM: I put a bid on the green-and-white-trimmed house.

BETH: See! See, you don't have one good . . . you did? *(Beat.)* You did?

TOM: Yeah. It was going to be a surprise present. It worked with Rosa. I knew you loved the place. I wanted to surprise you. I was hoping they'd give me an answer right there. Rosa told me her people will call us back tomorrow.

BETH: Oh, Tommy. *(She reaches her arms out.)* You're so wonderful. I love you so much. My little smooshy wooshy. *(Changing tone.)* But if you ever leave me waiting for fifty-four minutes again, I'll kill you! *(Beat.)* Let's have some Pu Pu.

RETURNING CARESSES

Edward, twenties, has come to Bath, Mat, Towels, Etc.
to return a foot massager that he purchased a few days
ago. Fearful of getting fired again, Molly, a clerk, is
overly friendly. She tries valiantly to handle Edward's
"little problem."

CHARACTERS
Molly: 20s, store clerk
Edward: 20s, a customer

SETTING
Bath, Mat, Towels, Etc. store

TIME
The present

MOLLY: *(Enthusiastically.)* Welcome to Bath, Mat, Towels, Etc. Happy Holidays and hello!

EDWARD: Hi. Happy Holidays? We haven't even celebrated Halloween yet?

MOLLY: Well, we don't care at Bath, Mat, Towels, Etc. We celebrate all holidays all year long!

EDWARD: Even when there isn't one?

MOLLY: Especially when there isn't one. That's what makes us special. And there's always a holiday on the way. If it's not Halloween, it's Thanksgiving, or Fourth of July, or Rosh Hashanah, or Ramadan —

EDWARD: OK, OK. I get the point. But don't your customers find that annoying?

MOLLY: It's in our employee handbook. In an adjunct memo entitled, "Hello."

EDWARD: *(Beat.)* I don't mean to be rude, and I know you don't write the policy yourself, but don't you think that customers find this holiday wishing all the time disingenuous?

MOLLY: Well I, I . . . Great weather today, huh?

EDWARD: There's a flood warning.

MOLLY: Oh. Well, perfect for towels then.

EDWARD: Look, I can tell you are trying to keep up the perfect store image, but look, lady, you can cut the crap with me.

MOLLY: I only wish I could, but I'm happy to serve you at Bath, Mat, Towels, Etc.!

EDWARD: Are you being watched?

MOLLY: I'm fine. I'm fine. I'm just not allowed to say certain things like *(Lowering voice for the "I don't know" part.)* "I don't know" because they are not part of our customer vocabulary.

EDWARD: You're not allowed to say "I don't know"?!

MOLLY: Shhh! *(She smiles, gestures. Whispering.)* Smile as I show you the Davenport pillow. *(He does. She gestures to another part of the room.)* Act natural as we turn toward the illuminated fairy rock relaxation fountain. *(He tries to act natural while looking at the illuminated fairy rock relaxation fountain.)*

EDWARD: *(Saying with fake enthusiasm for those watching.)* Umm, that is actually relaxing! *(Whispers.)* So you're not allowed to say, "I don't know"? *(She nods.)* What if you truly don't know? *(She rolls her eyes as if to say, "I don't know!!")* Wow. This place is tough, huh? Spies everywhere. *(She nods.)*

MOLLY: How can I help you on this fine day, sir? It's a perfect day to buy some berry clusters, don't you think? We have the Spice Autumn collection on sale today.

EDWARD: What are those things anyway? I mean, everywhere you go they have those now. Balls, cement balls, papier-mâché-ish balls, mesh balls. What are you supposed to do with all these balls?

MOLLY: Well, your imagination is the limit. *(Clears throat.)* But these particular balls are five-inch spheres of natural-looking berries, creating a colorful splash of warm hues. These are the pom-pom-style clusters.

EDWARD: As opposed to the melon-ball clump? What do you do with it exactly? Can you eat it?

MOLLY: No, no, but I'm glad you asked. 'Cause that would've been poisonous — *(Smiles.)* kills with incessant vomiting. These lovely berry balls provide a cheery seasonal accent to any room. A wonderful adornment in a centerpiece bowl on a buffet or mantel. And they're imported.

EDWARD: I bet. They'd have to be imported. Because no one in their right mind in any other country would display a bunch of expensive, inedible balls in a bowl on their buffet.

MOLLY: Well. Not manly enough? OK. Moving on.

EDWARD: Actually, I didn't come in here to buy anything, Miss. I just have a little problem.

MOLLY: Problem? Well, good. That's why we're here. We're here to solve problems. *(Showing her name tag.)* My name is Molly, and I'm a serve-you-first employee slash product advancer.

EDWARD: Product advancer?

MOLLY: *(Mumbling quickly.)* Stock and check-out girl.

EDWARD: Oh. I see. Well, the thing is I have this little problem with —

MOLLY: No problem is little. We make your problems as big as we can. I mean, we don't think of any of your problems as little, unless you do, which apparently you do. I don't think I got that right. Oh well. Is it, let's say, perhaps, a leaky faucet, nozzle, or hose?

EDWARD: No.

MOLLY: Do you have problems coordinating your towels, rugs, and accessories?

EDWARD: Well . . . yeah. But I don't consider that a problem.

MOLLY: Oh. OK. Do you have unrecognizable odors in your bathroom that you can't control?

EDWARDS: Well, sure I have odors there, but I don't think they're unrecognizable. I have a pretty good idea what they are.

MOLLY: We have pillar candles in assorted scents like peppermint, vanilla, and manly ginseng.

EDWARDS: No, no, no. It's something . . . I have already purchased here a few days ago.

MOLLY: Oh. Ohhh. And there's a problem?

EDWARDS: Yes! That's what I've been trying to say! There's a problem! *(Puts it on the table.)* I recently bought your Homedics Foot Massaging Spa. And I was really excited because I have this achy feet thing.

MOLLY: Oh me too! Oh my gosh! How could I be so stupid? You want the five extra interchangeable attachments with pedicure kit and pedi socks, don't you?

EDWARDS: No, no actually. The fourteen interchangeable attachments it comes with are just fine. I just want the massager to work as advertised.

MOLLY: Oh my gosh. It doesn't work?

EDWARDS: Well, no it works. I mean, it works partly, but not entirely.

MOLLY: Oh. Well, give me the sales slip and we'll exchange it right here and now, sir. We don't want it to partly work, we want it to completely work, don't we?

EDWARD: Yes, we do. *(Handing her the slip.)* Here's the slip.

MOLLY: Great. This paperwork will only take a sec. Now, the only thing I need to be sure of here, is that you didn't use the device with your feet at all, sir, right?

EDWARD: *(Beat.)* What do you mean?

MOLLY: Just checking to make sure that you didn't put your feet in the massager at any time. I just have to put a little check there to make sure this didn't happen. So just say *(Whispering quickly.)* you didn't, even if you did. *(Louder.)* So I can put a little X there.

EDWARD: But of course I did or I wouldn't know that it didn't work.

MOLLY: Well, see, that's kind of a little boo-boo. You see, we aren't allowed to take back pumice spa stones, paraffin manicure sets or foot-massaging merchandise if the customer has used them on their actual feet.

EDWARD: Well what would one use a *foot* massager on if not their feet?

MOLLY: Well, I, I . . . *(Quickly mumbling.)* I don't know. *(Louder.)* But I do know Bath, Mat, Towels, Etc. is concerned about spreading foot fungus, warts, and other hideous feetlike diseases to our customers. Not that that would be the case with you, sir, of course. Because you're obviously well kept. *(Smiles.) Very* well kept. In all regards. *(Giggles.)*

EDWARDS: Well, thanks . . . Molly. You too. And very customer . . . friendly. *(She smiles. He takes her in.)* But what are we going to do about this? I mean, I have a totally useless foot massager spa that I spent fifty bucks on that doesn't do what it is advertised to do in all of your Bath, Mat, Towels, Etc. catalogs. And you people won't take it back because I tried it out to find out it didn't work? What was I supposed to do, never use it, and just magically know it didn't work properly?

MOLLY: I see your point. But you see, this is how the employee rules work here. No matter how ridiculous, unreasonable, and excessive they may be, I have to follow them because otherwise I get written up as noncompliant and *(Tearful.)* I'll lose my job again. *(Putting hands together.)* Center.

EDWARD: *(Beat.)* I used "you people" very loosely there because I know you are extremely competent, Molly, and really very good — very, very good at what you do.

MOLLY: Bath Man — I mean, Mat, is not inflexible. Ohhh, we're flexible. We bend. We bow. We even grovel. I could send you to the merchandise superwitch upstairs and you could get an exception.

EDWARD: Superwitch?

MOLLY: *(Laughs.)* Did I say that? Supervisor. I mean supervisor. I've read somewhere in the manual we can send you up there, if it wasn't that you were just not pleased with the product, but there were some product errors — actual errors, big, bold, massaging errors that were misrepresented in all of our advertisements.

EDWARDS: But I have to go upstairs to do this? I just want a new massager where everything works as it's advertised to work. I'd rather deal with you. I enjoy dealing with you.

MOLLY: You do? Well, thanks, I . . . I like helping you too. Maybe. Maybe I could take care of the problem personally if you could explain the problem to me. I could then call upstairs or write something out and find out if perhaps they could send down a product exception ticket if the problem were compelling enough, which I'm sure it will be. So what was the problem with the Homedics Foot Massaging Spa, sir? Tell me everything.

EDWARD: Edward, please.

MOLLY: Edward. I like that. Edward.

EDWARD: Well, I'm not trying to be picky, but it was advertised, as you probably know, as a pulsing, vibrating, *caressing* foot massager. But when I got this home and tried it, it didn't —

MOLLY: It didn't pulse?

EDWARD: No, it pulsed. It pulsed. It was a good pulser.

MOLLY: Oh yeah? *(Laughing.)* I've always wanted one of those.

EDWARD: Yeah. Yeah. Me too.

MOLLY: *(Clears throat.)* Anyway, so, um then did the vibrating mechanism fail?

EDWARD: No, no, the vibrating was good too. It was good. It was good. It. Was. Good!

MOLLY: Good! Umm. Please, go on.

EDWARD: OK, OK, where was I?

MOLLY: Vibrating was — good! My God, I need one of those myself. My feet are killing me at the end of the day here.

EDWARD: Do it. Do it. It's worth it. Do it for yourself, Molly. You deserve it.

MOLLY: But wasn't there a problem?

EDWARD: Oh. Yes. *(Mesmerized by her eyes.)* It's, it's the, the other thing the —

MOLLY: Caressing?

EDWARD: *(Still out of it, looking at her.)* Uh-huh. It pulsed, it vibrated, but no caressing — not a bit of caressing.

MOLLY: Not even a semi-caress?

EDWARD: Not even a fondle.

MOLLY: Oh, how awful! How disappointing for you. How much we all need that.

EDWARD: I know, I know. I agree. It's almost everything. The caressing mechanism orb didn't even move.

MOLLY: Ohhh, the old orb problem. Sounds like a nightmare. I need to write all this down so I can convey this thoroughly to my soul-stealing supervisor.

EDWARD: I mean, let's not overstate it because like I said the pulsing and vibrating was out of this world, but . . . you know, without the caressing, it's just . . .

MOLLY: I know. I know.

EDWARD: Hey, maybe you ought to try it so you can explain completely.

MOLLY: Here?

EDWARD: Why not? It's charged and ready. *(He sets it on the floor.)* All you have to do is step right in. You can see what I mean personally. Besides, didn't you tell me your feet were killing you? Let me turn it on. It warms up right away. Come on. Try it.

MOLLY: It warms up? *(He nods.)* OK . . . Just a quickie. Just to explain things more thoroughly. *(She steps in.)* Ooooh . . . ummmmmm. Yes. I seeeeee. Um-hum. That's nice. That's nice. That's niiiiiicccccce!

EDWARD: You want me to turn up the pulse?

MOLLY: *(Shrugs, speechless.)* Well, I do need to understand the situatiooooon. Ooooohhhh! Yeah! That's nice, that's — yep! *(Laughs.)* OK, is it getting warm in here? I'm warm. Are you warm?

EDWARD: It's warmish. Now, here's the vibrating.

MOLLY: *(Vibrating.)* Uhhhhh! *(She covers her mouth with both hands. She smacks off the switch and quickly steps out. Pause. She gathers herself, fixing her hair.)* I can see what you mean. About the lack of caressing.

EDWARD: *(Massaging the air.)* You just need the squeezing or it's too much intensity on the soles of your —

MOLLY: Umm-hum. I agree one hundred percent.

EDWARD: So you see the problem?

MOLLY: Oh yeah. Oh yeah. Ohhhhhh yeah. A definite lack of . . .

MOLLY and EDWARD: *(Whispered.)* Caressing. *(Beat.)*

EDWARD: So when do you get off?

MOLLY: Oh . . . Now's good!

EDWARD: What about Bath, Mat, Towels, Etc?

MOLLY: Good idea! I'll grab some. Don't move.

CAT-TASTROPHY

Mathew and Bridget, late twenties, are newlyweds. They moved into their new home six months ago. So did their cats. Bridget and Mathew love each other. However, Bridget's two cats hate Mathew's cat. For six months now Bridget and Mathew have been trying everything possible to make them get along, including following a structured and laborious routine given to them by their cat therapist. It is now the middle of the night, and, once again, Mathew has been woken up by the cats fighting. He can't take it anymore.

CHARACTERS
Mathew 20s, Bridget's husband
Bridget: 20s, Mathew's wife

SETTING
The newlywed's home

TIME
The present

MATHEW: *(Very sincere and serious.)* Honey, I've been thinking about this all week.
BRIDGET: Oh no. I was afraid of this.
MATHEW: You and I both know we cannot go on like this.
BRIDGET: But Mathew, we just need to be a little more patient.
MATHEW: We've been extremely patient, Bridget. Six months worth of patient.
BRIDGET: The therapist was very optimistic.
MATHEW: Maybe at the beginning, but you heard what she said at our last visit. Not all personalities can make it work together.
BRIDGET: But we didn't try everything.
MATHEW: What? Well what didn't we try? We did therapy.
BRIDGET: We introduced them wrong. That was our fault. We

were supposed to blend their smells on the blanket first before we ever made them meet.

MATHEW: It's not our fault. It's no one's fault. Remember she told us that? And we reintroduced them and did the blanket thing. It still didn't make any difference.

BRIDGET: But that's not true, there was less anxiety. There was less twitching.

MATHEW: Yes, but we had to distract them with the crystal the whole time. Come on, Bridget, you have to accept this. We've done all we can.

BRIDGET: Have we? Have we really? Have we really done all we can?

MATHEW: Yes. We've done the group therapy. We've played classical music to soothe them. Family activity time. Creating self-space and seclusion for each of them. We've kept our play dates. We even drugged them! But it didn't work. It didn't work. Our cats cannot live together!

BRIDGET: Maybe we weren't liberal enough with the catnip? Maybe we didn't play enough on the play dates? Maybe we weren't really united in our front?

MATHEW: Maybe our cats just hate each other. Ever think of that? And besides, I was very united, even when you weren't. It was me who made sure everyone had Friskie treats at all merging times, right? I'm the one who had to spread the pheromones all over — me. You act as if you're the only one who bore the brunt of this.

BRIDGET: I was in charge of just as much as you. The secluded-room switching, I performed every day. The special playtime, almost always fell to me. I think they felt our resentment, our bickering. Maybe we weren't affectionate enough?

MATHEW: Well, it's kind of hard to be "affectionate" when your cats are under you bed, ripping each other's ears off, isn't it? It's hard to concentrate on making love when they're going *(Imitating the screech.)* "Reeoooooooowwww!" as they lunge over you and draw blood from your back as they graze it. Or listening to them knock every precious thing you've ever owned off the mantle.

BRIDGET: It's not that bad.

MATHEW: What? They've become positively acrobatic in their destruction. You saw them. They even dangled from the beads on the ugly lamp.

BRIDGET: *(Gasps.)* That's my grandmother's lamp. You told me you liked it.

MATHEW: See? See what's happening here? They're pitting us against each other.

BRIDGET: You *told* me you liked it. Maybe it's my fault I didn't keep their nails clipped short enough.

MATHEW: You clipped them twice a week. It didn't stop the bloodshed. They just bit each other. Don't you see? We can't keep pointing fingers at each other. This is the beginning of our life together and they are tearing us apart!

BRIDGET: But our therapist was so optimistic at the start.

MATHEW: So were we all, Bridg. So were we all. We wanted this very badly, but it just can't go on. I think you know it as well as I. We must *(Sighs.)* separate the cats.

BRIDGET: *(Beat.)* OK, but why today, Matt? What's so magical about today?

MATHEW: Nothing is magical about it. It's very sad. It's very, very sad. But they'll ruin us. We got very ugly last night. Very, very ugly. Uglier than we've ever been. Aside from the co-construction of the Ikea bookcase and the mounting-the-bike rack incident. Look at last night.

BRIDGET: I know. *(Beat.)* But was it really that bad?
(Cut to last night.)

MATHEW: *(Running throughout the house, yelling.)* Ahhhh-hhhhhhhhhhhhh!

BRIDGET: *(Just waking.)* Mathew?

MATHEW: *(Running throughout the house, yelling.)* Ahhhh-hhhhhhhhhhhhh!

BRIDGET: Matt?

MATHEW: *(Outside their bedroom.)* And stay in there you rotten little head bangers!!

BRIDGET: *(Looking at him.)* Oh no! Oh God, I thought the spray would do it.

MATHEW: Do it?! They love that Cat-Away Spray. They roll around in it. They bask in it saying ha, ha, ha!

BRIDGET: *(Handing it to him.)* Spray bottle?

MATHEW: It's over. I've closed the door and put them in their cat carriers for the night.

BRIDGET: The carriers? But there's no room for them to —

MATHEW: Exactly! It had to be done, Bridg. Do you realize what time it is?

BRIDGET: The usual I suppose?

MATHEW: No they started earlier tonight. Two instead of three. It is now four AM.

BRIDGET: Was it that loud?

MATHEW: *(Obviously out of control.)* You didn't hear it?! They were head-butting for the last two hours! I think they've moved to full-body slams. They just run and death-dive right into the door. They're possessed!

BRIDGET: Possessed?! Whoa. Time out.

MATHEW: OK, I'm sorry, that was spoken out of anger. That was unfair, honey.

BRIDGET: That's an awful way to put it! They're my cats you know? Remember the therapist said we need to stand united emotionally? We need to stay positive? I've had them since they were little kitties. They were there when you weren't. They helped me through getting fired and my breakup with Jeff.

MATHEW: I know. I know. But you have a job and Jeff is gone.

BRIDGET: You're so mean about it all sometimes. You act as if they're evil.

MATHEW: Honey, they *are* evil.

BRIDGET: Mathew?! They aren't evil!

MATHEW: They rip the soles from your shoes. They steal Dove chocolate from the counter. They steal toilet paper and scratch the paint off the doors *every* night.

BRIDGET: They just don't want to be away from us.

MATHEW: No, they just want to kill Miranda and me.

BRIDGET: Well, that too. But that's natural animal behavior. It's natural to hate the new things you aren't used to.

MATHEW: Well is it natural behavior for cats to open the refrigerator on a regular basis?

BRIDGET: OK, OK, so they're a little rambunctious.

MATHEW: A little? You live in denial, Bridget. They opened up your refrigerator at your old place for a whole two years, spoiling I don't know how much food, and you kept blaming the landlord's "bum" refrigerator. I had to make you witness it to believe it.

BRIDGET: A sight I never needed to see by the way. I would have believed your account.

MATHEW: I think you needed to see it. I think you had to see it.

BRIDGET: I sticky-taped the refrigerator door.

MATHEW: Oooh, and that really worked. *(Beat.)* I know you love them, honey. And I . . . know you love them, but we cannot keep this up. Somebody has to go.

BRIDGET: Well, what does that mean?!

MATHEW: I don't know. Maybe all of them. Maybe all of them should just go.

BRIDGET: Go where? Throw them out on the street?

MATHEW: Not a bad idea! *(She gasps.)* Oh honey, I don't mean to upset you. But one of your cats has to go.

BRIDGET: Oh, my cat? But you wouldn't want to give up your precious little neurotic Miranda who doesn't come out unless you spend an hour and a half cooing and ooohing and trying to coax her from under the bed.

MATHEW: Well, perhaps if she wasn't having her ear torn off by the brother-and-sister terror tag team, maybe it would be easier for her to come out?

BRIDGET: She eats plants and pees all over the bed.

MATHEW: One time! One time she peed. I can't believe you have the nerve to bring that up.

BRIDGET: Two times! I counted. Two! She's evil times two!

MATHEW: Well of course she peed, she was traumatized by them! She comes from an abusive kittenhood. She needs stability, we moved her here. She needs companionship, we brought her devils!

BRIDGET: Uh! And that's my fault? I told you from the beginning we should consult a cat specialist because introducing adult cats is no picnic.

MATHEW: Oh for them it is. A refrigerator feast! They don't even have to pack the basket. They don't even have to hit the park. They don't even —

BRIDGET: OK, OK!

MATHEW: I can't believe you honestly did not hear them tonight?

BRIDGET: Well, I didn't, but I couldn't miss *you* running down the hallway screaming "Ahhhhhhhhh!"

MATHEW: Well, what? You want to blame me now? I can't help it I'm a light sleeper. I'm afraid they'll wake the neighbors with all that. Our neighbors will hate us.

BRIDGET: And I suppose yelling "filthy runts" at the top of your lungs will endear them to us?

MATHEW: OK, OK, that's why we need to talk about this. This is not good. Do you see me? Do you see my hand? *(He holds out his hand.)*

BRIDGET: Yeah.

MATHEW: Don't you see that?

BRIDGET: What? Did they scratch you, honey?

MATHEW: No! I'm shaking with anger. I'm shaking violently with anger. I am not managing well in this environment. Valium opened the refrigerator again after both Dexedrine and Valium got out just now and I wanted to smash his head!

BRIDGET: *(Rubbing his back.)* But you didn't, honey. *(He nods.)* How's Miranda?

MATHEW: She fine. She's cowering under the sideboard as usual.

BRIDGET: Well that's a good sign. They didn't take a swipe at her?

MATHEW: Oh they swiped. They scratched. They swung. They got me!

BRIDGET: I think I didn't hear it that much because I had my earplugs in. You should break down and wear them too. It's the only way we're going to get through this, honey.

MATHEW: I don't want to wear earplugs! I don't want to get though this anymore, Bridg. I want to end this. I can't sleep through this.

BRIDGET: I'm painfully aware of that.

MATHEW: *(Offended.)* Oh.

BRIDGET: Well, you wake me up. *You,* not them. You say you want to sleep, but you won't wear earplugs. Sometimes we have to do things we don't want to, Mathew. Like I have to sit on your stomach when you're having that little gas problem. Do I want to do that all the time? No!

MATHEW: You never told me that.

BRIDGET: I'm just saying the earplugs work for me.

MATHEW: You said you liked to help me with my little problem.

BRIDGET: I don't. Sometimes, I don't mind. What I don't like is being woken up every night.

MATHEW: Well, I can't help it if I have sensitive eardrums. Maybe I should sleep on the couch if I wake you up so much?

BRIDGET: Is that supposed to make me feel guilty?

MATHEW: Yes! It's me or them, lady. Me or them!!

BRIDGET: Well, I resent that ultimatum. You know they were my little fuzz balls long before you. In fact, I resent *you* more than them right now. Sleep on the damn couch with your little sensitive eardrums if you want.

MATHEW: Fine! I will! And you know what, Bridg? Your grandmother's lamp? It's the ugliest thing I've ever seen in my entire life!! Ever!!

BRIDGET: *(She gasps.)* Well, you're the worse *cat daddy* in the world!

(Cut back to today.)

BRIDGET: *(Calmly.)* You're right, you're right, Matt. It was ugly. I guess I just wanted to forget. *(Tearfully.)* The lucky bamboo dying in the vase next to our picture was a sign like you said.

MATHEW: It's dying because they're eating it, Bridg. They're eating our love because it's sitting in the relationship sector. It's their fault it's dying. They're killing it. They're killing us.

BRIDGET: So what are you saying? *We* aren't working anymore?

MATHEW: No, we're not. And I'm saying maybe a separation is in order.

BRIDGET: *(Even more tearful.)* What?! Really? But I thought we were . . . just over this little . . . but we were just married, Mathew, in . . . when were we married again?

MATHEW: May. *(Patting her back.)* No, no, no, honey! Oh God, no! Not us. Them. The cats.

BRIDGET: Oh. *(Saddened.)* Oh. *(Beat.)* Ohhhh. They love each other too.

MATHEW: Now, now, listen I have a friend, Glenda, from work who just lost one of her kitties. She loves them. She's willing to be a foster care home for one. We could just, we could just see how it goes. She may be willing to adopt and give one of our little ones a nice and less hostile home.

BRIDGET: Oh. And which one will go? *(Beat.)* Valium? *(He nods.)* But he'll be so sad.

MATHEW: Now, this woman is very into Reiki and she'll make him feel so safe and protected.

BRIDGET: What's Reiki?

MATHEW: The laying on of hands.

BRIDGET: How do you know? Has Glenda been laying her hands on someone else I know?

MATHEW: What?! No, no, honey.

BRIDGET: Well, you've never mentioned this Glenda, the Reiki lady before.

MATHEW: Well, we just got to be friends.

BRIDGET: Friends? Um-hmm. Just like that?

MATHEW: Over the cat thing. Yes. Work friends. I'm not attracted to her in the least if that's what you're thinking. Look, it's just a possibility. Please just please, at least consider giving Val to her on a trial basis?

BRIDGET: Trial? Just give him to her. Let's not give her a way out. She may give him back. He'll open her fridge.

MATHEW: Yeah, he's kinda clever to figure that out, huh? *(Beat.)* Wow. That was so quick on your part. I wasn't thinking you'd be . . . I thought we wouldn't decide like right away exactly.

BRIDGET: Why? Are you having second thoughts?

MATHEW: No, no. You know, I hate it when he bugs me in the bathroom. I mean, you have business to do in there and he's always . . . duh-da-duh, walking around slipping and falling on the wet tile.

BRIDGET: Yeah, he's so cute. *(Mathew nods.)*

MATHEW: Especially when he rolls around and bumps your hand to get pet a couple of times. Oh poor Val.

BRIDGET: And she's some weirdo Reiki-freaky lady who's going to be laying her hands all over you — I mean, him.

MATHEW: Yeah. And he's my bud. He's my little big-dumb Valie. Oh. I can't give him away.

BRIDGET: You sure can't! What were you thinking?! *(She hits him.)* I can't believe you even considered such a thing!

MATHEW: I'm sorry, baby. I was just so sleep-deprived.

BRIDGET: I know, honey. But now we're all back together again. Right, baby? *(He nods.)* We'll figure a way through this period of adjustment.

MATHEW: We sure will. Kiss?

BRIDGET: *(She kisses him.)* Night.

(The both lie down. They both sit up straight as if they heard a loud noise.)

MATHEW and BRIDGET: Aaahhhh!

BRIDGET: Do you think that was my grandmother's lamp?

MATHEW: Oh God. We can only hope.

A BAD WEEK FOR THERAPY

Martha, late twenties, has come to see Harry, thirties, a therapist, because she is having trouble in her work and personal life. Martha is incredibly timid and needs help gaining the self-confidence that will make her a more effective human being. Harry, unfortunately, has had a bad week — his girlfriend and secretary left him, construction on his office building has begun, and his overbearing mother has dropped in unexpectedly. As the scene begins, Harry is trying to fill out standard forms with Martha.

CHARACTERS
Harry: 30s, a therapist
Martha: 20s, a new client

SETTING
Harry's office

TIME
The present

HARRY: Martha. *(Smiles.)* Good. Good. That's easy. *(Writes.)* Last name?
MARTHA: Anderson.
HARRY: Easy too. *(Writing.)* My handwriting is something else here. I used to have a secretary who did this.
MARTHA: What happened to her? Did you fire her?
HARRY: No, no. She quit Monday out of the blue. With no warning.
MARTHA: That's terrible.
HARRY: Yeah, she left me high and dry. My files were a mess, my life was even . . . ! Anyway, not that I should be telling you this, Martha. Who wants an angry therapist, huh? Not that I'm angry. I'm not angry. Actually very calm and col-

lected, usually, but when your . . . secretary up and leaves, well . . . ! What's your address?

MARTHA: 4567 Elmwood, Apartment 24B, Waltham, MA 02154. I thought you might have fired her for being too quiet or timid. You see, I'm a little —

HARRY: *(Furious.)* Ten years we were together! *(Claps his hands.)* Five, four, three, two, one. *(He inhales deeply and then exhales. To Martha.)* So, how are *you* doing today?

MARTHA: Fine. I had a little trouble getting a parking space, but I'm fine.

HARRY: Oooh, I'm sorry to hear that. It's a little tough around here right now. Course them deciding to reconstruct the whole building out of nowhere last week . . . No warning! Not a bit of warning. That made things a little challenging. And then of course, my overbearing mother decides to drop by from Pittsburgh and I just want to slam her face into the . . . *(Exhales sharply.)* Just a bad week. OK, um, welcome, Martha. I'm so glad you're here. I just want to say that I like to create in my office a warm and pleasant and safe environment for you so that you can explore — do you hear that banging?

MARTHA: Um, a little.

HARRY: A little? It sounds like the roof is caving in. *(Looking up to the noise.)*

MARTHA: Now that you mention it, but it's not bad. I could get used to it. I got used to my neighbor's child who screamed around the clock. Now, I even like it.

HARRY: *(Calling to the ceiling.)* Shut up!! I'm trying to work down here! *(To Martha. Smiles.)* It feels good to get help, doesn't it? *(Noticing her expression.)* Oh gosh. Did I scare you, Martha?

MARTHA: *(Cowering.)* No.

HARRY: I'm sorry. I apologize. Things aren't generally so tense. So um, do you have insurance?

MARTHA: Yes.

HARRY: OK. Good. *(Writes.)* It was just the abruptness of

everything that threw me really. It's not like I ever intended for us to become . . . Well, *(Laughs.)* I seem to be a bit distracted. I'm, I'm not usually distracted like this. OK, so um, so . . . um . . .

MARTHA: Did you break off your relationship with your secretary, Dr. Holden?

HARRY: Harry, please. Yes. Yes, Martha, we did. Actually, she did. *(He nods sadly.)*

MARTHA: I'm sorry to hear that.

HARRY: Thank you. Thank you, Martha. You just want a little kindness — a little sympathy. *(Wallowing in the moment, shaking out of it.)* OK. *(Claps.)* OK now. Um, let's not focus on me here. My focus is you. This is for you. This session is about you. Uh, let's talk about you. I'll just finish this form up and —

MARTHA: OK.

HARRY: Do you have insurance? *(She nods.)* Oh, you already told me that, didn't you? And, uh, the name of the plan?

MARTHA: Prudent.

HARRY: Terrific. *(Looking at the form.)* Oh gosh. Um . . . this form is quite long. I think that I should have my new secretary . . . *(Pausing because he's getting emotional. She pats his shoulder.)* when I hire her or him, fill the rest out with you next —

MARTHA: I could do it.

HARRY: Could you? No, no, no —

MARTHA: Sure, I'd like to. I could even straighten up those papers in the front office.

HARRY: Oh. *(Chuckles.)* Did, did you notice that? I just had a little accident with the filing cabinet. It's not usually on the floor like that.

MARTHA: I understand.

HARRY: Thank you for that. For all of this. So what brings you here today, Martha?

MARTHA: I really don't mind filling it out myself.

HARRY: Well thank you, but that's not necessary.

MARTHA: It's no trouble at all.

HARRY: Oh, no, really that's OK.

MARTHA: *(She reaches out for the form.)* I'll just take a second.

HARRY: *(Frustrated in general.)* I said no!! *(Martha pulls her hand back. Harry laughs.)* Ha. I'm sorry. I'm sorry, Martha. That wasn't about you. That was not about you. I'm experiencing a little frustration today, about my own personal, ya know, stuff. Are you OK?

MARTHA: Uh-huh.

HARRY: Well . . . good. OK, so what brings you here?

MARTHA: Well, I . . .

HARRY: Yes.

MARTHA: I, I, uh, have a problem.

HARRY: OK. And . . . ?

MARTHA: I tend to be a little . . .

HARRY: Yes? Yes. Feel free to expound.

MARTHA: Shy and non — well, you know.

HARRY: No, no, no, I think it's better if you put it right out there on the table, Martha. Just expose it and let it breathe.

MARTHA: I'm just non, non, just a little non . . . I kind of have a thing about being non, non —

HARRY: *(Screaming.)* Spit it out!

MARTHA: Aggressive! *(Beat.)* Oh.

HARRY: OK. OK, we can work with that. It's OK, Martha. That's very good. We're doing great here. Let's reel it in now. Both of us. Let's reel it in. Why don't we talk about your little nonaggressive issue in a positive way? Sometimes it's the connotation of the word that gets us. Let's make it . . . *(Waves hands.)* positive. What would be a positive way to say it?

MARTHA: *(Shrugs.)* Um. Uh. Well, well, let me think. Um . . . *(Harry is in his own world. He stares into space and sighs.)*

MARTHA: Assertive?

HARRY: *(Harry is still somewhere else. To himself.)* Why?

MARTHA: *(Seeking approval.)* I suppose because it doesn't

sound quite so mean? *(Beat.)* Is that not good? *(Beat.)* Doctor?

HARRY: Huh? Oh, yes. That's it! Very good, Martha. Assertive. Very positive. Now, um, tell me how you plan to work on that or something?

MARTHA: Well, I would like to work on being more assertive because my boss said I need to be more confident if I want to move up and be a real sales associate. And I would like to —

HARRY: *(Somewhere else.)* Uh-huh.

MARTHA: Be more confident in my life so I feel better about myself. *(Pause.)* Doctor?

HARRY: *(Startled.)* Yep!

MARTHA: Don't you think I should talk about my family of origin to gain some insight into why I have such a lack of self-confidence?

HARRY: *(Casually.)* Yeah, that sounds good. I mean, yes, I was just going to suggest that. Go ahead there, Martha.

MARTHA: Well, my parents split up when I was six and I think that really, really had a profound and terrible effect on me and the way that I am.

HARRY: Well, it's better than an overbearing mother who makes you sing in the boy's choir when you obviously can't sing. *(Beat.)* Go on.

MARTHA: My mother had to work three jobs once the divorce went through. We went to live with my grandmother who was very strict and cold. I don't just mean cold-cold. She was often really cold. She always fell asleep over the covered radiator. I used to bang around in the kitchen to wake her up. She would get all startled and say, "Oh, oh, oh." And then go back to sleep. She hated children, but she was the one raising me.

HARRY: *(Quietly.)* Whine, whine, whine.

MARTHA: I'm sorry. I didn't mean to —

HARRY: Not you, Martha! Everyone! Every one of my patients goes on and on — whine, whine, whine about their bad childhood. Do you think you're the only one? We all had bad childhoods. They sucked! I bet Cynthia had a bad childhood too. Well, so did I, Missy. So did I!

MARTHA: Who's Cynthia?

HARRY: Never mind. I'm sorry. Forget that. Please go on, Martha.

MARTHA: Anyway, um, my grandma was old-fashioned. She would say, "Children should be seen and not heard." At the dinner table every night, my mother and grandmother would talk about things that happened in their day and I was expected to be silent. I was so sad, but there was no point in speaking or I would be reprimanded by my grandma. Later, my mother would take a special moment to sit down on the couch and talk to me, but she always fell asleep because she was exhausted from all the jobs.

HARRY: *(Sniffing to himself.)* Yes, yes, she left you. Left you. You must accept that.

MARTHA: Well . . . she lives in Dedham. It's not that far. But I guess you could say figuratively she left me when she fell asleep when I was a child. I guess you're right, doctor. She left me. She did leave me. Anyway, I started to think that I had a dull voice because sometimes I was answering questions at school and it was like I could hear the other students dropping off to sleep. I'm not kidding. And my teachers seemed like they weren't listening most of the time because their eyes glazed over when I spoke. Soon, I started to feel there was no point in me talking at all because no one was listening. That's why I'm here. I'm so glad to finally come to therapy because finally I know that someone is truly listening to me. This is the main reason I think I'm not very assertive maybe, doctor. What do you think? *(Harry is out of it.)* Doctor?

HARRY: Huh? Oh yes, yes that's great.

MARTHA: Great? I just told you I had a very sad childhood because no one listened to me.

HARRY: Oh. Yes. Right. Well, the reason that's, that's, that's great . . . is because, we seem to have narrowed down the problem.

MARTHA: We? I don't think *we* have done anything. In fact, I don't think you were listening to me at all! *(Gasps.)* I didn't mean to yell.

HARRY: Yes, I was. Yes. I. Was.

MARTHA: What did I say then, Dr. Holden?

HARRY: Um, well, *(Clears throat.)* among lots of things, some things about people not listening and . . . in your childhood and . . . that kind of —

MARTHA: Well, aren't you supposed to be asking me questions as I go along? Making suggestions?

HARRY: *(Getting defensive.)* Well, yes. Of course. That's my job. I didn't realize you were so *aware* of all the steadfast rules and regulations of conducting therapy.

MARTHA: Well, I'm aware enough to know you are supposed to be focusing on me instead of your pathetic, adolescent relationship with your mother-replacing secretary Cynthia!! *(Realizing.)* Oh. I'm sorry. Good God. I'm so sorry.

HARRY: Adolescent? Mother-replacing? *(He starts to tear up.)*

MARTHA: I'm sorry. I'm sorry.

HARRY: *(Trying not to cry.)* I didn't realize you had so much background in psychology to know so much about my personal dysfunctionality with my mother and girlfriend. Shall we continue?

MARTHA: Oh, no, no, I don't think you have dysfunctionality. I don't think that at all. You're doing a great job with me.

HARRY: Just because I've had a lot of personal pain and agony in the last twenty-four hours, not to mention major reconstruction and the witch dropping in, doesn't mean I can't focus on your little problems, on your little . . . thingies. *(Starting to cry.)* It's just really, really, really, really, hard, ya know?

MARTHA: I know. I know. And I'm so, so sorry. I didn't mean to — wait a minute. What am I talking about? I'm not sorry. I'm paying you! Not the other way around.

HARRY: Well, maybe I'm doing something experimental? Something different? Something you didn't learn about in Pysch 101? Ever think of that? *(Calling up to the upstairs. Standing.)* Stop banging!! I'm creating an atmosphere that's calming!

MARTHA: Calming, my tushy! *(Points.)* Sit down! You heard me. Sit down. *(He does.)* Now, you listen to me, Whiney. She left! OK? Cynthia has left. Why? Probably because you never married her and treated her like she was a secretary.

HARRY: Well . . .

MARTHA: I am your patient. I paid for this session while you were out to lunch thinking about every other thing under the sun. Your mother, your girlfriend, the building's construction, your cat, your dog —

HARRY: We never had a dog —

MARTHA: *(Closing her hands together.)* Shhh! *(He's quiet.)* I will forget all this mess and won't go to the licensing board on the strict condition that you give me a free, completely-dedicated-to-me session next week! Do you understand?

HARRY: Yes. I understand. No problem. I will. No problem.

MARTHA: *(Realizing.)* Oh my God! *(Getting happy.)* Oh my God! I was . . . I was . . . assertive! Ha ha! You are good! You are so good, doctor!

HARRY: Oh. Yes. Well . . . you know, I like to . . . try new things . . . and this is a good day to toss away the old and make room for the *(Sniffs.)* new.

MARTHA: I can't believe this. I feel so empowered! I'm going to recommend you to everyone I know. *(Shaking his hand.)* Thank you! Thank you so much, Dr. Holden! How can I ever repay you?

HARRY: Well, you did offer to maybe help me clean up the filing cabinet out there a little.

MARTHA: Did I? I'm sure I did. *(Realizing.)* Ha! But I'm cured now! *(Firmly.)* Pick it up yourself. *(Pats his back.)* Ooh, I just love this! *(Exiting.)* Happy cleaning!

EBENEZER WHO?

Ralph, a grumpy college adjunct English teacher in his late twenties, is woken by a woman, twenties, in his bedroom. Since he is prone to neurotic phobias, it is not surprising that he thinks at first that she might be a drugged-up street lady breaking in to steal his belongings. She claims instead to be the new replacement for the Ghost of Christmas Past, coming to help redeem Ralph from his greedy tendencies. The only problem is that she does not seem to realize that she has the wrong "redeemee." In addition to having to convince her that he is not Ebenezer Scrooge and that they are in Cleveland, not London, Ralph fears that she might be just a little cuckoo. As the scene begins, Ralph has just woken up to find her in his bedroom window.

CHARACTERS
Ralph: late 20s
Ghost of Christmas Past: woman, 20s

SETTING
Ralph's apartment

TIME
The present, nighttime

CHRISTMAS PAST: *(Working to sound lofty.)* Hark! It is me, Mr. Scrooge, it is the Ghost of Christmas Past. *(Raising her arms awkwardly.)* But call me Chris, please.
RALPH: *(Terrified.)* Oh my God!
CHRISTMAS PAST: No, not God. I'm not God.
RALPH: *(Hiding behind his covers.)* How did you get in my window? This is the third floor, lady! *(Shooing her.)* Get out of here!
CHRISTMAS PAST: I have come from the heavens above, from the hearts of humanity.
RALPH: So what are you doing in Cleveland?!

CHRISTMAS PAST: I have come to transport you through time and —

RALPH: Oh God! You're on drugs!

CHRISTMAS PAST: Drugs?

RALPH: *(Scolding himself.)* I knew I should have locked my window, but I needed the air. I just opened it a crack. Can't breathe otherwise. Don't want to dehydrate. But no, leave a tiny crack and in flies a tiny cracked lady.

CHRISTMAS PAST: Now, wait, I don't think you understand, Mr. Scrooge. I am the coming that Marley warned you of. It *is* as you have been told.

RALPH: What is?

CHRISTMAS PAST: I is. I mean, I am. I mean, I am here, my Scrooge, to steal —

RALPH: Oh God! *(Pointing.)* All the stereo equipment is in there. OK?

CHRISTMAS PAST: What? No, no. I have appeared at your window to take —

RALPH: Take whatever you want, lady. I know you people on drugs get desperate. And I'm not being judgmental now, because I understand addiction. I quit smoking six months ago. That was tough. With the patch, and the gum, and the yoga, and the eating — I put on twenty pounds in the — What am I talking to you for?!

CHRISTMAS PAST: It's good to talk sometimes. But I am fearful you do not understand.

RALPH: Oh, I understand. I understand. I understand the whole . . . Ohhh! Myyyy! *(Backing up.)* There's something in your pocket that I don't need to know about, in the least! *(Extremely frightened.)* Especially if it's a ggu — !

CHRISTMAS PAST: *(Moving toward him.)* Gun?

RALPH: Stay away!

CHRISTMAS PAST: No. It's just my mittens. It's colder than a witch's you-know-what out there and then they only issue this robe. I'll just show you. *(Reaching into her pocket.)*

RALPH: *(Hiding his eyes. Screaming!)* Noooo!

CHRISTMAS PAST: Or not.

RALPH: No, no, no need! I'll do whatever you want. I have a TV and a DVD player.

CHRISTMAS PAST: Look, I'm not here to clean out the — you have a DVD player?

RALPH: It's a little broken. You have to pop it in and out a few times but it works. Take it!

CHRISTMAS PAST: Calm — calm — calm down. I was just interested in the behind-the-scenes interviews. I'm a real film buff. Now breathe, Scrooge.

RALPH: *(Quickly.)* I can't, I can't, I can't. *(Suffocating.)* I'm suffocating!

CHRISTMAS PAST: *(Patting him gently.)* Now, now, now it is a little stuffy in here.

RALPH: Isn't it? I have a little anxiety disorder.

CHRISTMAS PAST: I noticed that.

RALPH: *(Mortified.)* Is it *that* obvious?

CHRISTMAS PAST: Um . . . *(Getting higher pitched.)* No, no . . .

RALPH: I take a little pill for it. I'm claustrophobic. And I have a touch of hypochondria. Other than that it's just a terror of heights, dogs, crowds, and small children. *(Hyperventilating.)* But you flying in my window in the middle of the night in a robe took me over the edge.

CHRISTMAS PAST: Sure, sure, that could get to anyone. Now breathe. Breeeeeaaaaathe. *(Super sweet.)* It's OK now. *(Yells.)* Breathe!

RALPH: Ahhhhhhhhh! *(Ralph sucks in a quick breath..)* Wow. That's much better. Thanks.

CHRISTMAS PAST: Welcome. Oh boy, I can see what's going to happen when we get flying over childhood neighborhoods. I do have Dramamine. OK, now where was I? *(Looks at her arm beneath her sleeve.)* Oh. Right. My dear Scrooge . . . OK, so I have come to take you with me on a journey to a place far, far away —

RALPH: Scrooge? I don't mean to interrupt your robbery or anything, but did you just call me Scrooge?

CHRISTMAS PAST: Oh my. Maybe I should have referred to

you by your first name? How did the last guy do it? *(Ralph has no idea what she is talking about.)* It *is* more personal that way. The problem is that for some reason I can't seem to remember it.

RALPH: Well, I . . .

CHRISTMAS PAST: No, don't tell me. Don't tell me. I've been studying up on your whole life. Jeez . . . Ya know how sometimes the most important things just fly out of your mind, but silly things like the cat food jingle you heard once stays with you forever? *(He nods.)* Can you hold on a sec? *(She refers to her hand where she obviously has something written.)* Oh. That's right. *(She tries to rework her steps. Gets in place. Working to sound lofty.)* Hark! It is me, Ebenezer, it is the ghost of Christmas Past. *(Raising her arms awkwardly.)* I have come to take you on an important journey.

RALPH: *(Beat.)* OK, umm. You know, I think you have made a little mistake. Aside from being a little cuckoo too.

CHRISTMAS PAST: I'm not cuckoo. I'm here to help you cure your selfish ways, your disposition. I'll show you scenarios of your past and you'll have a catharsis.

RALPH: *(Beat.)* I'm calling the state mental facility.

CHRISTMAS PAST: No, now . . . If I were a mental case, how would I have managed to get in your window on the third floor?

RALPH: What, mental patients can't climb? Look, the only way you are *not* a mental case is if I'm dreaming. *(Realizing.)* That's it! This is a dream!

CHRISTMAS PAST: *(Again lofty sounding.)* You're not dreaming. I'm real. They who is a dream is unable to cast a shadow.

RALPH: I thought the loss of shadow was just a Peter Pan thing?

CHRISTMAS PAST: *(Waves it away with a hand.)* They who is a dream is unable to speak her own mind. They who is a dream is not me.

RALPH: You're right. My dream characters don't have so much trouble with subject-verb agreement. Maybe it's food poisoning.

CHRISTMAS PAST: I have come to, to liberate you . . .

RALPH: I told Shirley that artichoke dip was off.

CHRISTMAS PAST: From your greed and cold-heartedness and what's the word?

RALPH: Give me a hint.

CHRISTMAS PAST: Uh . . . It's kinda like when you're really mean to everybody.

RALPH: *(Thinks, folds his arms.)* Like jerky?

CHRISTMAS PAST: Yeah, but ghosts can't really say, "God, you're jerky."

RALPH: Yeah. It doesn't sound professional. How about moronic?

CHRISTMAS PAST: *(She shoots him a look of disgust.)* Uh, it's like a moron who is really, really cheap.

RALPH: Stingy?

CHRISTMAS PAST: Pretty good. But think polysyllabic. More ghost-speak.

RALPH: Avaricious?

CHRISTMAS PAST: (*Whispers with enthusiasm.)* Oh that perfect! That's great! You're good!

RALPH: Thanks.

CHRISTMAS PAST: So anyway, that's why I'm here. To sum things up, Ebenezer, I'm here to alter your avariciousness. We, there're a couple of other ghosts involved in this therapy, will take you on several journeys whereby you will go to the present, past and future, get a visual and multi-sensory, really, three-D tour, of all the kinds of nasty, rotten, Scrooge-like things you've done and you'll feel guilty enough to change your ways.

RALPH: Hmmm. Sounds fun. Though a bit familiar. Only one problem here, Chris.

CHRISTMAS PAST: What's that?

RALPH: I am not Ebenezer Scrooge.

CHRISTMAS PAST: *(Long pause while she thinks.)* What? *(Beat.)* What do you mean?

RALPH: I'm Ralph Meyers.

CHRISTMAS PAST: What are you talking about? You have to be Ebenezer Scrooge! I followed the directions. All the clouds, the quick right at the Mojave Desert. Don't tell me I flunked the interplanet navigation thing? Ralph? Are you sure?

RALPH: Sometimes I go by Ralphy.

CHRISTMAS PAST: And your last name is definitely not Scrooge?

RALPH: Meyers.

CHRISTMAS PAST: Middle name?

RALPH: Thadius.

CHRISTMAS PAST: Oh no! Your first boss wasn't a jolly, old man named Fezziwig?

RALPH: A slimy young guy named Guy.

CHRISTMAS PAST: Do you have a sister?

RALPH: Yes.

CHRISTMAS PAST: Good, good. Little Fan?

RALPH: Martha. She's a pharmaceutical sales rep.

CHRISTMAS PAST: She's still alive?

RALPH: Yeah, the big pain lives in a five-bedroom house on Avon Lake. You want me to call her and check?

CHRISTMAS PAST: No. And your fiancée Belle who left you because your passion for money outweighed your passion for her?

RALPH: Shirley? Are you kidding? *She's* the financial planner.

CHRISTMAS PAST: *(Biting her nails.)* This is terrible. I suppose there is no dilapidated schoolhouse where you were shunned by other boys and left alone for the holiday?

RALPH: No, but our house really needed new aluminum siding and my mom left me at my grandma's to help out one holiday because Gram had just had a hysterectomy. That was hell.

CHRISTMAS PAST: This is awful.

RALPH: By the way, aren't you supposed to be an old man ghost?

CHRISTMAS PAST: He retired. I've been in a training program.

RALPH: Ghosts retire?

CHRISTMAS PAST: Why shouldn't we? Don't we work hard too? And the benefits stink. Besides, do you know how redundant these jobs get? It's the same thing every year. The Ghost of Christmas Present went on a diet just to shake things up. They fired him. Just trying to get a little healthy. But noooo, "keep it traditional." They took a huge risk with me. They thought I had stilted ghost-speak.

RALPH: Yeah, I did notice that.

CHRISTMAS PAST: You did?

RALPH: Yeah, I'd cut the "Hark" thing. It sounds a little too "Angel of the baby Jesus" to me. And the "I have come from the heavens above, from the depths of blah-blah."

CHRISTMAS PAST: Oh my God. I suck! I'm terrible. And I've ruined Ebenezer's life. Christmas Past never came. He'll die unhappy and alone and, and —

RALPH: Rich as hell.

CHRISTMAS PAST: If Cratchit has to work Christmas, do you know what may happen?

RALPH: The company may make a profit? Just kidding. Don't worry. You can't be really worried. This is obviously a dream. And you're a figment of my imagination. I used to love this story so it's no wonder my subconscious would choose it. Too bad in the last ten years it's just an excuse for a bunch of money-grubbing Hollywood executives to regurgitate the same old story, "differently," in order to make a load of money from a bunch of over-sentimental, guilty-feeling, spendthrifts every Christmas season.

CHRISTMAS PAST: Exactly! A Christmas classic!

RALPH: This is the weirdest, most vivid dream I've ever had. It must be the ThermaFlu.

CHRISTMAS PAST: I'm not a figment. I can't be a figment. I'm, I'm, too committed. What a miserable failure I am!

RALPH: Wellll. Maybe you could change the story. Maybe the story is that you visit Ralph Meyers in Cleveland, Ohio, and you drag him around to the places of his youth where he can steal antiques from his youth and bring them back to resell on eBay for exorbitant prices all in the name of giving a lonely college adjunct a little extra cash cow.

CHRISTMAS PAST: *(She puzzles.)* What?

RALPH: You don't like it?

CHRISTMAS PAST: It's not very touching.

RALPH: What if he donates ten percent of the funds to public radio? *(She rolls her eyes.)* My point is that while I think this dream or hallucination is really interesting, I think you and all of this are just a bunch of hooey.

CHRISTMAS PAST: *(Crying out.)* Tiny Tim will die!

RALPH: Maybe he won't. Maybe Cratchit will kill Scrooge and take over his business.

CHRISTMAS PAST: He's a poor crippled boy!

RALPH: Don't you get it? The redemption story is out. We don't buy it.

CHRISTMAS PAST: What time is it now?

RALPH: Eight-fifteen.

CHRISTMAS PAST: And you were in bed already?

RALPH: Look, I was taking a nap. I thought I was getting a cold. I'm not "the ghost coming barging in on the wrong house in the wrong city, in the wrong country in the wrong century at the wrong hour."

CHRISTMAS PAST: OK! So I got a little confused!

RALPH: A little?!! Anyway, I think the story was overrated. I mean, come on, how many people do you know that change overnight?

CHRISTMAS PAST: It is the idea of the instant epiphany, the overnight repentance —

RALPH: Did Oprah keep off all the weight the first time? *(Beat.)* I rest my case.

CHRISTMAS PAST: But don't you think with our help Scrooge will discover that giving does not deplete the giver but rather enriches him?

RALPH: Look, Scrooge changes at the end, but what about day

two? He's probably duping Bob Cratchit on his health insurance plan and kicking Tiny Tim off his crutches.

CHRISTMAS PAST: You have a very warped and cynical view of things, Mr. Meyers.

RALPH: I was just kidding.

CHRISTMAS PAST: No, you weren't. I think you're worse than Scrooge.

RALPH: Worse?! So convert me. You can't help Scrooge then change me in one night.

CHRISTMAS PAST: You should be ashamed of yourself, you whiney academic. Here you are a lot younger than Scrooge, perfectly healthy, surrounded by people who obviously love you, and all you can think about on Christmas is reselling items from your past on eBay. Talk about money-grubbing. What about the hungry, the elderly, the, the, cell phoneless? I couldn't really think of a good third one.

RALPH: Well, I'm not that callous.

CHRISTMAS PAST: Will you go out of your way to help anyone this Christmas? Or will you just continue to see the world with that cynical view of yours?

RALPH: God, I didn't know I was actually all that bad. Am I?

CHRISTMAS PAST: You suck! Your heart is three sizes too small.

RALPH: I did pass up a lot of charities this year.

CHRISTMAS PAST: And there is no tree in your living room I see.

RALPH: The needles are such a pain.

CHRISTMAS PAST: *(Look of disgust.)* No poinsettia purchased for your mother?

RALPH: By God, she does love those. And they cost so little. But she told me they poison her cat.

CHRISTMAS PAST: A catnip toy might do the trick. And I'm sure your sister wouldn't mind if you at least stopped calling her a big pain for the holiday.

RALPH: I always considered it a term of endearment.

CHRISTMAS PAST: And Shirley . . . well, Shirley may appreciate a small stock investment. Would that be so darn hard?

RALPH: On my salary? Yes!

CHRISTMAS PAST: And she makes no sacrifices for you? She doesn't put up with your anxiety attacks regularly? She doesn't make sure you have plenty of, of, of —

RALPH: Room deodorizer?

CHRISTMAS PAST: See! So?!

RALPH: You're right. I under-appreciate my life. You know . . . I don't do enough for others less fortunate. (Thinking.) You know how you said, "Will you go out of your way to help anyone this season?" I just had a thought. I could help you find Scrooge. I'm great with directions. And London is about five hours ahead of us. If we left right this minute, we may be able to make it there by one.

CHRISTMAS PAST: Why this sudden change of heart?

RALPH: It's a bad TV night. Besides, I figure this whole trippy thing is better than most psychotropic drugs.

CHRISTMAS PAST: That would be a real gift, Ralphy. Especially since I know that you have fears.

RALPH: Well, we all do, don't we, of one kind or another?

CHRISTMAS PAST: Yes, but you seem to have more than your fair share.

RALPH: That's true. Maybe this is a bad idea. No, no I want to help you. I want to go. You're sure you have the Dramamine?

CHRISTMAS PAST: Positive. Just take my hand, Ralphy. And we'll jump out together.

RALPH: Jump? Out? The window, you mean?

CHRISTMAS PAST: I won't let you fall. I promise.

RALPH: Yeah, you bet you won't. My brother-in-law's a lawyer and he'll sue you're little white-robed butt if you so much as —

CHRISTMAS PAST: (Warning.) Uh-uh-uh, Scroogy-talk.

RALPH: (Through gritted teeth.) Merry Christmas. (He closes his eyes and braces himself in utter fear.)

MONOLOGUE MADNESS

Leslie and Bill, late twenties to early thirties, are teachers at competing high schools. Leslie teaches theater; Bill teaches U.S. history. Tonight, they have come to judge the annual Monologue Madness competition. All the high schools in the area come together to compete in this fiercely competitive event. As the scene begins, the competition is about to begin.

CHARACTERS
Leslie: late 20s to early 30s, theater teacher
Bill: late 20s to early 30s, history teacher

SETTING
The Monologue Madness competition at a local
    high school

TIME
The present

LESLIE: Don't you just adore these events?

BILL: Actually, this is my first time.

LESLIE: Really? Do you mean this is your first time attending or judging Monologue Madness?

BILL: Both.

LESLIE: Well, you must have a pretty impressive background in the theater. Do you teach theory as well as the usual classes?

BILL: No, I teach history.

LESLIE: Theater history, huh? No acting, voice, or speech?

BILL: *(Correcting her.)* No, no, no. I teach U.S. history.

LESLIE: You're a history teacher? *(He nods.)* How in the world did you end up as a judge in the annual Monologue Madness competition?

BILL: They needed teachers, and I thought it sounded interesting.

LESLIE: *(Annoyed.)* Oh, I see. Doesn't . . . which high school are you from?

BILL: Naperville Central.

LESLIE: Right. So Naperville Central doesn't have any acting teachers?

BILL: She's judging the History of Marlowe as Shakespeare debate.

LESLIE: Right. Makes perfect sense. I'm Leslie. *(Extends hand.)* From Wheaton North.

BILL: Bill. *(Shakes hands.)* From Naperville —

LESLIE: Central. Right. Well, Bill, if there's anything I can help you — ooh, looks like we're starting.

BILL: Yes, it does. And thank you.

(They both focus out at the "stage" and watch in silence for a moment.)

LESLIE: Oh, no! Not *Agnes of God* again. This piece is soooo overdone.

BILL: Well, there is such a thing as tradition in any culture.

LESLIE: *(Looking at Bill with disgust.)* This isn't Thanksgiving, it's a competition.

(They stare out for another beat. The actor has obviously ended. Leslie looks sickened. Bill is enraptured.)

BILL: That was wonderful. Very moving.

LESLIE: Yes. Just like after I eat prunes.

BILL: What?

LESLIE: Shhh. Here's the next one. *(Beat.)* Mamet. Brilliant playwright.

(They listen. Suddenly Bill looks horrified and Leslie looks pleased.)

BILL: He just cursed! And again! But the rules clearly state that cursing is cause for disqualification!

LESLIE: It's Mamet, Bill. You can't do it without cursing.

BILL: Well, he should have edited that out!

LESLIE: There would be nothing left! It's Mamet's trademark.

BILL: Well, then it worked. I am trading the mark to a zero. Oh, again! It's blasphemous!

LESLIE: It's truthful and passionate. It's real.

BILL: Maybe in your classroom, but not in mine!

LESLIE: Well, this is not your classroom, Bucko.

BILL: Well, it's not your classroom either.

(They stop arguing and smile at the actor who has just finished.)

LESLIE: Fabulous.

BILL: Appalling.

LESLIE: Maybe you should write *The Virgin Monologues*.

BILL: Maybe you should get yourself to church.

LESLIE: *(Laughs.)* Maybe you should get yourself to therapy!

(They cease fire at the introduction of the next actor's monologue.)

LESLIE: Ooohh, a piece I don't know. How refreshing.

BILL: Indeed. Maybe you'll be quiet and listen then.

LESLIE: Oh, stuff it, Your Prudeness.

(They watch. Bill is taken in, Leslie suddenly breaks out of it. The actor finishes the piece.)

BILL: *(Tearfully.)* Now that was superb. She actually cried. Did you see that?

LESLIE: Did I see it?? She emoted all over the stage. How could anyone miss it? Disgusting overacting. She had absolutely no objective whatsoever except to flood her dress . . . and her shoes . . . and the stage floor.

BILL: How does one teach acting when one is so unfeeling?

LESLIE: I'm feeling. I'm feeling all kinds of things, Bill. I'm feeling like punching your historical face!

BILL: Oh, violence as well as language. I can see why you liked that Mammy piece.

LESLIE: Mamet.

BILL: Whatever.

(Again they quickly stop talking as the next actor is introduced.)

LESLIE: *(Whispering, childlike bitterness.)* I wonder who George Washingtime is? *(Dumb giggle.)* I'm judging the presidency competition.

(Bill tries to ignore her. They both watch the actor. Suddenly, their eyes open wide. Leslie's in excitement, Bill's in horror.)

BILL: Did you see that?

LESLIE: *(Pleased.)* Yes!

BILL: He's standing on the chair! He jumped up on the chair!

LESLIE: Yes, bless his movement coach, he did.

BILL: You don't stand on people's furniture! This is an outrage! He's an animal!

LESLIE: He's an actor.

BILL: Synonymous! I'm disqualifying him!

LESLIE: What?! It was a beautiful move — fully motivated. It woke me up.

BILL: Naturally the destruction of school property would awaken you.

LESLIE: He didn't break it, he just used it.

BILL: Is that what you tell your unchaste actresses to say at confession?

LESLIE: Oooohhh, what a smutty thought from the preacher! Of course I don't tell them that. They don't go to confession! Being the wild, sexual, horrid beasts that they are!
(They both freeze and look out.)

LESLIE: *(Calling out.)* Uh, sorry. This is Bill's first time judging. He didn't realize the need to be quiet.

BILL: *(Whispering harshly to her.)* How dare you?!

LESLIE: Quite easily, I assure you. *(Calling out.)* Yes, please continue. Everything's fine.
(They both give angry, fake smiles. The next actor is introduced. Bill's jaw drops.)

LESLIE: Ahh! The dominatrix, moaning piece from the *Vagina Monologues*. And so, there is a God.

BILL: *(Hiding his head behind his hand.)* Uhh.
(They watch the monologue, Bill peeking through his hand. Leslie laughs on and off. Bill's jaw and body sink toward the floor. The actress finishes.)

LESLIE: That was brilliant.

BILL: *(Unable to speak.)* Hhhh . . .

LESLIE: Sorry, what did you say?

BILL: Hhhh . . .

LESLIE: You know, you really should take a class in voice and speech. Your articulation is the pits.

BILL: Hhhhedonist!

LESLIE: It speaks. Me or her?

BILL: Both of you!

LESLIE: Gee, thanks, Billy. *(She winks at him.)*
(They look out at the next actor.)

LESLIE: Hmmm. I never read that one. "The Lord's Prayer"?
(Beat.) Wait a minute. This is not a monologue, it's a prayer.

BILL: *(Smiles.)* Yes, it is.

LESLIE: Ridiculous, it's not from a play. There's no action — no objective, no change, or discovery.

BILL: Of course there is, she's talking to God. To ask for his help. That's her objective. At least it's more appropriate than all of that swearing. Now, shh.

LESLIE: Oh, Jesus, she's bawling like a fool.

BILL: *(Quietly speaking along with the actor.)* Lead us not into temptation.

LESLIE: Honey, you could use a little temptation. It would do you a world of good!

BILL: *(Clapping and teary-eyed.)* There's our winner, right there. That was so heartfelt and pure. So real, as you say.

LESLIE: In what world? I'm disqualifying her. The piece must be from a published and printed play.

BILL: Are you crazy? It's been printed and published many, many times.

LESLIE: Oh yeah? Who's the playwright, huh? Huh???

BILL: *(Beat.)* I'm beginning to understand why they call this the Monologue Madness competition. They invited you.

LESLIE: Actually, it's in reference to the fact that any inexperienced, naïve, prissy dimwit, who's clueless as to what good acting — or even, acting itself — is, can judge the bloody monologue competition. Even if they teach booga-wooga, thump bibles, and cry at info-mercials.

BILL: O, beware, my lord, of jealousy; / It is the green-ey'd monster which doth mock / The meat it feeds on.

LESLIE: You think I'm jealous? Of you???!! *(She laughs.)* Puhlease!! *(Beat. Realizing)* You just quoted Shakespeare.

BILL: Pretty impressive for a dimwit who teaches booga-wooga. You act like I'm some sort of ignorant conservative idiot!

LESLIE: Well, you act like I'm some sort of Medea-like, foulmouthed harlot! And besides, you are conservative!

BILL: No! Not entirely. I just happen to believe in God and think kids should stop swearing!

LESLIE: Well, see?! You're a goody-goody!

BILL: Well, at least I'm not wicked!! *(Beat.)*

LESLIE: *(Standing in her outrage.)* Wicked?! I'll show you wicked! *(Turning out to those in the competition who are all watching.)* Oh, would you shut up?! I'm talking! *(To Bill.)* I can be a real witch when I need to be.

BILL: I can see that.

LESLIE: Ohh, you have no idea. My second car is a broom. You stink!

BILL: Stink?! At least I'm not polluting my students.

LESLIE: Uhhhh! You priggish stick-in-the-mud.

BILL: And corrupting everyone who crosses my path!

LESLIE: Oooh, better wear your garlic!

BILL: No need. You aren't going to corrupt me, lady!

LESLIE: Oh yeah?! *(She grabs him and pulls him in close and kisses him passionately.)* What do you think of that?

BILL: *(Dazed and dizzy.)* That was . . . pretty corrupt. Um, do you think maybe when this thing is done, you might consider corrupting me some more?

LESLIE: *(Crossing her arms.)* No.

BILL: *(Puppy-dog.)* No?

LESLIE: I can't wait that long. Let's go!

(They both look out at the competitors who are giving them a standing ovation.)

BILL and LESLIE: Oh. *(Giggling, embarrassed. Waving.)* Hi. Thank you. *(Bowing.)* Thank you very much.

(They rush out.)

THE CUP

*Rosie, mid-thirties, has taken her precious family treas-
ure to the "Antiques Assembly," a TV show that trav-
els from town to town bringing several famous appraisers
to assess the quality of the items local folks bring to the
event. Rosie finally arrives at the front of the line. She
will be speaking with the famous, English-born Eric Silver, thirties, who works at Sotheby's in New York. Eric,
sick of his job, is in a rush to weed through the hordes
of people with worthless and uninteresting items.*

CHARACTERS
Rosie: mid-30s
Eric: 30s, an appraiser of antiques

SETTING
"Antiques Assembly" event and TV show

TIME
The present

ROSIE: Oh my God, my name's Rosie Blugoski, I can't believe
   I'm actually here on the "Antiques Assembly." I'm in in-
   credible shock! *(She lets out a little squeal.)*
ERIC: So is my entire nervous system at the moment.
ROSIE: I've seen you on the show as the "expert" appraiser so
   many times. It's incredibly bizarre that I'm actually, actu-
   ally talking to *you.*
ERIC: I find it equally disconcerting I assure you. *(Reaching out
   his hand.)* Eric Silver.
ROSIE: *(Wiping down her hand.)* Oh boy. I get sweaty when
   I'm a bit nervous and excited. *(She shakes his hand.)*
ERIC: Yes. *(Wiping the sweat off his hand.)*
ROSIE: Ah gee, Eric, I love your accent. It's even more amaz-
   ing in person. I just feel like my head is going to pop off.

ERIC: Oh, now don't you worry, dear, that might be an improvement. *(He laughs.)*

ROSIE: *(Laughs.)* Oh my God, that is so funny. I didn't know you had a sense of humor, Eric.

ERIC: Neither did I. I didn't realize I was joking. Now, hate to be all rushy even if I do have several screaming hordes of people behind you, but what little treasure do we have to show me today?

ROSIE: *(Laughs.)* Eric *Silver* — I always think that is so cute!

ERIC: Cute? Well, indeed, I've been called many things in my life — many, many things — but cute is generally not one of them. Thankfully.

ROSE: Well, I mean that you're an appraiser and your name's Silver. It's cute 'cause you could appraise silver. And then your name is Silver. See?

ERIC: Right. *(Beat.)* Anyway, I'm certain it took all of your creative juices to cook that up but let's conserve your energy for the displaying of your little . . . whatever.

ROSIE: *(Looking stiff suddenly and gesturing.)* Oooh. Is that the camera there?

ERIC: Yes, but the public has no worry as yet. We aren't filming at the moment.

ROSIE: Why not?

ERIC: Well, they only take footage of the rare and rather fascinating. And we are neither. Once we take a look at the item, we determine if it's worthy of a pitch. Which is why I'm encouraging taking a look at your item, any time now, or at any moment that feel you can possibly pull that gem out. If it is then determined to be of interest, then we film. It generally ends up being only about three percent of the people we see throughout the day. So please don't be too disappointed if it's not you because there's a ninety-seven percent chance, and perhaps even higher in your case, that it won't be. So hoorah, and on we go.

ROSIE: *(Beat.)* Well, that's cheating isn't it?

ERIC: *(Getting irritated.)* Cheating?

ROSIE: Well, it gives you a false perspective of things when you're at home watching. It makes you think like everybody who comes has something rare and fascinating rather than the fact that most of them are just lugging around a bunch of junk that you weed out.

ERIC: *(Beat.)* Well . . . true. And that very thought — people lugging junk here for me to weed through — torments my very soul as well. I assure you. However, *(Seriously.)* you don't grow a garden with weeds, do you, Ms. Ellis?

ROSIE: *(Pause, thinking.)* Oh my God! But all those poor people in line. Some had to bring their thing from miles and miles and miles and —

ERIC: I get the point. How awful for them.

ROSIE: And they won't make it on TV. When they find out how useless their family heirloom is, they'll be so, so sad.

ERIC: *(Falsely sympathetic.)* Oh, now, dear, no use feeling sorry for them, that could be *you.*

ROSIE: Oh no! My item is rare, and it's been in the family for years and years and —

ERIC: Quite.

ROSIE: Sorry. I just don't want those people who are so looking forward to this to realize they just have junk.

ERIC: Well, now, many could have a family piece of memorabilia that they love and cherish and only want to know more about. They don't really care if it's worth anything.

ROSIE: Really? Does that happen often?

ERIC: No, are you mad? They're looking for cold, hard cash. But anyway, I think a good majority of people have something slightly above junk.

ROSIE: Yeah, well, you weren't back there in line. *(Quietly.)* There was a guy back there with a table. It was so funny looking. Totally had these legs that were crooked.

ERIC: It had cabriole legs?

ROSIE: No, crooked legs. Bowlegs.

ERIC: Yes, I understand, assuming you are talking about the

table rather than the man. They are cabriole legs. Cabriole is the Italian word meaning "goat's leap."

ROSIE: Well, I don't know if the legs looked goatish. More like a bowlegged, midget, football player.

ERIC: Well, exactly. That's the Italians for you — very fu-fu and poetic. However, I don't imagine they have a poetic phrase for bowlegged midget football players — fortunately — so cabriole it is. It's an eighteenth-century style that brushed aside the straight William-and-Mary style.

ROSIE: Well, I don't care if the maker was straight or gay — the table was ugly. Don't tell that guy though, 'cause he seems very violent, you know what I'm saying?

ERIC: Well, ugly has nothing to do with worth, my dear. My aunt Eleanor is as ugly as a bulldog eating a wasp, but she's still worth several million. Besides, you don't understand. Cabriole legs are the signature of the Queen Anne style that swept the European salons.

ROSIE: Oh, OK. Well fine. I just thought a crooked-legged table was really the signature of one that wobbles so that you have to put sugar packs underneath it to keep it steady, but maybe I'm wrong, OK?! 'Cause I don't work at Southbees like you do. Anyway, it doesn't matter at this point because he threw it across the room and it broke.

ERIC: Sotheby's. Sotheby's, my dear. Why did he throw the Queen Anne table across the room may I ask?

ROSIE: I don't know. I might have offended him by calling his table bowlegged. It hit the lady with the tulip-shaped lamp.

ERIC: Oh dear. Tulip-shaped? *(She nods.)* Oh God, it was probably a Tiffany.

ROSIE: No, her name was Melanie, but boy, was she pissed. You know, if you people sold some hot dogs or something in that line, Melanie's lamp would have never gotten broken. It's probably a blood-sugar thing.

ERIC: Ms. Ellis, I understand your confusion with the show's policy on filming and hot dogs, and I apologize for the rather unruly line experience, that you apparently caused, but if you don't take out this item of yours, I'm going to have to do something I really, really rather not do.

ROSIE: What?

ERIC: *(Furious.)* Talk to you further!

ROSIE: Oh, you're funny. Fine. I was just building suspense.

ERIC: Yes, no wonder I feel in the midst of a horror film.

ROSIE: *(Puts it on the table.)* OK. Dah-da-da-dah! *(Sighs.)* There it is.

ERIC: Yes. *(Frozen. Looks at it hard from several sides.)* Well . . .

ROSIE: Now you understand, don't you?

ERIC: Oh, indeed . . . I'm beginning to . . . truly understand more about the table-throwing incident.

ROSIE: Pretty impressive. It's something, right?

ERIC: Well, it certainly is *something*.

ROSIE: Do you want to know a little more about it?

ERIC: Honestly? I . . .

ROSIE: It's a cup.

ERIC: *(Beat.)* Yes, this much I gathered. Fascinating.

ROSIE: It was my great, great aunt's originally who died.

ERIC: How tragic. She drank from it no doubt?

ROSIE: She received it from her grandfather who received it from his grandfather who fought in the Battle of Bunker Hill, which is a very famous battle fought in 1775 in Charlestown. Over hills. One of them being *Bunker* Hill.

ERIC: *(Acting surprised.)* Nooooo? And then they must have named it after the hill?

ROSIE: Really? You know the battle then?

ERIC: Vaguely. My degree from Oxford in American history seems *not* to have been a total waste after all.

ROSIE: So you can see the cup firstly has historical significance.

ERIC: In what way?

ROSIE: I told you. It was owned by my great, great aunt's grandfather's grandfather who fought in that battle.

ERIC: And is it connected to the battle in anyway?

ROSIE: Yes, there are several scratches and a dent in it that I'm told came from a bullet that almost hit my great, great aunt's grandfather's grandfather. The cup saved his life.

ERIC: How unfortunate. That it dented the cup of course. But the problem, my dear lady, is that these dents and scratches could be caused by someone dropping it in the mud several times, throwing it against someone's face, slamming a sledgehammer over its base, and running it over with a bus several times. One does not know that it has any connection to any battle, and particularly the Battle of Bunker Hill. Additionally, it does not appear to be that old. It *could* be because, in fact, tin is old, though worth almost nothing. But after careful examination for signatures, there is nothing to date it back to the seventeen hundreds or any battle at all.

ROSIE: But it is from that battle!

ERIC: Yes, that may be! Sorry. But with no proof, in the eyes of dealers, it is not. It is quite simply, a cup, with several unsightly dents and a rather brownish encrust . . . ment.

ROSIE: But Vincent Van Gogh drank out of it?

ERIC: Really? Perhaps this now explains why he went mad.

ROSIE: Are you being sarcastic with me?

ERIC: Oh no, Ms. Ellis. I'm simply saying it seems to be a bit . . . well . . . diseased. It also has an odd odor.

ROSIE: Well, I didn't want to ruin its patina. You always talk about ruining the patina if you clean it.

ERIC: Well, that's correct, that's absolutely correct in most cases, but in this case, the idea of ruining it is impossible, I'm afraid.

ROSIE: It's that good, huh?

ERIC: Let's just politely say again that ruining it is impossible.

ROSIE: I think the interest level increases for it with the Vincent Van Gogh connection.

ERIC: And how is it, my dear little irritant, that we would know that?

ROSIE: I was hoping you'd ask that!

ERIC: Oh jolly!

ROSIE: Because he painted it on his bedside table in the very famous painting *Vincent's Bedroom at Arles.* My great, great aunt was in Southern France in 1891 and met Van Gogh there, who she just called Go — He let her. Isn't that cute?

ERIC: Disgustingly so.

ROSIE: She let him borrow the cup for a full week.

ERIC: Oh, well, that is quite astounding! I had no idea! Now that you say that . . . well, that is something to behold!

ROSIE: See?! I told you!

ERIC: Yes, and this explains the little need to sanitize the cup. But one wonders how "Go" managed to paint it into the painting since that particular painting was completed in 1889, nearly a year before your great, great aunt's visit to France. In addition, and this is just a tiny bit more troublesome in the scheme of things, Van Gogh was . . . well, how do I put this politely . . . dead, at the time.

ROSIE: *(Beat.)* Dead? When my great, great aunt visited? Dead?

ERIC: Dead. Deceased. Departed. Defunct. Gone! Like I wish I were at this moment.

ROSIE: Oh God. Well, maybe I got the date wrong then?

ERIC: Oh, I'm afraid it's a bit more drastic than that.

ROSIE: What are you saying? That I'm lying?!

ERIC: No, no, dear, it's much more pathetic than that. I think you believe every word you've said. Your great, great aunt however is a lying cow. How much did she sell it to you for?

ROSIE: It's a family keepsake. We've passed it down. A value could not be placed upon it.

ERIC: Uh-huh. How much?

ROSIE: Five hundred dollars. *(Tearful.)* She said it was worth millions!

ERIC: Oh, dear, dear. Well, in the garden of life several poisonous flowers grow that choke the life out of the rest of us. Your aunt is your poisonous flower. You and people like you are mine.

ROSIE: I will be choking you for real in a second! I will!

ERIC: No need to bark. I believe you.

ROSIE: It must be worth something. At the least, it's very old.

You're supposed to give me an estimate! Where's my estimate?! I didn't stand in this godforsaken line since five AM in the morning for nothing, you snotty, prudish-faced, rotten meany!

ERIC: Ohhhh. Rudeness. I would think modestly it would be able to fetch . . . uh fifty cents to a dollar.

ROSIE: *(Screaming.)* What?!!

ERIC: I was being conservative! It could be a dollar fifty!

ROSIE: I can't believe this!

ERIC: Neither can I, my dear child. Neither can I!!

ROSIE: But only last week you talked to some stupid lady with this vile-looking bandoleer bag, you know that pouch, that was worth $40,000 dollars!

ERIC: I know, it was vile, but it was glass-beaded and it was Indian. Indian items are quite rare since everyone . . . well . . . killed them.

ROSIE: And the lady with the stupid fancy soap dish she paid fifty cents for?

ERIC: Yes, a bleeding bowl from the eighteenth century. Used to drain the veins of the unwell.

ROSIE: That's disgusting! Why would someone want a bowl some sick person bled in in the eighteenth century?

ERIC: That's a very good question. But why would someone want a Little Orphan Annie dress or Elvis Presley's undergarments or a table with bowlegged legs much like a midget football player for that matter? The answer is simply . . . because they do! Do you know that brat with the bleeding bowl didn't even give me a cut of her auction earnings? Well! Anyway, it was nice meeting you and your . . . cup. It's time to shove off. Ta, ta.

ROSIE: This experience was awful for me. I hate this show! I'll never watch it again!

ERIC: Oh my, what a threat to our ratings.

ROSIE: I don't like you a bit. I'm just going to put my cup away in my silly ceramic box *(She starts putting the cup away in the box.)* from China and take it home and bring it to a much more caring appraiser who will run proper testing that will prove it was in the Battle of Bunker Hill and painted by Go!

ERIC: Well, that's just — *(He notices the box.)* Wait, hold on, now. Let's not be too hasty. Where did you say you got that box?

ROSIE: Oh some great, great, great somebody in my family when he went to China in the sixteen hundreds. It's just a stupid old box that it fits in. I thought you wanted me to shove on? Now you want to look at my box?

ERIC: Oh my good God. Do you know what this is? That looks like the classic red-and-blue design from the Ming Dyna . . . *(Covering his excitement.)* No. Wrong. It's just a peasant box I'm sure. Very unsightly.

ROSIE: Is it worth something?

ERIC: No, no, no, don't be ridiculous. It's nothing. Very unpleasant actually. When was this person there again?

ROSIE: Sixteen hundreds, I think. But maybe that's a lie to you too. Why are you staring at it?

ERIC: Staring, no, I'm not staring. I'm simply watching you put away that lovely cup and thinking more and more about how interesting it is. It has the royal trinity: rarity, provenance, and beauty. It grows on you. Do you think maybe I could buy the whole kit and caboodle, cup and box, from you for a handsome . . . oh, four thousand?

ROSIE: *(Pause.)* Wait. But you said . . . and you told me . . . No. This is a precious family treasure that we have loved and cherished and passed down to each other throughout the years. We simply could not give it up for any reason. We wanted to find out a little more of its history and understand its worth. And then we will put it in a prized place in the hearth of our home, holding onto the history of those family members before us, so that we will pass down their strength and courage to my children and my children's children.

ERIC: Four thousand five hundred.

ROSIE: Sold!

ERIC: Oh, my dear, Ms. Ellis, how lovely it has been to meet you!

ROSIE: And you too, Mr. Silver. I'm glad you came around to the truth about my cup.

(He writes the check. She turns to the audience. Mumbling quietly.)

ROSIE: I knew he'd fall for the box. It's a great imitation. Works like a charm every time.

ERIC: What did you say?

ROSIE: I said it's worth quite a bit — every dime. You know, I was thinking about what you said about the garden of life. Many gardens do have poisonous plants, Mr. Silver, but you know what saves the lovely delicate flowers. Fertilizer. Lots and lots of cow dung. Well, have a great day!

THE WELCOME MAT

Seth, twenties, is taking care of a friend of the family's house and dog while she is away in Aruba. Seth, a college student, discovers that their family friend has an indoor Jacuzzi and sauna. He immediately wants to try it out and begins taking off his clothes to take a dip. Unfortunately, the dog needs to go out right at the moment Seth has taken off all his clothes. In the process of letting the dog out the back way, Seth gets locked out of the house with no clothes on. It's November and rather cold outside. He runs next door to the neighbor's house where he meets Erica, a college student herself, who has come to stay with her parents for the weekend. The scene begins as Seth is shivering and running up to Erica's front porch.

CHARACTERS
Seth: 20s, college student
Erica: 20s, college student

SETTING
Erica's parents' home; front door entranceway
  and porch

TIME
The present; cold morning in November

SETH: *(Wet and shivering like mad as he stands on a front porch. Seth rings the doorbell.)* Bbbbbbbrrrrrrrrr. Please, please, please God be home. *(Knocking.)* Anybody home? Hello? *(Calling.)* Hello?

ERICA: *(Opening the door.)* Hello, who is — *(Shocked as she takes him in.)* Oh my God.

SETH: *(Moving in slightly.)* Please, I know — but don't shut the —

ERICA: *(She slams the door hitting his nose.)* Ahhhhh!

SETH: *(His head knocks back in severe pain.)* Ow! *(He touches his nose.)* Door. *(Petting his nose.)*

ERICA: *(On the other side of the door.)* Get away! You pervert!

SETH: I'm not a pervert! I'm a, a, a, locked-out person!

ERICA: A what?!

SETH: I'm a locked-out-of-my-house person!

ERICA: What house? I've never seen you here!

SETH: I didn't mean it was *my* house exactly. I should have said I was locked out of *a* house. I was locked out of your neighbor's house.

ERICA: I bet you were. And for good reason. You're completely naked!

SETH: Well I know, but not on purpose.

ERICA: Get away from my porch!

SETH: Look, I know it looks bad, Miss. *(He bends down and picks up her welcome mat to cover himself.)*

ERICA: *(She gasps in horror as she peeps out the peephole.)* Get your filthy naked hands off of my welcome mat.

SETH: *(Dropping the mat.)* Sorry, I was just trying to —

ERICA: *(She gasps in horror.)* Pick it up, pick it up, pick it up!

SETH: OK! God, pick it up, put it down, pick it up, put it down . . . not very welcoming, is it?

ERICA: I'm calling the police. You get away now.

SETH: No, no, please, don't call the police!

ERICA: Why shouldn't I?

SETH: Because, I'll, I'll be in big trouble with my mom.

ERICA: Well, you should've thought of that before you decided to streak around the neighborhood in the buff!

SETH: I didn't do this on purpose! Please, I am so cold that a good portion of my body is actually turning several shades of purple at the moment.

ERICA: Well, good for you. I hear that color's in this season.

SETH: Come on! I could actually lose a limb. I think you already broke my nose. It feels like it could start bleeding any minute.

ERICA: And that's my fault, Pervo? Pinch it and put your head back! Off the porch! Off! Go away!

SETH: Look, I'm not a Pervo — pervert. I'm a, per-son, a normal person. I'm a student actually. I'm a grad student at the university.

ERICA: Oh yeah? *(Folding her arms.)* Then what are you studying? Perversion? Anatomy? Flashing?

SETH: No. *(Quickly.)* Abnormal psychology.

ERICA: Oh God!

SETH: I knew you'd say that! My family has teased me mercilessly for taking up psychology. This incident would certainly give them more fuel.

ERICA: Well *maybe* if you get off my porch this very instant, Dr. Freudenstein, I won't call the police and you won't suffer through that family nightmare.

SETH: Where am I going to go? I can't walk around. People will see me.

ERICA: Well what am I? It didn't seem to bother you when you came to my door. There you were — in all your glory.

SETH: Yes, but I don't know you. If I walk home, I might run into someone I know. I'd be embarrassed.

ERICA: As well you should be!

SETH: *(Looking down at himself, slightly hurt.)* What do you mean exactly?

ERICA: Oh please! Uck! I'm not participating in your pervyness.

SETH: Look, I'd be happy to clothe myself immediately. If you'd be kind enough to throw some clothing out to me, I'd be happy to put something of yours on — thrilled really.

ERICA: *(Disgusted.)* Oh God, I'm sure!

SETH: No, no, no! Not *thrilled* like that. Uhhh! Look, I'm a normal guy. I have a four point oh. I own pets. Please have mercy on me. Let me just explain to you why I'm this way.

ERICA: Please don't! Save it for therapy class, buddy! *(Picking up her cell phone, trying to get him to leave.)* I am now picking up my cell phone!

SETH: No, you don't understand! My mom will kill me for this!

ERICA: Well, I don't get involved in family affairs. I am dialing the number!

SETH: Rachel Miner is my mom's best friend. If the police call Ms. Miner all the way in Aruba, she'll think I'm some sort of freak!

ERICA: And right she is! I'm punching in a four!

SETH: Obviously I didn't intend on taking off my clothes. But then I saw the Jacuzzi and I don't know what came over me but — four?

ERICA: Yes, you idiot, Four, one, one.

SETH: *(Beat.)* You're calling information?

ERICA: No, I'm calling the police, you — Oh shoot!

SETH: What am I doing? I'm helping you end my life! Stick with the four. Or try a six. I hear one eight hundred is nice. And free!

ERICA: I'm punching in the nine!

SETH: See, I didn't know Ms. Miner's back door locked automatically or that Honey Bear would need to be let out at the precise moment that I got all my clothes —

ERICA: I'm punching in a one!

SETH: *(Knocking on her door.)* You must have met my mom at some point. I know she's over here with Ms. Miner all the time. Her name is Betty!!

ERICA: It's ringing! *(Erica thinks for a second, seems to remember this name.)*

SETH: Did I mention that I have never gotten in trouble in my life? Never! Not even for a traffic ticket. Besides dying my hair red and green for Christmas due to a peer pressure thing — a dare from Tina Watts when I was in the sixth grade — I have lead a near perfect existence. I have never gone nude anywhere. I never even tan. I don't even like being naked in the privacy of my own home! *(To himself.)* Oh my God, I can't believe I just told you that. That must sound kinda abnormal, but it's just I have this little extra weight around my . . . *(Stopping himself.)* OK, forget that. Shut up, Self — Seth.

ERICA: Are you having a conversation with yourself?

SETH: Yes.

ERICA: Right. Just checking.

SETH: Really, Miss, if you'll just look through that peephole of yours, you'll see, if you look in my eyes, I'm normal. *(Beat.)* Hello?

ERICA: Did you say Betty?

SETH: Yes, yes! Did you meet her? She's very normal. Sane. Just like me. *(Looking through the peephole.)* Hello?

ERICA: *(Moving toward, seeing eye up close.)* Ahh!

SETH: *(Startled.)* Ahhh!

ERICA: Get your eye out of my peephole!

SETH: Sorry! Sorry! I'm stepping away. My eye and I are stepping away.

ERICA: So let me get this straight. You were here because you were supposed to feed Honey Bear for Ms. Miner?

SETH: Yes.

ERICA: All right. And Ms. Miner's best friend, Betty, is your mom?

SETH: Right.

ERICA: So I have one question before the cops haul you and my poor welcome mat down to the county jail. Why are you naked?!!

SETH: Well, I admit it's odd, but I didn't know she had a Jacuzzi. You know one of those full-room, indoor Jacuzzis with the adjoining sauna?

ERICA: And you wanted to be in the Jacuzzi.

SETH: Yes! I just turned it on when — oh gosh, my nose is really starting to hurt.

ERICA: I told you, pinch and back! When what?

SETH: When Honey Bear started to . . . Well see, my parents don't have a Jacuzzi. We don't even have good water pressure.

ERICA: Anyway . . . *(She looks at him through the peephole.)*

SETH: I was looking at the hot water, bubbling in the Jacuzzi, and I don't know what came over me. I wasn't thinking. But it was so inviting. The windows were steaming up. It just looked so good. You know what I mean?

ERICA: *(Obviously, thinking he's kinda cute.)* Yeah. Yeah.

SETH: And then suddenly I was like taking off my clothes.

ERICA: Go on.

SETH: So I just got right in it. Without thinking. It was so nice.

ERICA: Um. Yeah, well.

SETH: But then Honey Bear started to cry to go out. Ms. Miner said when she has to go, she has to go. *(Wiping the blood from his nose.)* Uh. Ow. Eh.

ERICA: Oh God, I really made you bleed, huh?

SETH: Ah, it's not that bad. *(Realizing.)* Hey? Are you looking at me?

ERICA: *(Pulling away from the peephole.)* No! Why would you say that?

SETH: So how did you know I was bleeding?

ERICA: Just a guess. You said, "Ow." Go on. *(She moves to the peephole again.)*

SETH: So I let Honey Bear out the back door without —

ERICA: Putting your clothes on?

SETH: Yeah. And everything probably would have been fine if Honey Bear didn't head straight for the gate, which I realized was wide open. I thought she might wander into the street —

ERICA: There's a highway back there. She could get killed!

SETH: Exactly! *(Beat.)* So you believe me?

ERICA: *(Still staring, lost in watching him.)* I don't know. I guess.

SETH: You do?

ERICA: It's too detailed to make up.

SETH: You know what's really weird? I feel more comfortable talking to you through this door naked then most girls I talk to clothed and eye to eye.

ERICA: Yeah, well, don't get all sentimental on me. Uh, the welcome mat seems to be . . .

SETH: *(Noticing it's slipping.)* Ohh. I. Oop. Heeeeyyyy! You *are* watching me.

ERICA: Well I'm not going to leave a pervo on my porch unmonitored. You're the one who told me to peep way back when!

SETH: I'm not a pervo — and I didn't mean — I've just never been peeped on before. It feels kinda pervy.

ERICA: You're not being peeped on, you dorkhead! You're being monitored!

SETH: *(Singsongy.)* Whatever.

ERICA: I'm just making sure you're not freezing out there. That's all. So how are you doing? I mean with . . . your nose and . . . stuff?

SETH: Oh, it's OK. My nose is . . . fine. And besides losing feeling in every single limb in my body — I'm good. Thank you. But uh, I'm still feeling somewhat . . . underdressed.

ERICA: Hold on a sec! *(She grabs a robe.)*

SETH: Oh no, don't leave!

ERICA: Get out of the way. I'm opening the door. Now, don't try anything funny. I'm throwing you a robe and a pair of old shoes. *(She opens the door quick and tosses out the robe.)*

SETH: Oh thank you, thank you, thank you — purple?

ERICA: Hey streakers can't be choosers. Besides, it matches the color of your skin.

SETH: That's true. *(Putting it on.)* Aah. It's warm. Oh yes, warm. *(Bowing.)* I thank you. The style's not exactly me —

ERICA: Are you complaining?!

SETH: I love it. I love it. It's just a little . . .

ERICA: Eighties?

SETH: Uh . . . yeeaaah. And female-ish — which is not bad!

ERICA: It was my mother's. And you're wearing my dad's favorite old sneakers.

SETH: Oh God, please don't tell him!

ERICA: Don't worry. I won't. He'd kill you. The keys to Ms. Miner's door are in the pocket. We have an extra set. Good luck, uh, uh, naked . . .

SETH: Seth. And you're . . . ?

ERICA: Erica — fully clothed.

SETH: This is so kind of you. And I'll return this stuff right away.

ERICA: Please don't. I can smell those sneakers from here.

SETH: Well, I, uh . . . maybe we'll meet again under different circumstances. I hope. Minus your welcome mat.

ERICA: What?!

SETH: I mean plus clothes, plus clothes, I meant definitely plus clothes minus your welcome mat, we'd meet. God. Anyway . . . Thank you Erica!

ERICA: Well considering you're returning those keys and my mom's robe in a few minutes, we'd have to, wouldn't we?

SETH: Right. *(Beat.)* Or, I could just leave them on the steps? I don't want to bother you any more than I have already.

ERICA: Oh, no, it's OK. You can bother me — I mean, you know, knock. With clothes on. With clothes!

SMACK IT TO THE MOON

Rob and Catrina, both seventeen, meet unexpectedly in their senior year of high school. Rob is the introspective quiet newcomer with a melancholy bent on life. Catrina is the loud, outgoing, know-everyone-in-the-class type whose obsessive and spontaneous nature scares most peers away from getting too close. For some reason, these two characters just click. They go together like peanut butter and bananas.

CHARACTERS
Rob: 17, high school student
Catrina: 17, high school student

SETTING
Various locations; mostly Columbus High School

TIME
The present

ROB: *(To audience.)* When my father dragged us from Cherry Hill, New Jersey, to Columbus Junction, Iowa, two months before I was to graduate from my high school of nearly four perfect years, there was no way that I thought I could ever find happiness in this rotten, disgusting, pitiful world again.

CATRINA: *(To cafeteria lady.)* Apples are perfect and pears too. We need to eat more apples. I read that last night. *(Gesturing.)* And eggs! We need a pear, apple, and egg vending machine in here. And figs. Did you know that figs have fiber *and* protein, Maggie?

ROB: Until the bleak and dire day in which I met Catrina.

CATRINA: *(Nodding and pointing with her finger at Maggie as if to emphasize.)* Fiber. *(Shouting to her friend in the lunch line as she scoops up a bag of chips.)* Hey Mikey!

ROB: *(To audience.)* That's not really her name but in third grade she took it on as her pseudo name until college when she will adopt a brand new name of particular significance like Eleanor R., Armstrong N., or Yum Yum Dumpling.

CATRINA: Hey Mikey! He likes it! He likes it! *(Throwing up her fist.)* Ho, ho, ho! Eat a donut for me, Mikey!

ROB: She was everything I ever wanted in a woman. Outgoing, funny, sweet.

CATRINA: *(Speaking to someone else, with her own unique hand emphasis.)* Smack it!! Smack it to the moon!

ROB: And right from the start, I could tell she was attracted to me

CATRINA: *(Talking to another friend, looking back at him.)* Did you see that wacko talking to me in line?

ROB: It was instantaneous raw attraction on her part.

CATRINA: *(Pointing.)* The really funny-looking one. And he has that eye thing, that lazy-eye-potential-stalking-person eye thing. It's disgusting. But he has really good teeth.

ROB: We just, you know, clicked.

CATRINA: Did I spit at you?

ROB: I felt comfortable right from the start. I knew just what to say. *(To Catrina.)* No. *(To audience.)* And she was quite articulate herself.

CATRINA: I spit when I yell.

ROB: I wouldn't care if you did spit. My brother spits all the time and he does this really gross thing with mashed potatoes.

CATRINA: Cool! Big tip: Don't eat those here. They make the tater tots in reused lard grease. I'm not kidding. I have witnesses. *(Reciting mantra, covering eyes as she walks by the pudding.)* I hate chocolate pudding. It's disgusting. It's disgusting. I hate chocolate pudding. It's disgusting. It's disgusting. I hate chocolate pudding. It's disgusting. It's disgusting. *(To Rob.)* Am I past it?

ROB: Yes. *(To audience.)* It's like conversation just flowed from me, from us. More than any other woman I've known. Around her, profound thoughts flowed from me. *(To her.)* So do you like those Cruncha Cruncha Chips?

CATRINA: What chips?

ROB: The bacon-and-onion flavored Cruncha Cruncha — the stuff you're eating.

CATRINA: *(Looking down. Gasps.)* Oh my lands!

ROB: Oh my lands?

CATRINA: I'm not eating these. *(Handing him the bag.)* I'm not supposed to eat them. Take them.

ROB: Why can't you eat them?

CATRINA: Because they're not written in my notebook and today is not a whatever day.

ROB: Whatever day?

CATRINA: It's not an eat-whatever day! *(To cafeteria lady.)* How much, Ruby?

ROB: *(To audience.)* For some reason, she knew everyone everywhere. All the cafeteria staff, the school gardener, the religion teacher with the mentally retarded son, and I soon found out that she managed to be on a first-name basis with the principal of the school, his wife, and their pet dog, Sassy.

CATRINA: Put the open bag of chips on my tab even though I will not be eating any more of them. Ever. In my lifetime. *(To Rob.)* I have to warn you that I am on caffeine again. You have nice eyes.

ROB: Thanks.

CATRINA: *(Digging through her purse.)* I have a problem. Inadvertent eating. That's what I do. So I have to write things down. You'll eat my chips?

ROB: Well, I don't really like onion-and-bacon.

CATRINA: But you have to eat them. Eat them. Go on, eat them!

ROB: One sec. *(He hands the cafeteria lady money.)*

CATRINA: I wish I had a hand cream. Do you have any hand cream? *(He shakes his head no. To others.)* Does anyone have any hand cream?! *(To him.)* I refuse to be an inadvertent eater anymore. I refuse. It's a ninety-day plan. Do you think that's too long?

ROB: Well . . .

CATRINA: This cafeteria promotes inadvertency. Inadvertently, nonintended, accidental, involuntary, not part of the plan. We should have fig, pear, and apple vending machines. That's the definition, by the way, for inadvertent eating so mark me with an *I* and put me in a starving country. I think the cheese flavor's much better.

ROB: What?

CATRINA: The cheese-flavor Cruncha Cruncha Chips.

ROB: Yeah, I don't like mixing my flavors. If they were onion or bacon that would be fine, but onion *and* bacon well, that's just, you know, disturbing.

CATRINA: *(Taking him in.)* Yeah, I know what you mean. Do you talk to God or some like higher something?

ROB: I guess.

CATRINA: Well I already opened the bag. I've got to find someone to take them.

ROB: We could just throw them out.

CATRINA: *(Appalled at the idea.)* No, we could not. That would be wasting food.

ROB: Well, they aren't nutritionally sound anyway.

CATRINA: Yes, but pigs were killed for the bag. The bacon. I love your shirt. I love royal blue. It goes with your eyes. I can't deal with pigs being killed.

ROB: Well, not pigs with an *s*. I don't even think one pig. Maybe it's just bacon flavoring from a small portion of the —

CATRINA: Ahhh! I can't think about it. I'm a vegetarian from this time forward. I'm a vegetarian. *(Raising her hand to bear witness.)* I'm a vegetarian. Everything else, *(Snaps her fingers.)* out of here.

ROB: Just like that?

CATRINA: Well, sure because I can't deal with the pigs and the rabbits and things.

ROB: Where did the rabbits come from? There's no rabbit anything in these chips.

CATRINA: Yes, but there could be. And then we'd throw them out without regard. I can't think of the pigs anymore. I'm a vegetarian. I'm going to fill my notebook with broccoli and turnips and cantaloupe as soon as I sit down. Where are we sitting?

ROB: I, I . . . here? *(He throws away the bag of chips.)*

CATRINA: I saw you throw away the bag. *(Smacks her leg.)* I know, garlic-and-onion!

ROB: Garlic-and-onion —

CATRINA: Cruncha Cruncha Chip flavor.

ROB: Oh. Oh, well, yeah that might be OK — probably pretty good because they're complimentary.

CATRINA: Complimentary? They're giving them out for free?

ROB: No, I meant they go together. Like cheese and tomato. That's passionate. Like hot dog and mustard is classic. Like spaghetti and meatball. It's just natural.

CATRINA: Riiight. I'm sorry I'm thinking of the pig. And I can't eat the pig-free anyway. It's still fattening. So how often?

ROB: How often?

CATRINA: Do you speak to strange girls in cafeterias about God or higher beings or pigs or meatballs and mustard?

ROB: Well, I — I don't know. I guess just when taken off guard.

CATRINA: That's cool. I want to dive into the garbage and fish out the bag. Do you have urges like that?

ROB: Well, I guess. Look, the pig wouldn't have been fed at all if we hadn't bought the bag in the first place. He would be a wild pig and might have died in the cold far from the mud and good friends. Instead he led a nice, long, squeally pig life in the mud.

CATRINA: *(Beat.)* Do you mind if I leave?

ROB: What? Why?!

CATRINA: It's not you. It's the pudding and the tater tots and the pig bag. It's all just too much. I know you're new and probably insecure and all that, but I have to go.

ROB: Insecure? I'm from Cherry Hill, New Jersey! It's sophisticated and very wealthy

CATRINA: Meet me in the library by the Monet painting under the clock, three-thirteen PM after chemistry before oatmeal break. We can look at it — the painting. *(She starts to go, but turns around.)* Can I have one of your carrots? *(He nods.)*

ROB: *(To audience.)* Our compatibility was apparent immediately.

CATRINA: But I don't date guys under any circumstances. Ever! Uh! That's just a whole 'nother ball of wax. You have nice teeth by the way. *(She starts to leave.)*

ROB: *(To Catrina.)* Wait! What's your name? Three . . . ?

CATRINA: Thirteen. Catrina. Later, Rob.

ROB: *(To audience.)* I still don't how she knew my name. Once she left my presence, the Technicolor cafeteria blurred into a mass of gray. I admit that hearing, "I don't date guys under any circumstances. Ever!" may have sounded a bit disheartening, but I ignored it. I was distracted in my Values in Media class with the exception of making a small derogatory comment about the insensitive use of cows in milk commercials. Then I raced out of my final class — torturous swimming with our sadistic instructor, Mr. Toadstank who whipped each of us across the butt with a whistle. In order to properly impress, I was in the library at three-oh-six, quietly browsing the massive book *Impressionistic Painters of the World* under the Monet painting trying to look properly casual yet fairly fascinated in a cool way. She approached me and I was about to start expressing my delight of the colors and light emphasis in the Monet when —

CATRINA: *(Angrily, hitting him in the back hard.)* Son of a gun! *(Throws up her hands.)* You know what you made me do? I spent my entire chemistry class writing down flavors I felt were complimentary and flavors that were not. I put it in my notebook and you have to fill it out. You can mark your opinion in the boxes next to them.

ROB: Some people have said that Catrina is obsessive.

CATRINA: I made five columns. Super complimentary, somewhat, not at all complimentary, not sure, and sounds gross.

Use X's in the boxes, not checks. And do it in pencil, not pen because I don't expect you to be definite on the first try.

ROB: I just considered her thorough.

CATRINA: Put a plus in the super complimentary column if you think they cannot be separated under any circumstances. *(Grabbing his hand.)* Now, come on, we have to break into the cafeteria.

ROB: I was beginning to believe that "under any circumstances" was one of Catrina's standard expressions. But not one she created. Unlike . . .

CATRINA: *(To a friend in the distance.)* Smack it, Mr. Monet! To the moon!

ROB: *(To Catrina.)* What did you say?

CATRINA: *(Taking his hand.)* Come on. We're breaking into the cafeteria.

ROB: That's what I thought you said.

CATRINA: Don't worry. I'll do the breakin' in part, but I need you to watch. If anyone comes just start coughing. So you liked it, huh?

ROB: What?

CATRINA: The Monet?

ROB: Well, sure I — *(To audience.)* I didn't have the heart to tell her I was more like a Diane Arbus fan or a Salvador Dali type. I don't know why. I just felt more at home looking at art that was weird or depressing: melting clocks, purple stubs, contorted freaks of a downtrodden circus. *(Beat.)* Maybe they reminded me more of my relatives. Or maybe it's because I never met someone who enjoyed life like Catrina.

CATRINA: *(Picking the lock of the cafeteria.)* Do you ever want to jump into a painting or a book? I'd like to be in Monet's garden — the flowers are so brilliant. Just act like you're sick as dog if she comes by.

ROB: She?

CATRINA: Well, it could be a he too. Or it could be a them.

ROB: Why are we doing this?

CATRINA: To get the bag. *(Looks up as she's fiddling with the lock.)* I think talent is attractive. A lot more attractive than being really handsome.

ROB: *(To audience.)* Was I glad to hear this. Because though I am not ugly, I would rarely be considered really handsome. Cute sure, but never really handsome. But I am not without talents. I have many, many, many talents. None of which I can think of at the moment, but if need be I would be prepared to provide a Shakespearean performance of a sickened dog as good as any at Stratford.

CATRINA: Monet would be so attractive to me. He was really talented. So was Dr. Seuss.

ROB: Dr. Seuss? I thought it an odd pairing and I had never thought of Dr. Seuss's sex appeal. But it made sense. Monet and Dr. Seuss were both whimsical. I figured I could be whimsical too. I was whimsical — I am — in a male-Sylvia-Plath-Jerseyesque sort of way.

CATRINA: Oooooh. Got it!

ROB: We broke in with no need for my Oscar-worthy performance. *(To Catrina.)* Why are we getting the bag anyway? Are you that hungry?

CATRINA: Please! *(Playing with the lock.)* It's for the birds.

ROB: Oh. *(To audience.)* I pretended as if this all made perfect sense. It turns out we were to feed the chips to the birds in an abandoned field nearby, giving everything back to nature and in doing so, absolving any guilt about pigs. She headed immediately to the plastic garbage cans propped near the back door of the cafeteria.

CATRINA: *(Trying to do an accent.)* We're like on a magic quest to return the Cruncha chips to the snacking place on the fairy grounds.

ROB: *(To Catrina.)* Are you saying you want me to dig through the garbage?

CATRINA: Right.

ROB: *(To audience.)* I had visions of us throwing Cruncha Cruncha chips to the wind and the beautiful chirping birds floating sweetly down to gently catch them all around us. There

Catrina and I would be in the gorgeous green field that extended as far as the eye could see and suddenly we would be staring at each other. Her shirt whipping in the wind revealing the curve of her bosom and we would, in that moment, move into —

CATRINA: I did not break into the cafeteria to steal anything, Jerry — Mr. Holden! The truth has to do with my problem with inadvertent eating and a bag of chips because —

ROB: I'm a diabetic, sir. I needed something. Everything was put away. I could feel my blood sugar dropping rapidly. *(To audience.)* I couldn't believe I was saying any of this. I'd never lied so well in my life. Using the word *rapidly* was nearly genius. *(To Mr. Holden.)* Catrina was just trying to find something sweet for me. We apologize and will not ever do it again. *(To audience.)* It turns out the surveillance cameras did us in. Mr. Holden, our principal, believed every word I said.

CATRINA: *(Looking at Rob.)* Wow! Wow, you totally lied.

ROB: *(To Catrina.)* Yeah.

CATRINA: Son of a gun. You really lied! You seem all shy and then you lied!

ROB: *(Proudly.)* Yeah.

CATRINA: You shouldn't do that.

ROB: What?

CATRINA: Now I'll doubt everything you say.

ROB: No, no. I just didn't want to risk us getting in trouble in our senior year. It was a good cause. Doesn't that justify it? I've never done that before.

CATRINA: See, but how do I know that? Hmmm? So are you coming?

ROB: What?

CATRINA: To the field? I still have the chips. Then maybe you could come over for noodles and grapefruit juice.

ROB: *(To audience.)* And that's how it began. Noodles and grapefruit juice led to —

CATRINA: We can go swimming at the community center and

then we'll have peanut butter and jelly sandwiches, but it has to be low-fat peanut butter and you can only stay for a half an hour because I have to study and I have a play date with my cat Puppy.

ROB: Until we began doing homework together, which led to . . .

CATRINA: You can stay to help me with chemistry and we can watch *Animal Planet* and then you have to go home but you can call me at nine-twenty-five before I go to bed.

ROB: Which lead to a few movies and lots of talk all which got progressively slightly longer. I even got to . . . well, you know. Not sex.

CATRINA: *(To audience.)* Sex does not happen at this age under any circumstances. *(Turning around in dress. To Rob.)* I'm afraid my dress is falling down. I knew I couldn't do this strapless thing. Is it falling? My stomach sticks out in this. I don't want to look sleazy. Do I look sleazy? Don't answer that. Oh fiddlesticks! I forgot to get you a flower thing and I look ugly. I can't do these things right!

(Rob kisses her.)

ROB: You look beautiful.

CATRINA: *(Pause.)* You too. I mean handsome. I brought the list. *(She hands it to him.)*

ROB: Don't you think you can stray from the list for the prom?

CATRINA: No, because if I stray, I could get into a straying habit. I can't stray, Robbie. I told you that. You know I think I love you. I hope I'm not going to have gas.

ROB: What?

CATRINA: I can't stray from the list because it becomes a habit.

ROB: No, I . . . I — the other thing. I do too.

CATRINA: You have gas too?

ROB: No. I love you.

CATRINA: Oh, I thought you meant the gas thing. Oh my stars! I'm glad it's the other thing. Though it would be nice to not have gas alone. OK. So. Good. So we'll be late.

ROB: Did you hear me?

CATRINA: Sure. We've got to meet up with Page and Harry in front of the fountain at five-oh-four. *(Beat.)* Don't look that way. So . . . you call me every day at college but only once a day and we are not committed to each other unless we keep wanting to be. And e-mails are permitted as long as they are no longer than six sentences long. Now, stick that flowery thing on me and let's go have fun.

ROB: *(To audience.)* I never said the love you thing before to anyone in my whole life, minus my mother. And father and grandmother. And my sister Peggy when she had this wart removed. I relish the day that Catrina comes to visit my new college cafeteria this fall. We have both pears and apples in our vending machines. No figs yet, but there's always hope.

CATRINA: *(On the phone.)* OK, you won't believe this, Yum Yum. I'm putting on the swimsuit — it's this total . . . OK, I met this guy, Stewart, through this girl, Lee, who works at the aquarium and I talked to some big guy with a mustache and told him my lifelong dream is to go to the moon and swim with dolphins and maybe make friends with a gorilla and be a movie star. So, in exactly two minutes, I'm swimming with a dolphin! *(Talking to someone else.)* Get the bathing cap going. Smack it up! Do you want to talk to the dolphin?

ROB: That's fantastic! That's great — oh, before swimming off to paradise — "complimentary flavors of the day"?

CATRINA: Chocolate and potato chips?

ROB: Somewhat complimentary.

CATRINA: Tea and pretzels?

ROB: Umm, not-sure category.

CATRINA: Are you kidding? Tea goes with everything. So do pretzels.

ROB: Catrina N. Armstrong and Robert Yum Yum Dumpling?

CATRINA: Definitely complimentary. X in super to the moon complimentary.

ROB: *(Defiantly.)* In pen!

CATRINA: *(Beat.)* OK. Purple ink.

FAÇADE FACE-OFF

Nearly six months ago, Alexander, a Russian immigrant and a sculptor, moved from New York City to Seattle and bought a condo in Inez's building. The very organized Inez, an administrative assistant at a prestigious firm, is president of the condo association and a commanding force there. For the last few months, Inez and Alexander have been at each other's throats. At the monthly association meetings, the other residents hear how Alexander keeps Inez up at night with his music and his women. Alexander laughs it off, telling everyone she is too strict. Alexander is not happy with Inez, either. First, she is preventing him from building a new window that would give him a fabulous view of Alki Beach and, second,, she called the pound on his barking dog, Little Chekhov. Several of the other condo owners are now threatening to throw both of them out. Alexander and Inez have each responded to the other with a memo. In this scene, Inez confronts Alexander.

CHARACTERS
Inez: early 30s, the condo president
Alexander: 30s, a Russian painter

SETTING
Alexander's condo

TIME
The present

INEZ: *(Furious, but maintaining her cool.)* I received your memo about my abilities, Mr. Kurchov.
ALEXANDER: I got your memo about throwing me out, Ms. Busybody, and I don't like.
INEZ: You didn't like it? Well, I didn't exactly like being called a crazy lady either.

ALEXANDER: You know, I didn't like your memo so much, I didn't read. I put to other use.

INEZ: Well, being as I am, I read yours thoroughly, Mr. Kurchov, although I must admit it took me a while to get through it, given your inept attempt at the English language.

ALEXANDER: You're insulting! You think I should take remedial English course?!

INEZ: So you did read it then! Maybe I should have suggested that you just go back home to New York where it's probably not a problem.

ALEXANDER: My home is Russia, my dear crazy idiot, but at least back in New York people are not so rude. They are not preoccupied with people's business to stop them from making beautiful view window in own home.

INEZ: Well, in Seattle, and particularly, in this condo association, as I've told you many, many, many times, we have a process. I am not stopping you from making a window with your little "beautiful view" of Alki Beach. I was simply asking you to go through the already-existing process all of the residents go through when we make changes to our façade. It is a shared façade, so we must make shared-façade decisions.

ALEXANDER: Why?

INEZ: Why?! I don't know why! Because we do! Our façade is like our group face. You wouldn't want me changing your face without your permission, would you?

ALEXANDER: *(Thinks.)* Hmm. What kind of change we talking about?

INEZ: You get my point. And by the way, you incorrectly signed y*our* memo as if it were from "All Residents." That is grossly inaccurate, as suspected. I've talked to all the people in the building, and though they are all, well, let's say, annoyed by our bickering, none want to impeach me except you. But you cannot impeach a condo association president, Mr. Kurchov!

ALEXANDER: Why not? This is America! You do not impeach?

INEZ: This is ridiculous!

ALEXANDER: You are ridiculous! Look, I stop arguing on all this if you just let me make window in peace. I describe what kind of window. Ask everybody. Everybody shrugs, "OK." Easy. That's it. No three-meeting. Waste people's time.

INEZ: We have a shared process. A three-step shared process.

ALEXANDER: I cut it down. One step. I tell them. I do. Tell me, what are you afraid of? You afraid window will bring in too much light? Joy? Happiness? The façade will have too many opening in it? I have too much fashion for your taste? You might be outside and see me naked in window — what, what?

INEZ: I didn't say the window wasn't a good idea. I said you didn't follow the process.

ALEXANDER: Ah-ha, so you like to see me naked in window.

INEZ: Oh, now don't be . . . that's disgusting!

ALEXANDER: Not everyone think so. You are crazy woman, you know?

INEZ: Oh yeah?! Last time you did not follow proper procedure, we all had our water shut off for six straight hours.

ALEXANDER: I just put in little faucet. I did not know.

INEZ: Exactly you did not know because you did not examine the contractor's plans. The contractor had no references — none! He could have done a terrible job that caused leaks right over my head.

ALEXANDER: He didn't make any leaks. Any leaks in your head already exist.

INEZ: The point is that you didn't give a care about anyone else in the building. And it wasn't a little faucet. It was a jet-propelled-type bathtub used for God knows what and God knows who!

ALEXANDER: As soon as I realize about water, I tell everyone.

INEZ: With no warning. I was in the middle of dy — doing my hair.

ALEXANDER: Dying your hair? I noticed new color.

INEZ: Yeah? (Changes gears.) I'm not talking about my hair here.

ALEXANDER: It's beautiful.

INEZ: Really? *(Annoyed.)* Don't distract me. The point is we were all fine and happy and everybody followed the process until you moved in six months ago.

ALEXANDER: Maybe everybody followed process, Ms. Inez, but I don't think everybody was happy. Amanda tell me it was boring without Alexander.

INEZ: Well, we might have been bored, Alexander, but we were certainly fine.

ALEXANDER: No parties without *(Points to self.)* Alexander.

INEZ: No loud music all hours of the night either.

ALEXANDER: No cute little poodle.

INEZ: No constant reminders of poodle left on the lawn either. You better get a scooper.

ALEXANDER: Not necessary. I told you I put your memo to use. *(He winks.)*

INEZ: Ohhhhh! Don't you *dare* do that!

ALEXANDER: Do what? This? *(He winks.)*

INEZ: *(Points to him.)* Yes, that. Stop that!

ALEXANDER: *(Smiles. Winks.)* This is nothing.

INEZ: No, it's not nothing. You're a winker. One of those winking men types who thinks you can wink away at women in that way that you do, but I won't stand for it!

ALEXANDER: What does that mean? *(Realizing.)* Ohhhh. I see. Your boyfriend is angry that I winking at you? Ahhh. He doesn't satisfy you, so you don't like being remembered something sexual.

INEZ: Oh my God. You are — this — that is absolutely ridiculous!

ALEXANDER: I know. It's true. You're red. I know it's true.

INEZ: I'm red because I am — you are — I — you are disgusting. And I won't even dignify — Do you know that I work at a prestigious firm?

ALEXANDER: Ah-hah, that's why so grouchy. That is what it bubbles down to.

INEZ: This is derogatory — slander! Sort of, and I — my

boyfriend, even though I don't have one at the moment, is none of your business, do you understand me?!

ALEXANDER: You don't have boyfriend? But you are so pretty.

INEZ: Thanks. But that's not true at all. I mean . . . I don't know what I mean, but it's not your business and the idiom, the expression for your information is what it boils down to, Mr. Kurchov, not what it bubbles down to.

ALEXANDER: Boils, bubbles, burns up — whatever. Does it not make bubbles when it boils?

INEZ: Yes, but bubbles are nouns — well, you can bubble as a verb, but you can't blow boils because — the point is, I don't know what I'm talking about . . . *(Remembering.)* The expression! The expression is boiling down water, and you should learn English if you want to put in a window!

ALEXANDER: My God! You are extremely attractive when you get confused.

INEZ: What?

ALEXANDER: I think you hear me.

INEZ: Listen, I came up here tonight to say one thing and one thing only.

ALEXANDER: You say lot of things for only one thing, Ms. Inez.

INEZ: May I? Can I finish?

ALEXANDER: Fine. Say. Speak. Talk. My home is your stage.

INEZ: I am not going to stoop down to your level anymore.

ALEXANDER: *(Really noticing her.)* Too bad. I like how you stoop.

INEZ: See? I'm ignoring. I am not going to call you fifty million times a night to get you to turn down the music or tell the women you bring up here to stop clomping about at two AM when I need to get to work at six AM.

ALEXANDER: The women are my work. I have to work too. These women are my models. I am serious painter. With career. I have showing next week. *(Gesturing to his walls.)* This is what I should be concentrate on — my work! You act like I am playboy when I am always working.

INEZ: Oh, come off it. You are a total playboy. That's what you do. *(Pointing to the wall.)* Is that your work?

ALEXANDER: Yes!

INEZ: Oh my! It is? It's good.

ALEXANDER: Thank you. You seem surprised?

INEZ: Yes. Now, back to what I was saying. I am not even going to throw my weight around as condo association president, demanding you agree to my requests at our monthly meetings. I am not going to harass you like you have with me — throwing your junk mail in my box! I know that's been you.

ALEXANDER: I give for the coupons.

INEZ: I am not going to resort to name calling, or ridiculous idle threats.

ALEXANDER: Oh no, you take all interesting out of our relationship.

INEZ: I am simply and quietly going to kill your dog.

ALEXANDER: You are — what?!

INEZ: I said I am simply and quietly going to kill Little Chekhov.

ALEXANDER: Oh my God. You are *really* crazy. I would commit you right now if I not so curious what you will say next.

INEZ: You think I won't do it? Because I will. There are poisons that are undetectable. There are accidents that are unforeseen.

ALEXANDER: There are people who are *(Circles head with hand. Makes noise.)* Why you do this?

INEZ: Because you have made my life hell. I used to run this place, do you know that? People here totally respected me. I wasn't a nag. I wasn't a party pooper. I was organized, well-rounded, efficient, and I was almost engaged!

ALEXANDER: Engaged?

INEZ: I never said that.

ALEXANDER: Oh my — He leave you?! What a bad man! What a fool!

INEZ: You think? *(Beat.)* I don't really want to kill your dog,

OK? He is cute as can be. I just. I don't care if you obviously have immense talent, and an incredible smile, you're a royal pain!! And you don't listen to me — ever!

ALEXANDER: You look so sexy when your veins pop out like that.

INEZ: I was so crazy about this I was thinking of cyanide.

ALEXANDER: For the boyfriend or Little Chekhov?

INEZ: Little Chekhov originally, but now that you mention it . . .

ALEXANDER: This is the most strange feeling.

INEZ: I have an odd feeling too. I want to throw something of yours or break something. Do you have anything?

ALEXANDER: I have incredible desire to paint you.

INEZ: Don't be ridiculous. I was going to murder your dog. I'm obviously sick. *(Gesturing.)* You seem to only do nudes.

ALEXANDER: Well . . . so?

INEZ: I don't suppose you have a vase I could throw? It doesn't have to be anything nice.

ALEXANDER: Wait. Let me look. *(Looking.)*

INEZ: You know, I'm such a horrible person I thought about murdering your dog all night last night. Of wringing her little neck. I know she's cute, but that's not the point. And I know I would never do it, but I'll tell you, Mister, I really felt like killing her. And it felt good. It felt sooo good to really get you!

ALEXANDER: Maybe you didn't want to kill her. Maybe you just want to get me. *(He winks.)*

INEZ: *(Thinks.)* No, I wanted to kill the dog. But it's not as though I don't think you're occasionally attractive . . . mildly.

ALEXANDER: You look incredible right now. I see I never realize your passion.

INEZ: You better believe it, honey. I'm not this organized out of the blue. You have to love and hate things to organize the crap out of them.

ALEXANDER: I want you, Inez. I know this is strange because

you want to kill my dog, but I think we have always have something between us.

INEZ: We have. Anger. Did you find a vase?

ALEXANDER: Yes, but it is my parent's special gift. I want to give you my lips instead.

INEZ: But I want to break something, not kiss something.

ALEXANDER: OK, you break my lip, then you kiss.

INEZ: You are — You're — You are — OK, give me your lips.

ALEXANDER: Well, don't act bored — I am hot catch.

INEZ: Maybe I'll bite you instead.

ALEXANDER: Ohhh, you are spicy.

INEZ: Ohhh, shut up and kiss me!

ALEXANDER: You shut up!

INEZ: You!

ALEXANDER: OK, I shut up.

(He moves and kisses her passionately. Then he pulls her in tightly.)

INEZ: Just what do you think you're doing?

ALEXANDER: What? I hold you. Do I have to go through process for this too?

INEZ: Like you wouldn't believe. But being that I am condo president, perhaps I can make an exception just once.

ALEXANDER: I knew I like you. *(He growls at her.)*

SNIFF SNIFF, AHH AHH

Aaron and Kim, late twenties, work for a very young, up-and-coming advertising firm in Chicago. Aaron heads up a team in the creative area. Currently, he is working on the new Inhalo nasal spray campaign. Kim is the Inhalo account manager. Aaron and Kim have both moved ahead quickly — Kim for her selling abilities, Aaron for his success on last year's "feel the rush" mint copy. Aaron and his team, unbeknownst to the very busy Kim, have been stuck on the nasal spray copy. Kim has come to look at preliminary workups the night before the presentation is due, only to find that there is no copy written. Kim, who has always had a little thing for Aaron, enters his office in a "calm" panic.

CHARACTERS
Aaron: late 20s, a copywriter for an ad firm
Kim: late 20s, an account manager for an ad firm

SETTING
Aaron's office

TIME
The present; early evening through to the following
   morning

AARON: *(To audience.)* Five PM. End of the workday.
KIM: *(Containing her complete panic.)* Aaron, I just saw the
   Inhalo Pharmo campaign —
AARON: *(Overly friendly.)* Kim, hi! Oh good. That's good. Very
   good. Did you like it? I think Chuck did some bang-up work
   on it. He's so good. Isn't he good?!
KIM: He's good. Are you all right, Aaron?
AARON: I'm fine. I'm great! I'm good! Why?
KIM: You're about to down a mug of pencils.
AARON: *(Noticing.)* Oh. *(Laughs.)* That's no way to get the

lead out. Ha. Ha. I guess it's been a long week, huh? I just need a little java joe.

KIM: Yeah — so about the Inhalo campaign?

AARON: You look like you lost weight, Kim. You look terrific. Have you lost weight?

KIM: Thanks. I have been working out a little —

AARON: I wish I could get to the gym but my hours — whew.

KIM: Yeah, so anyway! It's not that I mean to be critical about the design of the campaign, Aaron, but it's just that —

AARON: How could you be? Chucky really got the misty green jungle thing in a hip urban sort of way like we described.

KIM: Yeah, he did, but it seems to be missing something.

AARON: Oh really? What could be missing?

KIM: Well, um, *words?!*

AARON: Oh. Oh yeah. That. Well, that's no problem, Kimmie.

KIM: No problem? Yes, Aaron, I think that is a problem, a big problem, especially since we are supposed to have Lisette Cole here tomorrow morning to review our preliminary ad design and *copy*. And you told me not to worry all week!

AARON: Oh, words are overrated.

KIM: She's a word person. A word lover. She sleeps with her Webster's CD ROM. She told us that the very first day we met her.

AARON: Well . . . So she's into words . . . you know, that doesn't mean we need a whole bunch of them. Less is more kinda thing. Besides, we have the design. We're halfway there. Ya got to look at the half-empty thing.

KIM: Don't you mean the half-full thing?

AARON: *(Beat.)* That too!

KIM: Aaron, she is going to see the sample of the nasal spray bottle sitting naked in the jungle with no words around it. She'll ask, "Where are the words? Where is the caption?" Then I will say, "I don't know." We have no context for this misty nasal spray thing in the middle of the jungle. "But isn't it wonderful? It's so nicely hipply green."

AARON: It's nasal spray, Kim. How much context do we need?

The bottle says it's nasal. It says it's spray. People automatically intuit that it's a bottle to sniff, to clear the nose. Will people think it's for their armpits? No. Will they mistake it for anti-anxiety medication? A brand new car? A VCR? No. Do we have to spell everything out?

KIM: In a word. Yes.

AARON: We need to teach people to think for themselves! Lead them away from their mindless MTV states of being! Let them ponder the sociological ramifications of the naked nasal spray! They'll talk about it on the buses, they'll muse at the watercoolers, they'll–

KIM: Ignore it completely.

AARON: No, no, it will inflame their tiny minds and override their stupefied senses! Then we'll follow it up with — something!! *(Beat. Kim stares at him.)*

AARON: If we really need words, why don't we get them from her in our brainstorming session tomorrow?

KIM: So what is she paying two hundred thousand dollars for?! She's not paying two hundred thousand to write her own ad!

AARON: Oh come on, she just wants support. She needs reassurance. We listen and give her two thumbs-up. It's all good. That's what she really wants. Does she not make us make it say what she wants it to say in the end anyway? Huh?! *(Kim is confused.)* Or we could come up with something like . . . now?

KIM: We? As in you and me?! You're the creative person. You're the one with the team.

AARON: Who have all been working till midnight every night on the Nifty-Swifty Mop! We are intellectually drained!

KIM: Why didn't you tell me before the end of the day today that you were stuck?

AARON: Stuck? I'm not stuck! Stuck? I've never been stuck in my life! I'm just a little . . . blocked.

KIM: OK then. Sure. I understand. I've been under amazing pressure myself. It does render one useless.

AARON: Useless? I'm not useless! I just need to get some ideas moving — to clear my head.

KIM: Well, then you better clear your head because I've been working my head off! *(She massages his shoulders.)* I had Reid Michaels and his pimple cream to deal with all week. You think my job's easy?! *(Starts pounding on his back.)* Just because I'm off to expensive dinners and lunches does not mean I'm not working. You talk about exhaustion. I have Harry breathing down my back to bring up the numbers, and keep the clients satisfied. But always keep it bubbly. They expect it. I have to be like *(Full of bubble.)* "Hey! How are ya?!" all the time. It's sick! And of course Reid wanted me to be incredibly enthusiastic about the intricacies of his Zit Zapper. I was eating. *(Squeezing his shoulders hard.)* He went on in detail about the sebaceous glands. That's against the rules!

AARON: What? No glandular talk during dinner?

KIM: Exactly. And I told him it made me sick. I told him but he still went on. I hate that!

AARON: Oww!! *(She stops.)*

KIM: Sorry. *(She begins massaging again.)* What I'm saying is of course you're . . . blocked a little, Aaron. Is there anything I can do to get the juices flowing?

(His eyes widen, but he is not sure how to respond.)

KIM: Oh my! I didn't mean —

AARON: No, no, of course not — nor do I . . . although, if you — I, uh . . . You want some coffee?

KIM: No. Thank. You. I think that's the problem. We've had too much. You're shaking from here to Kansas. Now, let's just sit down here and think things through. I'm sure if I go through the objectives, you'll come up with something brilliant in no time. You're the "feel-the-rush" breath mint guy!

AARON: *(Pridefully.)* That's true. You're right, Kimmie. With two heads bouncing around ideas, we'll be out of here in thirty minutes.

KIM: Sure. Or even less!

AARON: *(To audience.)* Three hours and a large pepperoni with double cheese later . . .

KIM: So let's go over what we have so far.

AARON: I hate how they cut pizzas in Chicago. In little squares like that. It ruins the experience! It's a pizza pie. It's round, no?

KIM: So the nasal spray is in the jungle. Mist happening. Caption reads "Feel the Mist."

AARON: So why do you people cut it in squares? Can you tell me that?

KIM: It's easier to eat. *(Saying it over.)* Feel, feel the mist.

AARON: For who? Then you have pieces with no crust and tons of gunk that get your hands all greasy and pieces that are heavy crust with no gunk.

KIM: It's got a decent depth to it.

AARON: If you are going to get all geometric about it, make square pizzas. Or do you actually like pieces that are gunk-heavy and crust-deprived?

KIM: Can we get back to "Feel the Mist"?

AARON: Sure. But it stinks!

KIM: It does?

AARON: Yes! And doesn't it sound just a wee bit familiar?

KIM: Familiar? Oh. Oh yeah. I didn't notice that. *(Thinking.)* Oooh, I got one! How about "Mist the Mist"?

AARON: Uh-huh. OK. Let's be sure to write that one down some time. Would you look in my third drawer? I have a new pen in there next to the big bottle of scotch.

KIM: OK, sure. Wait a minute! You are not drinking, Aaron!

AARON: Why not? It's my muse finder. I need it to come up with something amusing.

KIM: How's this? You just better think of something fast or you'll be out of a job, pal!

AARON: Well, that's inspiring. I've given you three perfectly good ideas tonight and you've shot them all down.

KIM: Well, forgive me if I'm not thrilled with, "Wow, Inhalo is amazing," or "Inhalo helps you inhale better," or "I inhale better with Inhalo." Come on, Aaron.

AARON: *(Looking at spray bottle.)* Have you noticed the side effects listed for this thing?

KIM: Yeah. So?

AARON: Do you know this could cause seizures and an oily discharge? What is that?

KIM: They're just little side effects.

AARON: Little? Side effects? No. Side effects are drowsiness, nausea. These aren't side effects; they're frontal attacks.

KIM: Well, you can address them in small print on the print ad and hide them in a deep, fast voice-over at the end of the TV spot.

AARON: How can you hide oily discharge and seizures?

KIM: Look, other companies have done it! I just saw an ad for Promac where people were dancing around and then suddenly in the voice-over, you find out you can get stomach cramps and bad breath.

AARON: Well, bad breath isn't as bad as a seizure.

KIM: They were dancing around, kissing.

AARON: *(Looks at her.)* At least they weren't spraying their noses and collapsing!

KIM: The drug sold.

AARON: Well, sure, if you were a depressed, suicidal person and suddenly you take Promac and you're dancing with Mr. Right and he kisses you and likes it, do you think you'd be upset about your bad breath?

KIM: These are *possible* side effects. Anyway . . .

AARON: I thought the grumpy gorilla with the cold was a great idea. But nooooo!

KIM: Gorilla with a cold? What grumpy gorilla?

AARON: I came up with the idea a week ago. I can see it now. It's part of the jungle theme. *(Acting it out.)* It's all misty and hot. Misty, misty, hhhot, hhhot. The grumpy, sniffily gorilla with the stuffed up nose growls *(Growls.)* at the poor chirping birds. *(Chirps.)* You be the birds, Kimmie. *(She has no idea what this entails.)* He scares them. *(Growls at Kim who jumps a bit, trying to be a bird.)* Then ta-da! He spies the Inhalo Nasal Spray among the coconuts. Curious, he smells the bottle and his strong hand squeezes it —

KIM: Do gorillas have hands or paws?

AARON: *(He looks at her.)* I'm on a journey here. And then he inhales. *(Inhales.)* Ahh. It is good. He sniffs again. Ahhhh, he can breathe again. Suddenly, he becomes this gorgeous tan Tarzan with bulging muscles. The birds gather round him, singing, and a scantily clothed woman smiles from behind a palm tree. The music. The caption. "Inhalo — get back to your real nature." *(He relishes the moment.)* Huhn? Huhn?

KIM: Well . . . it's humorous.

AARON: *(Insulted.)* Humorous?!

KIM: But when I think of colds, I don't really think of gorillas and Tarzan. And it has a sort of drug-induced weird thing to it.

AARON: Inhalo *is* a drug! Sure, shoot down my ideas, but can you think of anything? No! *You* come up with a jungle with nasal spray — oh, of course! But suddenly when I add a gorilla and Tarzan, it's all wrong!

KIM: Now, now, now, don't take offense. The jungle idea was about water or misting. The idea of trying to make our noses less dried up.

AARON: Less dried up? That's it? That's all you want?

KIM: More or less. With a little jungle.

AARON: OK. OK. How about this, the spray bottle stands in the mist and then begins to dance to like a *jungle* beat. And then we just hear the bottle squeeze and a man appears between the trees. He inhales the Inhalo and breathes. And he says, "Sniff, sniff. Ahh, ahh!"

KIM: Uh-huh. *(Pause.)* And then . . . ?

AARON: That's it.

KIM: "Sniff, sniff, ahh ahh?" That's the end? That's the entire copy?

AARON: I thought you just wanted less dried up with a little jungle?

KIM: "Sniff, sniff, ahh ahh." I see the jungle, but where's the less dried-up part?

AARON: *(As if obvious.)* The ahh ahh! It's simplistic, but it has a ring to it. Say it with me. *(He encourages her.)* Come on.

AARON and KIM: "Sniff, sniff, ahh, ahh." *(He nods as if to say, see?)*

KIM: Are you trying to tell me that we are announcing to Lisette Cole, the marketing director of Pharmo, a billion dollar pharmaceutical company, that she is spending over two hundred thousand dollars on copy that reads "Sniff, sniff, ahh, ahh?!"

AARON: You think it's a little flat?

KIM: Flat? I think it's flatter than a thirteen-year-old Calista Flockhart! To be honest, I think it sucks. I think it blows. I think it's the worst thing I've ever heard!

AARON: But it's catchy, right?!

KIM: In a diseased kind of way! And why is the man in the jungle?

AARON: Because you picked the jungle! I'm weeding through your jungle!

KIM: *(To audience.)* Closing in on the three AM hour.

KIM: *(A little drunk.)* Can you pour me another glass of that scotch?

AARON: *(A little drunk.)* You're supposed to be the sober one.

KIM: Oh, you take all the fun out of it.

AARON: You're cute when you're like this.

KIM: You're cute when I'm like this too.

(Aaron laughs with what's left of his energy.)

KIM: You were so good on that mint thing . . . what was that thing?

AARON: "Oooh, ahh. It's massive mint. Oooh —

AARON and KIM: *(Lifting their arms.)* "Feel the rush!"

AARON *(Realizes.)* That was good.

KIM: It was fantastic! It was incredible! It was — *(She suddenly grabs him and kisses him.)*

AARON: *(To audience.)* Several scotches and a few Inhalo sniffs later . . .

AARON: I think you're discarding the "sniff sniff" thing too quickly. Sometimes things have to grow on you.

KIM: I don't like things to grow on me. And neither do most people or we wouldn't have a multibillion dollar market for Nair.

AARON: I know it sounds simple, but simplicity is the root of all good advertising. "Coke Is It." "Pepsi Is." "Do the Dew." These are classic. They are not complicated. You know how much that firm probably paid for "Pepsi Is"?

KIM: Yes, but those are beverage campaigns. This is medication. It's serious!

AARON: It's nasal spray! We're not talking about curing cancer.

KIM: Oh Aaron, we talked about this! We aren't emphasizing the truth here. We want the fantasy.

AARON: Oh my God! It's almost eight AM.

KIM: What?! Lisette will be here any minute.

AARON: Don't panic! We just need to work a fantasy around nasal deblockage!

KIM: Oh my God! Go for the little purple pill kinda thing.

AARON: But it's not purple and it's not a pill.

KIM: Oh God! This is terrible!

AARON: Don't worry. We can tell them it temporarily relieves the swelling of nasal membranes!

KIM: People don't want membranes in their ads! Just like I don't want glands during dinner!

AARON: Well, what do you want? A crowd of various people staggered on the tops of jagged rocks out in mountainous terrain reciting testimonials to the Inhalo Nasal Spray with Enya playing in the background?!

KIM: *(Beat.)* My God! That's it! That's brilliant! That's what I want! *(Beat.)* But in a jungle!

AARON: What?!! But what about the copy? What about the words?

KIM: Ah, words are overrated!

AARON: All right done. Let's do it. Jungles and Enya it is. I'm too tired to live.

KIM: *(To audience.)* Of course Lisette listened to the entire Enyaesque presentation. She was not impressed. Aaron quickly segued to the gorilla-Tarzan concept. She thought gorillas had paws. Finally, in desperation, I spouted out "Sniff, sniff, ahh, ahh."

AARON: *(To audience.)* She loved it. She said "Sniff, sniff, ahh, ahh" was the best ad campaign she had heard since "Plop, plop, fizz, fizz." She only made one adjustment.

AARON and KIM: "Sniff, sniff, ahh, ahhhhhhhhhhhh."

THTICK 'EM UP

Out of desperation Troy, mid-twenties, decides to mug someone tonight to pay for a few Christmas gifts for his young son. Recently divorced and out of work for months, Troy is frantic to bring his son some happiness and some much-asked for presents when the boy comes into town for a short visit. Unfortunately, Troy picks Janice, also mid-twenties, to mug this evening. She is a very angry lady who has just lost her job due to her hot temper. As the scene begins, Troy watches Janice from the alley in a tough neighborhood in Chicago. Janice lags behind the crowd as she gets off the El train.

CHARACTERS
Troy: mid-20s, a mugger
Janice: mid-20s, an angry commuter

SETTING
Urban street near the subway station

TIME
The present; evening

(Suddenly, Troy jumps out of the alley.)
JANICE: *(Screams.)* Ahhhhhh!
TROY: Shh, shh, shh!
JANICE: Don't shhh me! What is your problem? You shouldn't jump out of alleys in front of people.
TROY: I'm thorry. I'm thorry. I wasn't thrying to sare you, sare you — *(Shaking his head.)* scare you!
JANICE: OK. Fine. Apology accepted. *(Mumbling to herself.)* Be patient. Do not blow up. Obviously from the state facility.
TROY: *(Following.)* Hey, I juth need to athk you thomething.
JANICE: Oh great. Look, I can tell you right now, you will not

get my hard-earned cash. What's left of it anyhow. You want a handout? Go back to school. *(She walks faster.)*

TROY: *(Running after her, following, whispering.)* Give me your furth.

JANICE: *(She stops and turns.)* What?!

TROY: *(Getting close. Clearing throat. With emphasis.)* I said give me your furth?

JANICE: *(Walking.)* Ferth? *(Pointing.)* Oh. It's three streets down toward the —

TROY: No, no.

JANICE: *(Stops.)* No, what?! What do you want then, you crazy idiot?

TROY: Give me your *furth*!

JANICE: My wh — what?!

TROY: Furth! Furth! You hearf me!

JANICE: Well, I may have "hearf" you, but I didn't understand you. Do you understand this? *(Pretending to do sign language.)* I do not understand *furth*. *(Opening and closing hands toward him.)*

TROY: Wewl, you know what I mean!

JANICE: No, I don't! Maybe if you'd take that ski mask off your face, idiot, you could. *(Overenunciating.)* Enunciate your words and I'd understand.

TROY: Your muh-ey! Your muh-ey!

JANICE: Muh-ey? Yeah. Muh-ey. OK!

TROY: I'm not k-kidding, lady! I want your muh-ey! *(Holding out his hand in his pocket.)* I have a kun in my focket!

JANICE: *(Beat.)* Uh-huh. Good for you.

TROY: *(Very serious.)* I have a kun in my focket!!

JANICE: "Kun in your focket?" Uh-huh. Oh, I think there's a kun across the street. Go get it. *(Pointing.)* It's over there.

TROY: No! *(Points down to his pocket.)* A kun, a kun, a ga — ga — gaaan!

JANICE: Gaaa — Gun? Are you trying to say you have a gun in your focket?!

TROY: Yeth!

JANICE: Are you trying to say . . . are you trying to rob me?

TROY: Yeth!

JANICE: Oh. So Furth is purse?

TROY: Yeth!

JANICE: And Muh-ey is money?

TROY: Yeth!

JANICE: Kun in your focket is gun in your pocket? Oh honey, that one's really — Oh my God! Help, help!

TROY: *(Quickly.)* Shhh! I haf a kun!

JANICE: *(Even louder.)* Help! He wants my purse!

TROY: *(Putting his finger to his lips.)* Shhhhhhhhhhhhhhth!!

JANICE: *(Calling across the street.)* Sir, oh sir, help! *(To Troy who doesn't know what to do.)* See, he sees me! *(Looking across the street.)* Heeeelllllp! *(Beat.)* Where are you going? Can't you see this man is . . . ? *(To man across the street.)* You suck, you . . . bad man!!! *(To Troy.)* Did you see that? He just walked on by. This neighborhood blows. Nobody ever helps anybody.

TROY: You should be sare. I could take you in the alley.

JANICE: And do what?! Take my three dollars and two maxed-out credit cards?

TROY: Thwee? Dat's all?

JANICE : Yeah! And a box of feminine hmm-hmms. Which you cannot have! Those things cost an arm and a leg.

TROY: Are you thure you're not wying to me about the thwee bucks?

JANICE: You want to count it, you little defect?

TROY: Defect? Dat's not nithe. I have a kun. You should be sare.

JANICE: *(Imitating him, making him sound whiney.)* "You should be sare. You should be sare." I'm not sare!

TROY: *(Grabbing her arm.)* I'll take you in the alley if you keep theaming.

JANICE: I'm not theaming! And I'll cut your head off if you take one more step. How do you like that threat? *(Annoyed.)* Now, let go of my arm. Let go!

TROY: *(He does.)* I'm thorry.

JANICE: You should be. *(Rubbing it.)* That hurt my arm.

TROY: I'm thorry!

JANICE: There was no need to grab my arm like that. I just told you I have my little friend right now. I'm iron deficient.

TROY: OK. God. But you're juth thapposth to give me your furth. And I'll go. I'll go.

JANICE: You'd bother for thwee bucks? You must be hard up.

TROY: It's tha frinthcifal of it.

JANICE: Well, I told you I also had my hmm-hmms in there.

TROY: Wewl, take them out then. I don't care.

JANICE: And carry them where? Out in the open?

TROY: Well, don't you have a focket?

JANICE: You know what, buddy, I'm sorry to disappoint you, but I'm keeping my purse. Hmm-hmms and all. You picked the wrong lady to rob tonight. OK? You know why? I don't care if I die. In fact, I don't think I will. I think it's more likely that *you* will die!

TROY: I don't have time for thith!

JANICE: Ohhhhhh, well, *you* may not, but I have time. I have *plenty* of time. You know why?

TROY: No.

JANICE: Because I was fired today.

TROY: Oh no.

JANICE: *(Screaming at him.)* Fired!

TROY: *(Jumping.)* You don't haf to theam everything.

JANICE: I'll theam when I want to theam! You see, I don't have control. I'm not "good with authority." I "fly off the handle." I have "poor anger-management skills." I don't get along with others. *(Doing flaky imitation.)* "I create a negative climate!"

TROY: *(To himself.)* I don't know what I'm doing wong.

JANICE: *(Sighing.)* So I get a little crazy one time and dent the kitchen wall of the Burnstein's with my head? That's why we have extra two by fours. That's why we have cement filler. *(Screaming.)* That's why we have white paint!

TROY: You dented a wawl with your head?

JANICE: Do you have something to say about that?

TROY: No. Juth making thure I got dat whight.

JANICE: Well, at least I'm not inept like you. You know you're a total disaster at this thing?

TROY: Disahter? What am I doing tho wong?

JANICE: What are you doing *right* is the question?

TROY: Well, I got a kun in my focket. It'th not my fault you have a death width and you are not sare.

JANICE: Get out. You do not have a gun.

TROY: I have a kun!

JANICE: Well, you may have a kun, but you don't have a ga-ga-gun. Gun. Enuciate — Guh, guh —

TROY: Hey, don't teathe me. How do you know?

JANICE: Because you would have pulled it out sooner, when I started screaming.

TROY: Oh. Wath that a teth?

JANICE: Yes. But it was obvious from the beginning that you'd never done this before.

TROY: It wath?

JANICE: Yes, for one, saying you're sorry for jumping out at me didn't help.

TROY: Yeah? Yeeeahh. *(Beat.)* Tho how do you know tho muth about thith, huh?

JANICE: Because I did it a couple of times.

TROY: *(Very surprised.)* What? Wobbed people?!

JANICE: Mugged. I prefer mugged. It's less offensive.

TROY: Wheally? You did not.

JANICE: Wheally. *(He gives her a look.)* Sorry. I couldn't resist. Just a couple of times.

TROY: No waay.

JANICE: Yeah! Back in high school. But never with a kun.

TROY: Oh.

JANICE: No offense. But you have to sound a tiny bit confident to get action.

TROY: I did, I did! Didn't I?

JANICE: Are you kidding? And you got to look like you know what you're doing.

TROY: I did.

JANICE: Well, now, don't get insulted!

TROY: I'm not! I juth want to know what I did wong.

JANICE: Well . . . the ski mask is a dead giveaway.

TROY: Wheally?

JANICE: Yeah. How early-seventies-*Dog-Day-Afternoon* can we get? Take it off! Nobody wears a ski mask when they rob people anymore. It's just . . . out. Muggers know darn well that cops aren't going after one person who mugs someone for a couple of bucks. They're going after huge gangs — hell, drug dealers, terrorists, CEOs. They don't have time for schmucks like you.

TROY: Yeah?

JANICE: So the ski mask just makes you look really unprofessional and you're probably all hot under it. It's safe to take it off. Go ahead.

TROY: You think? *(She nods.)* I do feewl a wittle fainty. *(He takes it off.)*

JANICE: That's better. And this gun threat of yours? Really dangerous. You're lucky I came by. In this neighborhood, somebody else might have taken one look at you and your little "kun in your focket" and pulled out an Uzi and blown your head off. *(Doing imitation.)*

TROY: *(Cringes.)* You're whight.

JANICE: And not to get into what I imagine is probably a sore subject there, but you do have a little . . . speech —

TROY: I know . . .

JANICE: Well, it's an issue! You can't mug people if they can't understand you.

TROY: Well, it's not dat bad when I'm not nervouth.

JANICE: Well obviously, you were nervous. OK? I can see you're nervous from the fountain of sweat dripping off your forehead.

TROY: You underthood me.

JANICE: Eventually. But there was a major communication block with *purse, money,* and *gun in your focket — pocket.* You know what I mean? These are important words to communicate during a mugging.

TROY: Yeah, yeah. Twue. But I've been wooking on my wissp thing for yearth now. What am I thuppothed to do?

JANICE: Keep practicing. *(Looking at him.)* You know you look very familiar now that I look at you.

TROY: Oh gweight. You gonna turn me in now?

JANICE: Nah. This was nothing. I mean, what was I going to do tonight anyway? But maybe throw a few bookcases across my living room? I'm just saying you look familiar. And that lisp of yours reminds me of this dweeby kid I had a crush on back in grade school. I used to pick on him so bad because he was a little skinny, short guy, but when we were in gym class he sweat like a pi . . . oh my . . . Troy F-f-franklin?!

TROY: Janithe Afterbirth?!

JANICE: Alberts, Alberts! Oh my God!

TROY: Wow! *(Laughs.)* Oh yeah, thorry. That's juth what I youth to call you.

JANICE: *(Slightly hurt.)* You used to call me that?

TROY: Juth to myself. I was a kid. You ficked on me all the time.

JANCIE: Yeah. I did. So how the hell are you?

TROY: Well . . . not so good as you can thee.

JANICE: Hey, you know, it happens to all of us at one time or another. Everybody wants to say the hell with it, and go out and rob someone.

TROY: Yeah? You fink?

JANICE: Sure. Heck, at least you suck at it. That's a good thing. Keep you out of trouble. Me? Now, I was good at it. And, of course, my father would always say I was cut out to be a hoodlum or a bank robber or a postal worker or something.

TROY: Well, dat's not nithe. And not twue.

JANICE: Thanks.

TROY: Actually, I only rethorted to this because of my thon.

JANICE: You have a son?

TROY: Yeth.

JANICE: So you got married?

TROY: Yeth.

JANICE: *(Disappointed.)* Oh.

TROY: Yeah, but we're divorth.

JANICE: *(Interested.)* Oh. *(Trying to cover.)* Oh, that's too bad.

TROY: Yeah. We got mawied whight out of high school. It was too early. I wanted thomeone with a wittle more sthability. Bethides, I don't wheally think she liked me.

JANICE: How could she not like you? You're so sweet.

TROY: Thank you. Are you mawied?

JANICE: No.

TROY: *(Happy to hear this.)* Oh. Well, it'th alwayth better to wait. You'll find thomeone.

JANICE: Yeah. If I want him. It's good being single. So what have you been up to job-wise?

TROY: Well, I thudied to be a twavel wep at this little speciality thool and I got a job whight away, and was working as a customer service wep for this small travel agency, booking tickets. Nobody said they couldn't understand me, but then this recession hit.

JANICE: Oh boy, don't you know it. Who wouldn't resort to mugging people?

TROY: It's wheally no excuse though. Really. I just wanted to get a little extra cash to pay for this electronic game little Carl wanted for Chrithmath tho bad. I juth thought if I could peacefully wob one nithe lady who was wobbable and had a wad of cash, I could get him thome stuff.

JANICE: Yeah. Hey, you thought I looked nice? Robbable?

TROY: Yeah. Real nice. Real Robbable.

JANICE: God. Thanks. That's really nice to hear.

TROY: You know, I wheally don't understand this anger-management problem this boss says you have. You seem really in control and sane.

JANICE: Thanks. I've been using a kettledrum at home to get a handle on it.

TROY: Must drive your neighbors crazy.

JANICE: Well who cares about what they think. We're talking about my sanity.

TROY: Right.

JANICE: By the way I'm sorry I threatened to cut your head off earlier.

TROY: Hey, like you said, it happens.

JANICE: You know, your lisp is barely noticeable now.

TROY: Yeah, it tends to gets worse when I get all nervous. Robbing people is not a good way to show off my enunciation work. I've been seeing a speech therapist.

JANICE: That's great. Oh gosh. I used to tease you sooooo bad.

TROY: Oh. You were OK. No worse than anybody else.

JANICE: Yeah, but all that teasing made you start stuttering like mad.

TROY: I don't recall that.

JANICE: Are you kidding? Oh yeah. You used to stutter like crazy. That's why we called you F-f-franklin.

TROY: I d-d-don't remember that. At all.

JANICE: Oh. Well, I'm in therapy too. I have been ever since I ran over Mitzy Hamilton's rocking chair. Long story. Anyway, it's good I ran into you like this.

TROY: Yeah, no kidding. Glad I decided to stick you up tonight, even though you didn't understand a word of it.

JANICE: Yeah, well, I'm glad I had you take off your mask.

TROY: Yeah, you too. *(She nods.)* I mean, I'm glad I took it off too.

JANICE: So. *(Beat.)* Umm . . . Well . . . cool. I'll just see you around?

TROY: Wait. Uh, uh so what are you up to tonight, Janice? Besides thwowing a few bookcases across the living woom?

JANICE: I don't know. Maybe get out the kettledrum. It's not like I have money to burn.

TROY: Oh. Yeah. Me neither. But I do have thome hot chocolate back at home. And a few old ugly plates you could definitely throw.

JANICE: Yeah? Are you asking me to . . .

TROY: Well, maybe, I, I, I'm — if, if, if — but if not —

JANICE: You know, I always thought that was so cute.

TROY: Thanks. (*Looks down.*)

(*She takes his arm.*)

THE AUTHORS

Barbara Lhota is an award-winning playwright as well as a screenwriter. The Studio's production of her play, *Third Person,* was selected by the *Boston Herald* as one of the top ten plays of the 1993–1994 season. She was awarded the Harold and Mimi Steinberg for *Hanging by a Thread* at the Crawford Theater at Brandeis University. *Green Skin*, her most recent collaboration, was staged at the Producers' Club with Theatre Asylum in New York.

Her plays have been produced at various theaters across the country including the Ritz Theater in New Jersey, the American Stage Festival in New Hampshire, the New England Theater Conference, and the Wang Center in Boston. In addition, her shows have been performed at several Off-Off Broadway theaters including Tribeca Lab, Madison Avenue Theater, Love Creek Productions at the Nat Horne Theatre, and the Phil Bosakowski Theater.

She received her MFA in dramatic writing from Brandeis University, where she was an artist-in-residence and taught playwriting. Barbara now lives in Chicago, where she has had the opportunity to see *Strangers* and *Romance* performed at the Athenaeum Theatre with the Jupiter Theater Company, *Family Portrait* at the Bailiwick's Directors' Festival, *Third Person* through Symposium at National Pastime, and *Morbid Curiosity* with the Women's Theater Alliance at Chicago Dramatists and with Writers' Block at the Theater Building. At present, Barbara is collaborating with Ira Brodsky on a screenplay called *The Long Shot*. Barbara's plays, *Strangers* and *Romance,* can be found in Smith and Kraus's *Women Playwrights: The Best of 2001.*

If you would like to contact Barbara, you can e-mail her at BLhota@aol.com. Barbara is lucky to have Janet as a collaborator and friend.

Janet B. Milstein is an actor, acting teacher, and private monologue coach. She received her MFA in acting from Binghamton University in New York, and her BA with Distinction in theater from the University of Delaware. Janet has an extensive background in theater, having performed at numerous theaters with a variety of companies, including the Milwaukee Repertory Theater, the Organic Theater, ImprovOlympic, Bailiwick Repertory, Writers' Block at the Theatre Building, Tinfish Productions at the Athenaeum Theatre, National Pastime Theater, Stage Left Theatre, Mary-Arrchie Theatre, the Women's Theatre Alliance at Chicago Dramatists, Theatre Q, and more. Janet has appeared in a number of independent films, as well as working in industrials and voice-overs.

Janet has taught acting to undergraduates at Binghamton University, to apprentices at Fort Harrod Drama Productions, to students at John Robert Powers, Chicago (where she was named Best Instructor), and to children and adults in various acting workshops. In addition, Janet has trained more than four hundred fifty talent contestants for competition at the International Modeling and Talent Association conventions in New York and Los Angeles.

Currently, Janet works as a private acting coach in Chicago, training beginning and professional actors in monologues and cold readings.

Janet is thrilled to have had the opportunity to collaborate with the talented Barbara Lhota from whom she learned a great deal about writing and unlearned everything about grammar! Janet is the author of *The Ultimate Audition Book for Teens: 111 One-Minute Monologues* and *Cool Characters for Kids: 71 One-Minute Monologues*.

If you would like to contact Janet, you can e-mail her at Act4You@msn.com.